BIBLE PROPHECY ANSWER BOOK

RON RHODES

HARVEST HOUSE PUBLISHERS
EUGENE, OREGON

Cover by Dugan Design Group

Cover image © dell / Fotolia

BIBLE PROPHECY ANSWER BOOK

Copyright © 2017 Ron Rhodes
Published by Harvest House Publishers
Eugene, Oregon 97402
www.harvesthousepublishers.com

ISBN 978-0-7369-6429-6 (pbk.)
ISBN 978-0-7369-6430-2 (eBook)

Library of Congress Cataloging-in-Publication Data

Names: Rhodes, Ron.
Title: Bible prophecy answer book / Ron Rhodes.
Description: Eugene, Oregon : Harvest House Publishers, 2017. | Includes
    bibliographical references.
Identifiers: LCCN 2016030265 (print) | LCCN 2016037180 (ebook) | ISBN
    9780736964296 (pbk.) | ISBN 9780736964302 (ebook)
Subjects: LCSH: Bible—Prophecies. | Bible—Prophecies—End of the world. |
    End of the world—Biblical teaching. | Eschatology—Biblical teaching.
Classification: LCC BS647.3 R43 2017 (print) | LCC BS647.3 (ebook) | DDC
    220.1/5—dc23
LC record available at https://lccn.loc.gov/2016030265

Printed in the United States of America

17 18 19 20 21 22 23 24 25 / BP-SK / 10 9 8 7 6 5 4 3

To my beloved wife, Kerri

Acknowledgments

A heartfelt thanks goes to the late Dr. John F. Walvoord and the late Dr. J. Dwight Pentecost, both of whom were my mentors in biblical prophecy at Dallas Theological Seminary in the early 1980s. (Seems like yesterday!) Their insights played a significant role in shaping my views on biblical prophecy.

As always, my heart continues to overflow with gratitude for my wife, Kerri. What an awesome gift God has given me in her. From the very beginning, she has faithfully stood by me and my work. I am truly blessed.

Most importantly, I remain ever grateful to the Lord Jesus Christ, not only for His wondrous gift of salvation but also for the opportunity He has given me to serve Him during this short earthly life. Come soon, Lord!

Contents

Introduction: The Blessing of Biblical Prophecy 7

1. Understanding Prophecy 9
2. God and Prophecy 19
3. Rightly Interpreting Prophecy 25
4. Understanding the Book of Revelation 33
5. The Covenants and Biblical Prophecy 45
6. The Distinction Between the Church and Israel 53
7. Israel's Rebirth and Rising Anti-Semitism 59
8. The Signs of the Times 69
9. America in Prophecy 81
10. The Ezekiel Invasion 91
11. The Rapture of the Church 105
12. The Judgment Seat of Christ 123
13. The Tribulation Period 129
14. The Antichrist and the False Prophet 141
15. God's Servants: The 144,000 Jews and the
    Two Prophetic Witnesses 157
16. Religion During the Tribulation Period 165
17. The Campaign of Armageddon 171
18. The Second Coming and Subsequent Judgments 179
19. The Millennial Kingdom 187
20. The Great White Throne Judgment 197
21. The Lake of Fire 205
22. The New Heavens, New Earth, and New Jerusalem 213
23. Blessings of the Eternal State 227
24. Death Finally Conquered 237

Postscript: An Eternal Perspective 243
Bibliography 247

The Blessing of Biblical Prophecy

The study of prophecy can change your life. It has mine. In fact, my exposure to biblical prophecy was a strong contributing factor to my becoming a Christian back in the 1970s.

Fulfilled prophecy demonstrates the following:

- God knows the future.
- The Bible really is the Word of God.
- God is in sovereign control of all that occurs in the world.
- God has a plan for humanity—and a plan *for you.*
- God will one day providentially cause good to triumph over evil.
- A new world is coming—a new earth and new heavens (and new resurrection bodies).
- The Lord is coming *soon!*

Through the years, as I've engaged in the work of Christian ministry, I've discovered that Christians have many questions about biblical prophecy. Some questions relate to the timing of end-time events. Others relate to the proper interpretation of prophetic Bible verses—whether in the Old or the New Testament. Still others relate to prophetic paradigms such as premillennialism, amillennialism, and postmillennialism. Such questions are the reason I wrote this book. I've compiled the most common questions people ask about prophecy and have provided concise, easy-to-understand answers. My prayer is that you will find this book educational, enriching, and exciting.

The prophetic truths in this book are not just for the *head* but also for the *heart*. Theology that does not touch the heart—that does not resonate with your inner spirit so that it changes you—has failed at its task. My prayer is that this book will cause a paradigm shift in the way you view this present world *and your place in it*. Scripture itself says prophecy ought to have a life-changing effect on us (see, for example, Titus 2:11-14). So, this book—full of scriptural answers to commonly asked prophecy questions—is ultimately engineered to make a difference in the way you live your Christian life.

May it be so!

1

Understanding Prophecy

What is a prophet?

The word "prophet"—from the Hebrew word *nabi*—refers to a spokesman for God who either declares God's message to humankind regarding a contemporary situation or foretells the future based on divine revelation. While the predictive role is often stressed, the Bible equally emphasizes the teaching function. Both aspects require communication from God to the prophet (see 2 Samuel 7:27; Jeremiah 23:18).

What is prophecy?

Prophecy can be defined as God's revelation regarding history in advance. The backdrop is that only God—who is omniscient (or all-knowing)—knows the future. In Isaiah 46:9-11, God affirms:

> I am God, and there is no other; I am God, and there is none like me, declaring the end from the beginning and from ancient times things not yet done, saying, "My counsel shall stand, and I will accomplish all my purpose"...I have spoken, and I will bring it to pass; I have purposed, and I will do it.

This means that our sovereign God controls human history, and He is the only one who can reveal the future to us.

What does "end times" mean in the study of prophecy?

"End times" is a general term that embraces a broad spectrum of events that will take place in the last days. This includes the rapture, the judgment seat of Christ (for Christians), the seven-year tribulation

period (and all the events included in that period, such as the emergence of the antichrist and Armageddon), the second coming of Christ,
Christ's 1000-year millennial kingdom, the great white throne judgment (for the wicked), a destiny in hell for the wicked, and a destiny
in heaven for believers.

Some of these terms may be unfamiliar to you. Don't be concerned.
I'll explain them all in this book.

What does "last days" mean in the study of prophecy?

A number of New Testament passages use "last days," "last times,"
and "last time" to refer to the present church age in which we now live.
For example, the writer of Hebrews said, "Long ago, at many times and
in many ways, God spoke to our fathers by the prophets, but in these
last days he has spoken to us by his Son" (Hebrews 1:1-2). We also see
this in 1 Peter 1:20, where we are told that Christ, in the incarnation,
"was made manifest in the last times for the sake of you who through
him are believers in God." This means that people in New Testament
times up to the present day—*all* who have lived and are now living in
the church age—are, in one sense, in the "last days."

It is critical to recognize, however, the distinction between how
"last days" is used in the New Testament in reference to the church age
and how the term is used in Old Testament prophecies in reference to
Israel. The Old Testament use of "last days" (and similar terms) refers
to the time leading up to the second coming of the Messiah to set up
His millennial kingdom on earth. Among the many verses that substantiate this is Deuteronomy 4:30, where we read: "When you are in
tribulation, and all these things come upon you in the latter days, you
will return to the Lord your God and obey his voice." Contextually,
this verse equates the future tribulation with the "latter days." The Old
Testament usage of such terms as "latter days," "last days," "latter years,"
"end of time," and "end of the age" all refer to a time when Israel is in
her time of tribulation. Deuteronomy 4:30 will find its ultimate fulfillment in the final restoration of Israel, which will take place at the second coming of Jesus Christ.

Taking all the biblical data into account, it seems that in regard to

Israel, "last days" probably embraces a seven-to-ten-year period, which would span the time from the rapture* through the end of the tribulation period, as well as the "glorious appearing" of Jesus Christ. The reason it could be up to ten years is that there could be a few years between the rapture and the beginning of the tribulation period, which starts with the signing of the covenant between the antichrist and Israel (Daniel 9:27).

What does "eschatology" mean in the study of prophecy?

"Eschatology" is derived from two Greek words—*eschatos*, meaning "last" or "last things," and *logos*, meaning "study of." Eschatology is the study of last things or of the end times, particularly as related to the second coming of Christ and the events preceding and following this great event. It is a more formal theological term for the study of prophecy.

Why is it important that Christians study eschatology?

The importance of eschatology is found in the fact that about 25 percent of divine revelation was prophetic when originally written. In other words, one out of four verses in the Bible are prophetic in nature. Such prophetic verses typically deal with Jesus Christ, Israel, the church, the Gentiles, Satan, the antichrist, the signs of the times, the various judgments, Armageddon, the second coming, the millennial kingdom, the eternal state, and much more.

Is there a difference between personal eschatology and general eschatology?

Yes. Personal eschatology concerns such things as a person's death, his or her future judgment, and his or her destiny in either heaven or hell. General eschatology, by contrast, concerns more general matters such as the rapture, the tribulation period, the second coming, and the millennial kingdom. Both types of eschatology are important.

---

* Later in the book we will see that the rapture is that glorious event in which the dead in Christ will be resurrected and living Christians will be instantly translated into their resurrection bodies—and both groups will be caught up to meet Christ in the air and taken back to heaven.

Can the study of eschatology affect the way we live as Christians?

Yes, indeed. God doesn't tell us the future just to show off. He doesn't give us prophecy to teach us mere facts about the end times. It is highly revealing that many prophetic passages in the Bible are followed by an exhortation to personal purity. As we study Bible prophecy, it ought to change the way we live. It ought to have an effect on our behavior.

An analogy is found in ancient Jewish marriages. In biblical times, a betrothed woman would eagerly await the coming of her groom to take her away to his father's house in marriage celebration. During this time of anticipation, the bride's loyalty to her groom was tested. Likewise, as the Bride of Christ (the church) awaits the coming of the messianic Groom (Jesus Christ), the church is motivated to live in purity and godliness until He arrives at the rapture. Key passages related to living in purity in view of biblical prophecy include Romans 13:11-14; 2 Peter 3:10-14; and 1 John 3:2-3.

Did Jesus ever speak about prophecy?

Yes, He did—mostly in His Olivet Discourse, though also in His other discourses. As a backdrop, Jesus—the divine Messiah—fulfilled the three primary offices of prophet, priest, and king. As a prophet, Jesus gave major discourses such as the Upper Room Discourse (John 14–16), the Olivet Discourse (Matthew 24–25) in which Jesus speaks about the end times, and the Sermon on the Mount (Matthew 5–7).

The Olivet Discourse is so named because Jesus was sitting on the Mount of Olives when He delivered it (Matthew 24:3). The disciples had come to Him and asked, "Tell us, when will these things be, and what will be the sign of your coming and of the end of the age?" The entire Olivet Discourse should be viewed as a response to this question.

Highlights of Jesus' teaching in this discourse include His prediction of the signs of the end of the age such as the appearance of false Christs, wars, earthquakes, famines, the profaning of the Jewish temple, and cosmic disturbances (verses 4-28), the sign of His coming (verses 29-31), and how the end times will be much like the days of Noah (verses 36-39). Jesus also provided parables that stress being ready when He returns (24:32-35,45-51; 25:1-13,14-30) and prophesied the judgment of the nations that will take place following the second coming (25:31-46). Prophecy obviously constitutes an important and significant part of the teachings of Jesus.

Did God's prophets ever make mistakes?

No, not when speaking for God. Some, however, have tried to argue that Jonah made a mistaken prophecy. Jonah proclaimed that in 40 days Nineveh would be overthrown by God. But Jonah's prediction of Nineveh's destruction did not come to pass. So—did he make a mistake?

Not at all. Jonah told the Ninevites exactly what God told him to say (see Jonah 3:1-2). It is important to recognize that there was apparently a repentance clause built into Jonah's prophecy. The Ninevites understood that Nineveh would be toppled in 40 days *unless they repented* (Jonah 3:5-9). Based on how the Ninevites responded in repentance to Jonah's prophecy, God withdrew the threatened punishment—thus making it clear that He Himself viewed the prophecy as hinging on how the Ninevites responded.

This is quite obviously related to something God said in the book of Jeremiah: "If at any time I declare concerning a nation or a kingdom, that I will pluck up and break down and destroy it, and if that nation, concerning which I have spoken, turns from its evil, I will relent of the disaster that I intended to do to it" (Jeremiah 18:7-8). This principle is clearly illustrated for us in the case of Nineveh. It is noteworthy that God is often seen showing mercy where repentance is evident (Exodus 32:14; 2 Samuel 24:16; Amos 7:3,6).

The biblical prophets were always 100 percent accurate. If a prophet was less than 100 percent accurate, he was stoned to death as a false prophet (Deuteronomy 13; 18:20-22).

Have many prophecies in the Bible already been fulfilled?

Yes. More than 100 messianic prophecies were fulfilled in the first coming of Jesus Christ. From the book of Genesis to the book of

Malachi, the Old Testament abounds with anticipations of the coming Messiah. Numerous predictions fulfilled to the crossing of the "t" and the dotting of the "i" in the New Testament relate to His birth, life, ministry, death, resurrection, and glory.

Among the literally fulfilled prophecies are that the Messiah would be born of a virgin (Isaiah 7:14), from the line of Abraham (Genesis 12:2-3), from the line of David (2 Samuel 7:12-16), in the city of Bethlehem (Micah 5:2), would be betrayed for 30 shekels of silver (Zechariah 11:12), be pierced for our sins (Zechariah 12:10) and crucified with criminals (Isaiah 53:12), and would be resurrected from the dead (Psalm 16:10). Jesus literally fulfilled these and many more messianic prophecies in the Old Testament.

All this gives us strong confidence to expect that those prophetic utterances that are not yet fulfilled—or not yet completely fulfilled— will also end up being fulfilled just as literally as the earlier prophecies. The fulfillment of past prophecies establishes an unbroken pattern of literal fulfillment. The precedent has been set!

Why is it important for us to be aware of world events and how they may relate to biblical prophecy?

Jesus' words to some Jewish leaders in Matthew 16:1-3 give us some perspective on this issue:

> The Pharisees and Sadducees came, and to test him they asked him to show them a sign from heaven. He answered them, "When it is evening, you say, 'It will be fair weather, for the sky is red.' And in the morning, 'It will be stormy today, for the sky is red and threatening.' You know how to interpret the appearance of the sky, but you cannot interpret the signs of the times."

Jesus was rebuking these Jewish leaders. They were the religious elite of the time and were supposed to know the Scriptures—including prophetic Scripture. Yet they were completely blind to properly discerning the signs of the times.

More specifically, the Pharisees and Sadducees were blinded to the reality that the Messiah was in their midst. The miracles Jesus wrought were just as clear a sign to His divine identity as dark clouds in the sky are a sign of impending rain. Specific kinds of miracles had been prophesied of the Messiah in multiple Old Testament verses (for example, Isaiah 35:5-6). The Pharisees and Sadducees—experts in the Old Testament—should have seen Jesus as being the fulfillment of these messianic verses. In their blindness, however, they could not "interpret the signs of the times."

The lesson we learn is simple: Don't make the same mistake as that of the Pharisees and Sadducees. We ought to be educated in the prophetic Scriptures so that we can discern whether the stage is being set for the fulfillment of end-time prophecies.

Jesus also urged: "From the fig tree learn its lesson: as soon as its branch becomes tender and puts out its leaves, you know that summer is near. So also, when you see all these things, you know that he is near, at the very gates" (Matthew 24:32-33). Jesus indicates in these verses that certain things God has revealed in prophecy ought to cause people who know the Bible to understand that a fulfillment of prophecy is taking place—or perhaps the stage is being set for a prophecy to be fulfilled. Jesus is thus informing His followers to seek to be accurate observers of the times so that when biblical prophecies are fulfilled, they will recognize it (see also Luke 21:25-28).

Why should we as Christians seek to improve our world if biblical prophecy says it will get worse and worse in the end times?

I sometimes hear people say, "Why polish the brass on a sinking ship?" The idea is, why should we make sustained efforts to make things better if the biblical prophets indicate that things will get worse and worse in the end times?

However, as Christians, you and I are not to contribute to things getting worse and worse; we should always be about the business of seeking the betterment of our fellow human beings and conditions in the world. One cannot read Jesus' Sermon on the Mount for long before seeing that He taught that you and I—as "salt" and "light" in the world—ought to seek to positively influence society around us (see Matthew 5–7). We ought to be consistent bright lights in a world that is getting darker and darker.

Don't some people get a bit sensationalistic when studying Bible prophecy?

Sad to say, *yes*. Contrary to sensationalism, 1 Peter 4:7 urges us: "The end of all things is at hand; therefore be self-controlled and sober-minded for the sake of your prayers." The Holman Christian Standard version translates the relevant part of the verse, "be serious and disciplined." The New King James Version puts it, "be serious and watchful." The New Living Translation says, "be earnest and disciplined." The Amplified Bible puts it, "keep sound minded and self-restrained." The Expanded Bible says, "think clearly [be serious/alert] and control [discipline] yourselves."

The best way to stay self-controlled and sober-minded is to regularly feed our minds on the Word of God. Keeping our minds stayed upon the Scriptures will keep us on track in our thinking and in our life choices in the light of biblical prophecy.

Why is it wrong to set dates on specific prophetic events?

While it's fine for Christians to be excited to be living in the general season of the Lord's return, they should never set dates on specific events. Here's why.

1. First, date-setters tend to be sensationalistic, and sensationalism is unbefitting to a Christian. As noted above, Christ calls His followers to live soberly and alertly as they await His coming (Mark 13:32-37).

2. Over the past 2000 years, the track record of those who have set specific dates for end-time events has been 100 percent wrong. The history of doomsday predictions is little more than a history of dashed expectations.

3. Those who succumb to date-setting may end up making harmful decisions for their lives. Selling one's possessions

and heading for the mountains, purchasing bomb shelters, stopping education, leaving family and friends—these are destructive actions.

4. Christians who succumb to date-setting—for example, by expecting the rapture to occur by a specific date—may end up damaging their faith in the Bible (especially prophetic sections) when their expectations fail.

5. If one loses confidence in the prophetic portions of Scripture, biblical prophecy ceases to be a motivation to purity and holiness (see Titus 2:11-14).

6. Christians who succumb to date-setting may damage the faith of new or immature believers when predicted events fail to materialize.

7. Christians who get caught up in date-setting can do damage to the cause of Christ. Humanists and atheists enjoy scorning Christians who have put stock in end-time predictions—especially when specific dates have been attached to specific events. Why give ammunition to the enemies of Christianity?

8. The timing of end-time events is in God's hands, and we haven't been given the precise details (Acts 1:7). As far as the second coming is concerned, it is better to live as if Jesus were coming today and yet prepare for the future as if He were not coming for a long time. This way we are prepared for time and eternity.

What is "prophetic agnosticism," and why has it emerged in our day?

The word "agnosticism" comes from two Greek words: *a*, meaning "no" or "without," and *gnosis*, meaning "knowledge." Agnosticism literally means "no knowledge" or "without knowledge." More specifically, an agnostic is a person who claims he is unsure (having "no knowledge") about the existence of God.

There are some today who seemingly have succumbed to prophetic agnosticism, claiming they are unsure about the specifics of prophecy. For example, they might say that because there are so many views of the rapture—pretribulationism, midtribulationism, posttribulationism, the partial rapture theory, and the pre-wrath view—one cannot be sure about the timing of the rapture. Likewise, because there are different views of the millennium—premillennialism, amillennialism, and postmillennialism—one cannot be sure about the nature of the millennium.

The antidote to prophetic agnosticism is a literal approach to interpreting biblical prophecy. Just as all the prophecies relating to the first coming of Christ were literally fulfilled, so I believe the prophecies relating to the second coming of Christ will be literally fulfilled. A literal approach naturally leads to premillennialism and pretribulationism. (I'll address the literal approach to interpreting Bible prophecy in chapter 3.)

It is my hope and prayer that the rest of this book will help you avoid succumbing to prophetic agnosticism.

2

God and Prophecy

Is God the only one who can truly predict the future?

Yes, indeed. God's ability to foretell future events separates Him from all the false gods of paganism. Addressing the polytheism of Isaiah's time, God Himself affirmed in no uncertain terms:

- "Who is like me? Let him proclaim it. Let him declare and set it before me, since I appointed an ancient people. Let them declare what is to come, and what will happen. Fear not, nor be afraid; have I not told you from of old and declared it? And you are my witnesses! Is there a God besides me? There is no Rock; I know not any" (Isaiah 44:7-8).

- "Who told this long ago? Who declared it of old? Was it not I, the LORD? And there is no other god besides me" (Isaiah 45:21).

- "I alone am God! I am God, and there is none like me. Only I can tell you the future before it even happens. Everything I plan will come to pass" (Isaiah 46:9-10 NLT).

- "The former things I declared of old; they went out from my mouth, and I announced them; then suddenly I did them, and they came to pass...I declared them to you from of old, before they came to pass I announced them to you" (Isaiah 48:3,5).

Of course, anyone can make predictions—that is easy. But having them fulfilled is another story altogether. The more statements you make about the future and the greater the detail, the better the chances are that you will be proven wrong. But God has never been wrong. This is born out in the more than 100 very specific messianic prophecies in the Old Testament pointing to the first coming of Jesus Christ (see, for example, Genesis 3:15; 12:3; 49:10; Psalm 2:7-9; 16:9-10; Jeremiah 23:5-6; Isaiah 7:14; 40:3; 53; Micah 5:2; Zechariah 9:9; 12:10; Daniel 9:24-25). Why did God get them all right? Because He knows the future just as clearly as He knows the past. Our God is an awesome God! He knows all.

Is God's accuracy in prophetic statements related to His omniscience?

Yes—and this is extremely important because in some Christian circles today, it is fashionable to deny that God is all-knowing or knows the future. In this view, known as "open theism," there is no predetermined end toward which we are directed. Open theists say God does not foreknow future contingent events. At any moment in time, He knows as much as can be known—embracing the past up to the present moment—but His knowledge continues to grow as future unforeseen events unfold. Every moment, new unforeseen events take place that then and only then become "known" by God.

Such a view is absolutely contrary to the Bible. Because God transcends time—because He is *above* time—He can see the past, present, and future as a single act. God's knowledge of all things is from the vantage point of eternity. In view of this, we can infer that the past, present, and future are all encompassed in one ever-present "now" to Him.

Scripture reveals that God knows all things, both actual and possible (Matthew 11:21-23). He knows all things past (Isaiah 41:22), present (Hebrews 4:13), and future (Isaiah 46:9-11). Because He knows all things, there can be no increase or decrease in His knowledge. Psalm 147:5 affirms that God's understanding is "beyond measure." His knowledge is infinite (Psalm 33:13-15; 139:11-12; Proverbs 15:3; Isaiah 40:14; Acts 15:17-18; 1 John 3:20). Hence, contrary to open theism, Scripture is clear that God knows all things *simultaneously*—past, present, and future.

There are plenty of examples in Scripture where God indicates He knows the freewill decisions human beings will make. One example is John 13:38, where Jesus told Peter that before the cock crowed, Peter would disown Jesus three times. Notice the specificity of Jesus' prediction. He did not say Peter would disown Jesus a few times, or many times, or even two times or four times, but specifically three times. One must wonder how there can be such specificity in Jesus' prediction if God (and hence Jesus) is unaware of the future freewill actions of humans? Of course, things unfolded just as Jesus predicted.

Jesus also knew that Judas would make the freewill decision to betray him (John 13:18-19). This was not a mere educated guess on Jesus' part. Jesus omnisciently knew what Judas intended to do.

Jesus' omniscience is also illustrated in John 11:7,11 when He omnisciently pronounced to His disciples that Lazarus had died. No one came up to Him and told Him this. Rather, Jesus in His divine all-knowingness—*His omniscience*—simply knew that Lazarus had died.

We further observe that as God, Jesus could read the hearts of every man and woman (Mark 2:8; John 1:48; 2:24-25; 4:16-19; Acts 1:24; 1 Corinthians 4:5; Revelation 2:18-23). Jesus knew just where the fish were in the water (Luke 5:4-6; John 21:6-11), and He knew which fish contained the coin in its mouth (Matthew 17:27). Jesus was truly omniscient.

Why do I speak so much about Jesus and His omniscience? The answer is simple. First Peter 1:11 reveals that the spirit of Christ spoke through the biblical prophets. And because Christ is all-knowing—because He is *omniscient*—His prophecies of the future are always laser-accurate.

If the past, present, and future are simultaneously known to God, what is God's relationship to time?

Scripture is not clear about the relationship between time and eternity. Some prefer to think of eternity as time—a succession of moments—without beginning or end. However, Scripture indicates that time itself may be a created reality—a reality that began when God created the universe.

The book of Hebrews contains some hints regarding the relationship between time and eternity. Hebrews 1:2 tells us that the Father "has spoken to us by his Son, whom he appointed the heir of all things, through whom also he created the world." The last phrase of this verse is rendered more literally from the Greek, "through whom also he created *the ages*." Likewise, Hebrews 11:3 tells us, "By faith we understand that the universe was created by the word of God." This is more literally from the Greek, "By faith we understand that *the ages* were formed by a word of God."

Scholars have grappled with what may be meant here by "the ages." Some conclude that this is a clear indication that time came into being when the creation came into being. Some believe it refers to not just vast periods of time but all that transpires in them as well. Many modern theologians have thus concluded that church father and philosopher Augustine was right in saying that the universe was not created in time but that time itself was created along with the universe. If this is correct, as Scripture seems to suggest, then it would not be correct to say that time already existed when God created the universe. Rather, the universe was created *with* time rather than *in* time.

When God created the earth and put human beings upon it, He Himself set boundaries for day and night (Job 26:10) and divided the year into seasons (Genesis 1:14). These are handles by which temporal humans can orient themselves as time passes. As the days pass, so seasons eventually pass; and as seasons pass, so years eventually pass; and as years pass, we eventually die and enter into eternity—either an eternity with God in heaven for believers or an eternity in hell for unbelievers (see Matthew 25:31-46). The decision we make about Christ during our short time on temporal earth thus becomes all-important.

Now, most crucial to our study is the reality that God *transcends* time. He is above the space-time universe. As an eternal being, He has always existed. He is the "King eternal" (1 Timothy 1:17 NASB), who alone is immortal (6:16). He is the "Alpha and Omega" (Revelation 1:8) and is the "first and the last" (Isaiah 44:6; 48:12). He exists "from eternity to eternity" (Isaiah 43:13 NLT) and "from everlasting to everlasting" (Psalm 90:2). He lives forever from eternal ages past (Psalm 41:13; 102:12,27; Isaiah 57:15).

What all this means is that while events transpire daily here on earth—and while prophecies are fulfilled temporally—God Himself remains beyond time altogether. Because God transcends time—because He is *above* time—He can instantly see the past, present, and future. That's why His prophecies of the future are always spot-on accurate.

What should our daily attitude be toward the passing of time?

Scripture indicates that no matter what comes our way in life, *our times are in God's hands* (Psalm 31:15). Hence, we are to "trust in him at all times" (Psalm 62:8). We are urged to make "the best use of the time, because the days are evil" (Ephesians 5:16). And because God is in sovereign control of the universe, we must ever be mindful that our plans for tomorrow are subject to God's will (James 4:13-17). We should constantly be about the business of doing what is right "at all times" (Psalm 106:3).

Did the prophets and apostles write down God's prophecies on their own accord, or were they instructed to do so by God?

God instructed them to write down His prophetic word. God told the apostle John: "Write what you see in a book and send it to the seven churches" (Revelation 1:11). The Lord instructed Isaiah, "Take a large tablet and write on it" (Isaiah 8:1). It has always been God's will for His revelations to be written down for future generations (see Exodus 24:4; Joshua 24:25-26; 1 Samuel 10:25). You and I ought to be thankful that we have the Word of God, over a fourth of which is prophetic in nature.

How do we know that God's prophets accurately recorded His prophecies?

The Holy Spirit made sure the prophets and apostles got it right. Second Peter 1:21 provides a key insight regarding the human-divine interchange in the inspiration of Scripture. This verse informs us that "no prophecy was ever produced by the will of man, but men spoke from God as they were carried along by the Holy Spirit." The Greek phrase translated "carried along" in this verse literally means "forcefully borne along." Even though humans were used in writing down God's prophecies, they were all "borne along" by the Holy Spirit. The human wills of the authors were not the originators of God's message. God did not permit the will of sinful human beings to misdirect or erroneously record His message. Put another way, God *moved* and the prophet *mouthed* these revelational truths. God *revealed* and man *recorded* His Word to humankind.

Interestingly, the Greek word for "carried along" in 2 Peter 1:21 is also found in Acts 27:15-17. In this passage the experienced sailors could not navigate the ship because the wind was so strong. The ship was being driven, directed, and carried along by the wind. This is similar to the Spirit's driving, directing, and carrying the human authors of the Bible as He wished. The word is a strong one, indicating the Spirit's complete superintendence of the human authors.

Yet, just as the sailors were active on the ship (though the wind, not the sailors, ultimately controlled the ship's movement), so the human authors were active in writing as the Spirit directed. This assures us that the prophetic Scriptures truly did derive from God and not from mere humans.

You can trust the prophecies recorded in the Bible!

3

Rightly Interpreting Prophecy

Is the literal method the best approach for interpreting prophetic Scripture?

I believe so. The word "literal" as used in hermeneutics (the science of interpretation) comes from the Latin *sensus literalis*, which refers to seeking a literal as opposed to a nonliteral or allegorical sense of the text. It refers to the understanding of a text that any person of normal intelligence would get without using any special keys or codes.

Another way to describe the literal meaning of Scripture is that it embraces the normal, everyday, common understanding of the terms. Words are given the meaning they normally have in common communication.

The literal approach allows for a secondary (allegorical) meaning when demanded by the context. Notice, however, that when the biblical text specifically identifies the presence of an allegory (as in Galatians 4:24), it thereby indicates that the Bible's ordinary meaning is a literal one. Why qualify things with the word "allegory" unless the normal approach is literal?

Moreover, a literal approach is the only sane and safe check on the subjectively prone imagination of humans. And it is the only approach in line with the nature of inspiration—the idea that *the very words* of Scripture are "God-breathed."

Is the literal approach most in keeping with God's purpose for language?

I believe so. The biblical backdrop is found in the book of Genesis. When God created Adam in His own rational image, He gave Adam the gift of intelligible speech. This enabled him to communicate objectively with his Creator and with other human beings through sharable linguistic symbols—*words* (Genesis 1:26; 11:1,7). Scripture shows that God sovereignly chose to use human language as a medium of revelation, often through the "Thus saith the Lord" pronouncements of the prophets (Isaiah 7:7; 10:24; 22:15; and many others).

Here is something to keep in mind: If God created language in order to communicate with humans and to enable humans to communicate with each other, He would undoubtedly use language and expect humans to use it in its normal and plain sense. This view of language is a prerequisite to understanding not only God's spoken word but His written Word (Scripture) as well.

So—when the plain, literal sense of Scripture makes good sense, seek no other sense. For example, when God says in His Word that human beings are fallen in sin, we need to accept that harsh reality (Isaiah 53:6). When God says in His Word that He loves us so much that He sent His Son to die for us (Romans 5:8), let's accept that literally and give thanks to God for it. When God says in His Word that His gift of salvation comes only by faith in Christ (Acts 16:31), let's accept that literally and respond accordingly. When God says in His Word that those who reject this gift will spend eternity in hell (Matthew 25:41), we need to accept that literally, without trying to spin Christianity into a "kinder and gentler" religion. Likewise, when God says an invasion will be launched into Israel by a massive northern military coalition in the last days (Ezekiel 38–39), let's accept that and then determine what we can learn from Scripture about it.

Do we find examples of a literal interpretation illustrated in the text of Scripture itself?

Yes, indeed. Later biblical texts often take earlier biblical texts as literal. A good example is how Exodus 20:10-11 (a later text) interprets as literal the earlier creation events in Genesis 1–2. This is likewise the case regarding the creation of Adam and Eve (Matthew 19:6; 1 Timothy 2:13), the fall of Adam and his resulting death (Romans 5:12-14), Noah's flood (Matthew 24:38), and the accounts of Jonah (Matthew

12:40-42), Moses (1 Corinthians 10:2-4,11), and numerous other historical figures. Even within the text of Scripture itself, we find that the normal means of interpreting God's Word was a literal approach.

Were messianic prophecies in the Old Testament fulfilled literally in New Testament times?

Yes. Over a hundred predictions about the Messiah were literally fulfilled in Jesus' first coming, including that He would be (1) from the seed of a woman (Genesis 3:15); (2) from the line of Seth (Genesis 4:25); (3) the offspring of Abraham (Genesis 12:3); (4) from the tribe of Judah (Genesis 49:10); (5) the son of David (Jeremiah 23:5-6); (6) conceived of a virgin (Isaiah 7:14); (7) born in Bethlehem (Micah 5:2); (8) the heralded Messiah (Isaiah 40:3); (9) the coming King (Zechariah 9:9); (10) the sacrificial offering for our sins (Isaiah 53); (11) the One pierced in His side at the cross (Zechariah 12:10); (12) "cut off" or killed about AD 33 (Daniel 9:24-25); and (13) the One who would be resurrected from the dead (Psalm 2; 16).

This sets a strong precedent for how we are to interpret prophecies of the second coming of Christ and all the events that lead up to it. Here is a wise policy: *If you want to understand how God will fulfill prophecy in the future, examine how He has fulfilled it in the past.*

How does the literal method of interpreting Scripture deal with symbols in prophetic books?

Many symbols are found in prophetic Scripture. It is important to note, however, that each symbol is emblematic of something literal. For example, in the book of Revelation John said the "seven stars" in Christ's right hand were "the seven angels [messengers] of the seven churches" and "the seven lampstands" were "the seven churches" (Revelation 1:20), "the bowls full of incense" were "the prayers of the saints" (5:8), and "the waters" were "peoples and multitudes and nations and languages" (17:15). Clearly, then, each symbol represents something literal.

Textual clues often point us to the literal truth found in a symbol—either in the immediate context or in the broader context of the whole of Scripture. In the book of Revelation many of the symbols are defined within the text of Revelation itself. Others are found in the Old Testament. One of my former professors at Dallas Theological Seminary, Dr. J. Dwight Pentecost, once said that if you have six months to study the book of Revelation, you should spend the first three months studying the Old Testament because many of the symbols in Revelation are found in the Old Testament.

The basic rule of thumb is that when you encounter a symbol you are unsure about, consult other Scriptures that relate to that symbol. For example, if you want more information about Jesus being called "Lamb" in Revelation 5:6, look up other verses relating to sacrificial lambs (for example, Exodus 12:1-13; 29:38-42; Isaiah 53:7; Jeremiah 11:19). That way, you can discover the intended literal meaning of the symbol (in this case, that Jesus was a substitutionary sacrifice for our sins).

How does the literal method of interpreting Scripture deal with figures of speech?

When the Bible speaks of the eyes, ears, arms, or wings of God (Psalm 34:15; 91:4; Isaiah 51:9), these should not be taken as literally true. God does not really have these physical features since He is pure Spirit (John 4:24). Likewise, He cannot literally be a rock (Psalm 42:9), which is material. But we would not know what *is not* literally true of God unless we first know what *is* literally true.

For example, if it were not literally true that God is pure Spirit and infinite, then we would not be able to say that certain things attributed to God elsewhere in the Bible are not literally true, such as having material body parts. When Jesus said "I am the true vine" (John 15:1), the literal method of interpretation does not take this as physically true. Rather, we understand this as a figure of speech that communicates that believers derive their spiritual life from Christ, our spiritual vine. It is important to understand all this because apocalyptic literature, such as the books of Daniel and Revelation, make heavy use of figures of speech.

I grant that it may sometimes be difficult to determine when a passage should not be taken literally, but certain guidelines are helpful in making this determination. Briefly put, a text should be taken figuratively...

- when it is *obviously* figurative, as when Jesus said He was a door (John 10:9)
- when the text itself authorizes the figurative sense, as when Paul said he was using an allegory (Galatians 4:24)
- when a literal interpretation would contradict other truths inside or outside the Bible, as when the Bible speaks of the "four corners of the earth" (Revelation 7:1).

In short, as the famous dictum puts it, "When the literal sense makes good sense, seek no other sense, lest it result in nonsense."

How does the literal method of interpreting Scripture deal with Jesus' parables, many of which address prophetic issues?

Jesus often used parables that are not to be taken literally. Yet, there is always a literal point that each parable conveys. That Jesus wanted His parables to be clear to those who were receptive is evident in the fact that He carefully interpreted two of them for the disciples—the parable of the sower (Matthew 13:3-9) and the parable of the weeds (13:24-30). He did this not only so there would be no uncertainty as to their correct meaning, but also to guide believers in properly interpreting the other parables. The fact that Christ did not interpret His subsequent parables indicates that He fully expected believers to understand the literal truths intended by His parables by following the methodology He illustrated for them. I will address some of these parables a bit later in the book.

What are some good interpretive principles to keep in mind as we study prophecy?

Aside from what I've already stated in this chapter, five additional principles have guided me through the years:

Submit all "preunderstandings" to Scripture. Theological "preunderstandings"—doctrinal opinions we have previously formed—should not bias our interpretation of Scripture. Of course, all interpreters are influenced to some degree by personal, theological, denominational, and political prejudices. None of us approaches Scripture in a "chemically pure" state. For this reason, preunderstandings must be in harmony with Scripture and subject to correction by it. Only those preunderstandings that are compatible with Scripture are legitimate.

Pay close attention to the context. Every word in the Bible is part of a sentence; every sentence is part of a paragraph; every paragraph is part of a book; and every book is part of the whole of Scripture. The interpretation of a specific passage must not contradict the total teaching of Scripture on a topic. Individual verses do not exist as isolated fragments but as parts of a whole. The exposition of these verses, therefore, must involve understanding them in right relation both to the whole and to each other. Scripture interprets Scripture.

Consult history and culture. The interpreter of Scripture must seek to step out of his Western mindset and into an ancient Jewish mindset, paying special attention to such things as Jewish marriage rites, burial rites, family practices, farm practices, business practices, the monetary system, methods of warfare, slavery, the treatment of captives, the use of covenants, and religious practices. Armed with such detailed historical information, correctly interpreting the Bible becomes a much easier task because we better understand the world of the biblical writers.

Keep the "law of double reference" in mind. According to the law of double reference, prophetic Scripture may refer to two events separated by a significant time period but seemingly blended into one picture, masking the intervening time period. While the time gap is not evident within that particular text, the gap becomes clear in consultation with other verses.

An example is Zechariah 9:9-10, which refers to both the first and second comings of Jesus Christ: "Rejoice greatly, O daughter of Zion! Shout aloud, O daughter of Jerusalem! Behold, your king is coming to you; righteous and having salvation is he, humble and mounted on a donkey, on a colt, the foal of a donkey…He shall speak peace to the nations; his rule shall be from sea to sea, and from the River to the ends of the earth." The first part of this passage deals with Jesus' first coming ("having salvation…mounted on a donkey"), while the latter part of the passage deals with Christ's second coming and subsequent millennial kingdom ("his rule shall be from sea to sea").

Always be watching for insights about Jesus. From beginning to end, from Genesis to Revelation, the Bible is a Jesus book. Jesus once told some Jews, "You search the Scriptures because you think that in them you have eternal life; and it is they that bear witness about me, yet you refuse to come to me that you may have life" (John 5:39-40). The Jews to whom Jesus spoke knew the shell of the Bible but were neglecting the kernel within it. It is not the Book that saves but the Savior of the Book.

We must ever keep before our minds that Jesus said the Scriptures were "concerning himself" (Luke 24:27), were "written about me" (verse 44), and were "written of me" (Hebrews 10:7). So always be watching for Jesus as you study Bible prophecy. And as you study, *let Jesus be exalted in your heart!*

4

Understanding the Book of Revelation

Why did the apostle John write the book of Revelation?

John had been imprisoned on the isle of Patmos, in the Aegean Sea, for the crime of sharing Jesus Christ with everyone he came into contact with (Revelation 1:9). It was on this island that John received a revelation from God. The book was apparently written around AD 95.

The original recipients of the book were Christians who lived some 65 years after Jesus had been crucified and resurrected from the dead. Many of these were second generation Christians, and the challenges they faced were great. Life as a Christian had become increasingly difficult because of Roman hostilities toward Christianity.

The recipients of the book were suffering persecution, and some of them were even being killed (Revelation 2:13). Unfortunately, things were about to get even worse. John therefore wrote this book to give his readers a strong hope that would help them patiently endure in the midst of relentless suffering.

At the time, it seemed like evil was prevailing at every level. However, Revelation indicates that evil will one day come to an end. Sin, Satan, and suffering will be forever banished in heaven. For believers, there will be no further sorrow or death, and fellowship with God will be perpetual and uninterrupted. This was good news for the suffering church back in John's day. It's good news for our day too!

In what way is the book of Revelation a "revelation"?

The opening words of the book label it as "the revelation of Jesus Christ" (Revelation 1:1). The word "revelation" carries the idea of "uncovering" or "revealing." The book uncovers and reveals prophetic truth.

The phrase "revelation of Jesus Christ" can refer to revelation that *comes from* Jesus Christ or a revelation that is *about* Him. It seems likely that both senses may be intended in this verse.

Why is the book of Revelation classified as "apocalyptic literature"?

Apocalyptic literature is a special kind of writing that arose among the Jews and Christians in Bible times to reveal certain mysteries about heaven and earth, especially regarding the world to come. This type of literature is often characterized by visions, the necessity of making ethical and moral decisions or changes as a result of such visions, and a pervasive use of symbols. The symbols in the book of Revelation are either defined in the context of Revelation or are found in or alluded to in the Old Testament.

Certain themes are common to apocalyptic literature. These include: (1) a growing sense of hopelessness as wicked powers grow in strength; (2) the promise that the sovereign God will intervene; (3) heavenly visions, which provide readers with a heavenly perspective that helps them endure present suffering; (4) the intervention of God in overcoming and destroying evil; (5) the call to believers to live righteously; (6) the call to persevere under trial; and (7) God's final deliverance and restoration, with the promise to dwell with His people. We see such themes illustrated throughout the book of Revelation.

In what way does the book of Revelation bring a special blessing to those who read it (Revelation 1:3)?

Revelation is the *only* book in the Bible that promises a blessing to the person who reads it and responds to it in obedience. There are seven specific pronouncements of blessing in the book (1:3; 14:13; 16:15; 19:9; 20:6; 22:7,14). The word "blessed" means "spiritually happy." Those who read Revelation are spiritually happy because they come to see that God controls human history—and that in the end, believers will enjoy a blessed eternity in heaven.

What is the historicist approach to the book of Revelation?

The historicist approach holds that the book of Revelation provides a panoramic sweep of church history from the first century to the second coming of Christ. This approach emerged in the fourth century AD when some interpreters saw parallels between current events and the prophecies in Revelation. Later, Joachim of Fiore (1135–1202) developed the approach by dividing history into three primary ages. Still later, some of the Reformers were attracted to this model, viewing the Roman Catholic pope as the antichrist of Revelation 13.

Among the shortcomings of this view is that a comparison of the prophecies in Revelation with other prophetic Scriptures—for example, Daniel 9:25-27; Matthew 24–25; 1 Thessalonians 4:13–5:11; 2 Thessalonians 2:1-12; and Titus 2:13-14—reveals that these prophecies point to the future tribulation period, the antichrist, the second coming, Christ's millennial kingdom, the great white throne judgment, and the eternal state.

Another problem with historicism is that this model has led to endless speculation and subjectivity in dealing with specific details in the book of Revelation. It is difficult if not impossible to arrive at a consensus in identifying people and events in Revelation. Historicist interpreters tend to view the events of their own day as relating to prophecies in the book.

What is the idealist approach to the book of Revelation?

The idealist approach holds that the book of Revelation contains a symbolic description of the ongoing battle between God and the devil, between good and evil. In this view, Revelation does not relate to any historical or future events at all.

The problem with this understanding of Revelation is that it would not likely bring any genuine comfort to the original recipients of the book, who were suffering through great persecution and martyrdom under the Romans. A more literal understanding of Revelation—one that points to God's absolute control of human history with a blissful afterlife for believers—is much more satisfactory in this regard.

Furthermore, idealism ignores the specific time markers within the book. For example, John is instructed to "write therefore the things that you have seen, those that are and those that are to take place after this" (Revelation 1:19). Such words indicate a definite sequence of events. We also read of time-limited events in Revelation. For example, the holy city is to be trampled for "forty-two months"—which is three and a half years (11:2). The Jewish remnant is to find refuge in the wilderness for "1,260 days"—which again is three and a half years (12:6). These Jews will be "nourished" in the wilderness for "a time, and times, and half a time" (12:14). "Time" is one year, "times" is two years, and "half a time" is half a year, totaling up to three and a half years. Idealism ignores such time-delimited events in Revelation.

The idealist may rebut that there are many symbols in the book of Revelation. That is true. However, as we have seen, these symbols are often defined in the immediate context (Revelation 1:20; 5:8; 17:15). They typically point to real personalities and real events. The idealist approach fails to account for this.

What is the futurist approach to the book of Revelation?

The futurist approach to interpreting the book of Revelation holds that most of the events described in the book will take place in the end times, just prior to the second coming of Jesus Christ. This view honors the book's claim to be prophecy (see Revelation 1:3; 22:7,10,18-19). Moreover, as noted previously, Jesus informed John that "I will show you what must take place *after this*" (Revelation 4:1). The events that "take place after this" pertain to futuristic prophecy.

This view holds that just as the more than 100 prophecies of the first coming of Christ were fulfilled literally, so the prophecies of the second coming, and the events that lead up to it and follow it, will be fulfilled just as literally. Futurists believe, based on a literal interpretation, that there will one day be a literal tribulation period with literal judgments and a literal antichrist, followed by a literal second coming and a literal millennial kingdom (see Daniel 9:25-27; Matthew 24–25; 1 Thessalonians 4:13–5:11; 2 Thessalonians 2:1-12; Titus 2:13-14).

The early church took a futurist view of the book inasmuch as it saw the tribulation, second coming, and millennium as yet-future events.

Later writers who took a futurist approach include Francisco Ribera (1537–1591) and John Nelson Darby (1800–1882). As we examine specific prophecies throughout Revelation, we will see that a futurist approach makes very good sense.

What is the preterist approach to the book of Revelation?

The word "preterism" derives from the Latin *preter*, meaning "past." In this view, the prophecies in the book of Revelation (especially chapters 6–18) and Matthew 24–25 (Christ's Olivet Discourse) have already been fulfilled. More specifically, the prophecies were fulfilled in AD 70 when Titus and his Roman warriors overran Jerusalem and destroyed the Jewish temple. Hence, the book of Revelation does not deal with the future.

Are there different kinds of preterism?

There are two forms of preterism—moderate (partial) preterism, and extreme (full) preterism. Moderate preterism is represented by modern writers such as R.C. Sproul, Hank Hanegraaff, and Gary DeMar. While they believe the literal resurrection and second coming are yet future, the other prophecies in Revelation and Matthew 24–25, including prophecies about the antichrist, were fulfilled when Jerusalem fell in AD 70 (some relate the antichrist to General Titus). Extreme or full preterism goes so far as to say that all New Testament predictions were fulfilled in the past, including those of the resurrection and second coming.

What's the problem with preterism?

A primary problem with preterism is that Revelation claims to be prophecy (see Revelation 1:3; 22:7,10,18-19). Also against preterism are the many key events described in the book of Revelation that simply did not occur in AD 70. For example, in AD 70 "a third of mankind" was not killed as predicted in Revelation 9:18. An invasion of 200 million soldiers from the East did not occur as predicted in Revelation 9:13-15. Nor has "every living thing died that was in the sea" as predicted in Revelation 16:3. In order to explain these and many other such texts, preterists must resort to an allegorical interpretation of prophecy.

How does the dating of the book of Revelation relate to preterism?

Preterists often claim that the book of Revelation was written prior to AD 70, and hence the book must have been fulfilled in AD 70 when Rome overran Jerusalem. Futurists point out, however, that some of the earliest Church Fathers confirmed a late date (AD 90 or later), including Irenaeus who claimed the book was written at the close of the reign of Domitian (about AD 96). Victorinus confirmed this date in the third century, as did Eusebius (263–340). Since the book was written well after AD 70, it could hardly have been referring to events that would be fulfilled in AD 70. This deals a significant blow to preterism.

What is the eclectic approach to understanding the book of Revelation?

The eclectic view mixes and combines the features of all the other views. It says there is both a present and a future fulfillment of the prophecies contained in Revelation. Or perhaps some of the events described in the book were fulfilled in the past while others will be fulfilled in the future. This is not a widely held view.

Are there any contextual clues in the book of Revelation regarding how the book is to be understood?

Yes. We discover a contextual outline of John's prophetic book in Revelation 1:19—and it supports a futurist approach to understanding Revelation. The Lord instructs John: "Write therefore the things that you *have seen*, those *that are* and those that are to *take place after this*." The "things that you have seen" is a reference to Revelation 1, where we find a description of Jesus in His present majestic glory and an introduction to the book of Revelation. The things "that are" relates to the then-present circumstances of the seven churches of Asia Minor recorded in Revelation 2 and 3. John directed his book to these seven churches. The things "that are to take place after this" refers to futuristic prophecy of the tribulation period, the second coming, the millennial kingdom, the great white throne judgment, and the eternal state described in Revelation 4 through 22.

Does Matthew 16:28 support preterism?

In Matthew 16:28 Jesus affirms to His disciples, "There are some standing here who will not taste death until they see the Son of Man coming in his kingdom." Preterists claim that prophecies of the second coming must have been fulfilled during that generation—apparently in a metaphorical way in AD 70 when Rome overran Jerusalem.

Contrary to the preterist view, many evangelicals believe that when Jesus said this, He had in mind the transfiguration, which happened precisely one week later (Matthew 17:1-13). The transfiguration served as a preview of the kingdom in which the divine Messiah would appear in glory. Moreover, against the idea that this verse refers to AD 70 is the pivotal fact that among the disciples, all but John had been martyred by AD 70 and hence wouldn't have been around to witness the events of AD 70.

Does Matthew 24:34 support preterism?

In Matthew 24:34 Jesus asserts, "This generation will not pass away until all these things take place." Preterists claim this verse proves the prophecies would soon be fulfilled.

Contrary to this view, many evangelicals believe Christ was simply saying that those people who witness the signs stated earlier in Matthew 24—the abomination of desolation (verse 15); the great tribulation, such as has never been seen before (verse 21); and the sign of the Son of Man in heaven (verse 30)—will see the coming of Jesus Christ within *that* very generation. Since it was common knowledge among the Jews that the future tribulation period would last only seven years (Daniel 9:24-27), it is obvious that those living at the beginning of this time would likely live to see the second coming seven years later (except for those who lose their lives during this tumultuous time).

Other evangelicals hold that the word "generation" is to be understood in its basic usage of "race," "kindred," "family," "stock," or "breed."

If this is what is meant, then Jesus is here promising that the nation of Israel will be preserved, despite terrible persecution during the tribulation, until the consummation of God's program for Israel at the second coming. Many divine promises have been made to Israel, including land promises (Genesis 12; 15; 17) and a future Davidic kingdom (2 Samuel 7). Jesus could thus be referring to God's preservation of Israel in order to fulfill the divine promises to the Jews (see Romans 11:11-27). Whichever view is correct, the verse is perfectly compatible with futurism.

What about Revelation 22:12,20, where Jesus says, "I am coming soon"?

The Greek word for "soon" often carries the meaning "swiftly," "speedily," "at a rapid rate." For example, in Luke 18:7-8, Jesus stated, "Will not God give justice to his elect, who cry to him day and night? Will he delay long over them? I tell you, he will give justice to them *speedily.*" In the context of Revelation 22, it appears that the term indicates that when the predicted events of the tribulation period first start to occur, they will progress speedily, in rapid succession.

The Greek word can also mean "suddenly." The catastrophic events described in Revelation may descend upon humanity suddenly, taking them off guard.

Both usages of the Greek word are perfectly compatible with futurism.

Questions on Millennialism

The book of Revelation teaches that following the second coming of Christ, He will personally set up His kingdom on earth. In theological circles, this is known as the millennial kingdom. The primary passage on this kingdom is Revelation 20:1-6 (see also Psalm 2:6-9; Isaiah 65:18-23; Jeremiah 31:12-14,31-37; Ezekiel 34:25-29; 37:1-13; 40–48; Daniel 2:35; 7:13-14; Joel 2:21-27; Amos 9:13-14; Micah 4:1-7; Zephaniah 3:9-20).

The nature of the millennial kingdom is an issue of great debate among Christians. The debate is largely rooted in what hermeneutical approach one uses in interpreting the prophetic texts involved. Those who take an allegorical approach to Revelation 20:2-7 (and other passages) generally uphold amillennialism or postmillennialism. Those who take a more literal approach embrace premillennialism. If these are foreign words to you, fear not. I explain them below.

What is the biblical case for premillennialism?

Premillennialism teaches that following the second coming, Christ will institute a kingdom of perfect peace and righteousness on earth that will last for 1000 years. Two forms of premillennialism have emerged. Dispensational premillennialism, championed by scholar John F. Walvoord (1910–2002) among others, draws a distinction between the church and Israel and holds that the millennium will be a time of fulfillment of unconditional promises made to Israel. Historic premillennialism, espoused by George Eldon Ladd (1911–1982) among others, more generally rests its case on a literal interpretation of Revelation 20:1-6.

Among the biblical arguments offered in favor of premillennialism are that this view...

- naturally emerges from a literal interpretation
- best explains the unconditional land promises made to Abraham and his descendants (the Jews), which are yet to be fulfilled (Genesis 13:14-18)
- makes the best sense of the unconditional Davidic covenant, which promises that one of David's descendants (Jesus) will reign on a throne in Jerusalem (2 Samuel 7:12-16)
- is most compatible with numerous Old Testament predictions about the coming messianic age (millennial kingdom)
- is consistent with the Old Testament ending with an expectation of the messianic kingdom (for example, Isaiah 9:6; 16:5; Malachi 3:1)

- best explains the scriptural teaching that Jesus and the apostles would reign on thrones in Jerusalem in the future (Matthew 19:28; 25:31-34; Acts 1:6-7)

- is most consistent with the apostle Paul's promise that Israel will one day be restored by God (Romans 9:3-4; 11:1)

Since a plain (literal) reading of Scripture naturally leads to this view, and since this view makes perfectly good sense, I see no good reason to allegorize Revelation 20:1-6 (the primary passage about the millennial kingdom). Many throughout church history have held to premillennialism, including Church Fathers Justin Martyr (AD 100–165), Clement of Alexandria (150–215), and Tertullian (155–225). Augustine (354–430), early in his theological career, held to this view. Other theological luminaries who held to this view include John Nelson Darby (1800–1882), Griffith Thomas (1861–1924), Lewis Sperry Chafer (1871–1952), and James Montgomery Boice (1938–2000).

What is the biblical case for amillennialism?

Amillennialism takes a spiritualized approach in interpreting biblical prophecy. It teaches that when Christ comes, eternity will begin with no prior literal thousand-year reign of Christ on earth. "Amillennial" literally means "*no* millennium." Instead of believing in a literal rule of Christ on earth, amillennialists typically interpret prophetic verses related to the reign of Christ metaphorically and say they refer to Christ's present (spiritual) rule from heaven. Old Testament predictions made to Israel are viewed as being spiritually fulfilled in the New Testament church.

The following arguments are suggested in favor of amillennialism:

- The Abrahamic and Davidic covenants were conditional, and hence do not require a future fulfillment because the conditions were not met. (Premillennialists rebut that these covenants were *unconditional*, resting upon God alone for their fulfillment.)

- Prophecy should be interpreted symbolically, for apocalyptic literature is highly symbolic in nature.

(Premillennialists rebut that prophesy ought to be interpreted literally, for all the prophecies dealing with the first coming of Christ [over 100] were fulfilled literally. Though there are symbols in Revelation and Daniel, these symbols point to literal truths, and Scripture itself guides us in how to interpret them.)

- Israel and the church are not two distinct entities but rather one people of God united by the covenant of grace. (Premillennialists rebut that the church and Israel are viewed as distinct all throughout the New Testament [for example, 1 Corinthians 10:32, Romans 9:6, and Hebrews 12:18-24].)

- This view is most compatible with the idea that the Old Testament is fulfilled in the New Testament. (Premillennialists rebut that the Old Testament promises to Israel were unconditional and await a future fulfillment. God does not break His promises!)

This view was held by the later Augustine, as well as by Reformers Martin Luther (1483–1546) and John Calvin (1509–1564). Most Puritans were amillennial, as are most Roman Catholics. Famous proponents of the view in more recent history include Oswald Allis (1880–1973), Louis Berkhof (1873–1957), and Anthony Hoekema (1913–1988).

There is much debate on amillennialism. My approach has always been rather simple: When the plain sense makes good sense, seek no other sense lest you end up in nonsense. To me, premillennialism makes great sense. I see no justification for allegory-rich amillennialism.

What is the biblical case for postmillennialism?

The postmillennial view also takes a spiritualized approach in interpreting biblical prophecy. It teaches that through the church's progressive influence, the world will be Christianized before Christ returns. The millennium will involve a "thousand years" of peace and prosperity that precedes Christ's physical return. (The "thousand years" is viewed as a metaphor for a very long time period.) Famous proponents of this view include A.A. Hodge (1823–1886), B.B. Warfield (1851–1921), A.H. Strong (1836–1921), Loraine Boettner (1932–2000), and R.J. Rushdoony (1916–2001).

The following arguments are suggested in favor of postmillennialism:

- A universal proclamation of the gospel is promised in Scripture (Matthew 28:18-20).
- People from all nations will come to salvation (Revelation 7:9-10).
- Christ's throne is in heaven, and it is from this throne—not a throne on earth—that He rules (see Psalm 9:7; 11:4; 47:8; 103:19).
- Jesus' parable of the mustard seed indicates there will be a continual advance of Christianity in the world (Matthew 13:31-32).
- World conditions are improving morally, socially, and spiritually—all due to the church's influence.

Premillennialists challenge each of these points. For example, it hardly seems that the world is getting better and better. In fact, the world seems to be plummeting ever deeper into sin, darkness, and utter apathy toward God. Moreover, postmillennialism seems to contradict clear biblical passages that predict a massive apostasy in the end times prior to Christ's return (Matthew 24:3-14; Luke 18:8; 1 Timothy 4:1-5; 2 Timothy 3:1-7). Further, the unconditional Davidic covenant and other biblical passages clearly point to a *literal* future reign of Christ on earth (2 Samuel 7). Finally, it requires a leap in logic to claim that simply because there will be a universal proclamation of the gospel prior to the Lord's return (Matthew 28:18-20) that this means the world will get better and better, and that the world will be Christianized. The truth is that despite this universal proclamation, many will continue to reject it. (Any who doubt this should take a hard look at Jesus' sobering words in Matthew 7:13-14.)

I believe premillennialism best reflects the teachings of Scripture on the millennial kingdom.

5

The Covenants and Biblical Prophecy

What is a covenant?

A covenant is simply an agreement between two parties. Covenants were used among the ancients in the form of treaties or alliances between nations (1 Samuel 11:1), treaties between individual people (Genesis 21:27), friendship pacts (1 Samuel 18:3-4), and agreements between God and His people.

In the Bible, God made specific covenant promises to a number of people. These include Noah (Genesis 9:8-17), Abraham (Genesis 15:12-21; 17:1-14), the Israelites at Mount Sinai (Exodus 19:5-6), David (2 Samuel 7:8-16; 23:5), and God's people in the new covenant (Hebrews 8:6-13).

What does the Bible say about God being a promise keeper?

Numbers 23:19 asserts, "God is not man, that he should lie, or a son of man, that he should change his mind. Has he said, and will he not do it? Or has he spoken, and will he not fulfill it?" Prior to his death, an aged Joshua declared, "I am about to go the way of all the earth, and you know in your hearts and souls, all of you, that not one word has failed of all the good things that the LORD your God promised concerning you. All have come to pass for you; not one of them has failed" (Joshua 23:14). Solomon later likewise proclaimed, "Blessed be the LORD who has given rest to his people Israel, according to all that he promised. Not one word has failed of all his good promise, which he spoke by Moses his servant" (1 Kings 8:56; see also Joshua 21:45). *God truly is faithful!*

What is the Abrahamic covenant, and what is its significance to Bible prophecy?

God made a very famous covenant with Abraham (Genesis 12:1-3; 15:18-21), and it was later reaffirmed with both Isaac (17:21) and Jacob (35:10-12). In this covenant, God promised to make Abraham's descendants His own special people. More specifically, God promised Abraham: (1) I will make you a great nation; (2) I will bless you; (3) I will make your name great; (4) You will be a blessing; (5) I will bless those who bless you; (6) I will curse those who curse you; (7) All peoples on earth will be blessed through you; and (8) I will give you the land of Canaan.

Were God's promises in the Abrahamic covenant unconditional?

Yes. As a backdrop, there were two kinds of covenants in biblical days: conditional and unconditional. A conditional covenant was enacted with an "if" attached. This type of covenant demanded that the people meet certain obligations or conditions before God was obligated to fulfill what was promised. If God's people failed to meet the conditions, God was not obligated in any way to fulfill the promise.

An unconditional covenant depended on no such conditions for its fulfillment. There were no "ifs" attached. What was promised was sovereignly given to the recipient of the covenant apart from any merit (or lack thereof) on the part of the recipient. Some scholars refer to this type of covenant as a "unilateral covenant," a "one-sided covenant," or a "divine commitment covenant." The covenant God made with Abraham was unconditional, and was characterized by God's "I will," indicating that God was determined to do just as He promised.

According to ancient custom, the two parties of a conditional covenant would divide animals into two equal parts and then walk between the two parts, indicating that both were responsible to each other in mutually fulfilling the obligations of the covenant (see Jeremiah 34:18-19). In the case of the Abrahamic covenant, however, God alone passed between the animal parts after Abraham had been put into a deep sleep. This indicates that God made unconditional promises to Abraham in this covenant (Genesis 15:17).

What is the significance of the Davidic covenant to biblical prophecy?

God made a covenant with David in which He promised that one of his descendants would rule forever (2 Samuel 7:12-13; 22:51). This is another example of an unconditional covenant. It did not depend on David in any way for its fulfillment. David realized this when he received the promise from God, and he responded with an attitude of humility and a recognition of God's sovereignty over the affairs of humankind.

The three key words of the covenant are "kingdom," "house," and "throne." Such words point to the political future of Israel. The word "house" here carries the idea of "royal dynasty." This covenant finds its ultimate fulfillment in Jesus Christ, who was born from the line of David (Matthew 1:1) and will one day rule on the throne of David in Jerusalem during the future millennial kingdom (Ezekiel 36:1-12; Micah 4:1-5; Zephaniah 3:14-20; Zechariah 14:3-11).

When the angel Gabriel appeared to Mary to inform her that she would give birth to the Messiah, he told her, "The Lord God will give to him the throne of his father David, and he will reign over the house of Jacob forever, and of his kingdom there will be no end" (Luke 1:32-33). To describe this future rule of Christ, Gabriel used three significant words: "throne," "house," and "kingdom." Notice that each of these words is found in the covenant God made with David in which God promised that one from David's line would rule forever (2 Samuel 7:16). Gabriel's words must have immediately brought these Old Testament promises to mind for Mary, a devout young Jew.

What is the new covenant?

The new covenant is an unconditional covenant God made with humankind in which He promised to provide for forgiveness of sin, based entirely on the sacrificial death and resurrection of Jesus Christ (Jeremiah 31:31-34). Under the old covenant, worshippers never enjoyed a sense of total forgiveness. Under the new covenant, however, Christ our High Priest made provisions for such forgiveness. When Jesus ate the Passover meal with the disciples in the upper room, He spoke of the cup as "the new covenant in my blood" (Luke 22:20; see also 1 Corinthians 11:25). Jesus has done all that is necessary for the forgiveness of sins by His once-for-all sacrifice on the cross. This new covenant is the basis for our relationship with God in the New Testament.

How does the classical covenant system of theology interpret biblical prophecy, including the prophetic elements in the covenants?

The classical covenant view rejects a strict literal interpretation of prophetic Scripture. Jesus is viewed as an allegorical fulfillment of Old Testament promises made to Israel, including the land promises in the Abrahamic covenant (Genesis 13:14-17) and the throne promises in the Davidic covenant (2 Samuel 7:12-16). The New Testament church is viewed as spiritual Israel, a continuation of Old Testament ethnic Israel. Hence, there will be no literal fulfillment of land promises (or other Old Testament prophecies) to Israel.

In my view, this theological model involves more *eisegesis* (reading a meaning into the text) than *exegesis* (deriving the meaning out of the text). A consistent use of the historical-grammatical method demands that the unconditional land and throne promises be literally fulfilled in Israel. Moreover, from the perspective of Jesus Christ Himself, the church was in no sense a continuation of Old Testament Israel; rather the church was yet future from the time He spoke (Matthew 16:18; see also Ephesians 3:1-10). It was the advent of the Holy Spirit on the day of Pentecost that inaugurated the church (Acts 2:1-12; 1 Corinthians 12:13). Let us not forget that the apostle Paul affirmed that national Israel will be restored before Christ returns in the end times (Romans 11:1-2,29).

How does the modified covenantal view deal with biblical prophecy?

The modified covenantal view rejects a strict literal interpretation of biblical prophecy, but it also modifies things a bit by allowing for a future literal fulfillment of land and throne promises made to Israel. There will allegedly be an initial spiritual fulfillment of these promises in the church, but the future will provide a more fully realized and literal fulfillment in which both Israel and the church share.

This view is built upon a faulty and inconsistent hermeneutic that ultimately allegorizes Old Testament promises made strictly to Israel (Genesis 13:14-17; 2 Samuel 7:12ff.). This view also fails to recognize the church's status as a "new creation" of God (2 Corinthians 5:17; Ephesians 3:3-5,9; Colossians 1:26-27).

What is dispensationalism, and how does it deal with biblical prophecy?

Dispensationalism is a system of theology that is characterized by (1) a consistent literal method of interpreting the Bible, (2) a clear distinction between Israel and the church, and (3) the glory of God as God's ultimate purpose in the world. The word "dispensation"—from the Greek *oikonomia* (meaning "stewardship")—refers to a distinguishable economy in the outworking of God's purpose.

This system of theology views the world as a household run by God. In this household, God delegates duties and assigns humankind certain responsibilities. If human beings obey God during that dispensation, God promises blessing; if humans disobey, He promises judgment. In each dispensation, we generally see (1) the testing of humankind, (2) the failure of humankind, and (3) judgment as a consequence. As things unfold, God provides progressive revelation of His plan for history.

The present dispensation is the church age. Prior to that was the dispensation of the law. A future dispensation is the millennial kingdom (see Ephesians 1 and 3; John 1:17; Romans 6:14; Galatians 3:19-25). These three dispensations might be categorized as Old Testament, New Testament, and kingdom.

Dispensationalism recognizes that God deals differently with people in different ages or economies, as illustrated in how God related to people in Moses' time, in our day, and in the future millennium.

What are all the dispensations in Scripture?

There are seven dispensations according to traditional dispensationalism:

1. *Innocence (Genesis 1:28–3:6)*. This dispensation relates to Adam and Eve until the time they fell into sin at the Fall.

2. *Conscience (Genesis 3:7–8:14)*. This dispensation describes the time between the Fall and Noah's flood (see Romans 2:15).

3. *Human Government (Genesis 8:15–11:9)*. Following the flood, God began a new dispensation when He instituted human government to mediate and restrain evil on the earth.

4. *Promise (Genesis 11:10–Exodus 18:27)*. This dispensation relates to God's call of Abraham and the specific promises God made to him and his descendants, both physical and spiritual.

5. *Law/Israel (Exodus 19–John 14:30)*. This dispensation is characterized by God's giving of the law to Israel as a guide to live by, governing every aspect of their lives. The law was not presented as a means of salvation. The law was temporary, lasting only until the coming of—*and fulfillment by*—Jesus Christ.

6. *Grace/Church (Acts 2:1–Revelation 19:21)*. In this dispensation, the rule of life in the church is grace.

7. *Kingdom (Revelation 20:1-16)*. This dispensation relates to Christ's future millennial kingdom, over which He will rule for 1000 years on the throne of David. The church will rule with Christ as His bride.

How is revised dispensationalism different from traditional dispensationalism?

Both traditional dispensationalism and revised dispensationalism use a literal hermeneutic in interpreting Bible prophecy, and thus both believe in a national fulfillment of the Abrahamic covenant for Israel. Traditional dispensationalists, however, hold that there are two new covenants—one for Israel (yet to be fulfilled) and one for the church (presently being fulfilled). As well, Israel and the church are viewed as two separate peoples with different destinies: one in heaven (the church) and the other on earth (Israel).

Revised dispensationalists, by contrast, hold that there is only one new covenant. While this new covenant has a later literal fulfillment in national Israel, it has a present application to the church. Even though revised dispensationalists see distinctives between Israel and the church, both are viewed as collectively composing one overall people of God who share in the spiritual redemption wrought by Christ.

What is progressive dispensationalism?

Progressive dispensationalism, an off-shoot of traditional dispensationalism, is somewhat open to allegorism in interpreting Bible prophecy in that it rejects the idea that there is a fixed objective meaning of the biblical text. Rather, it holds that a biblical text may have many meanings and we ought to seek a deeper understanding than the author's expressed meaning. This view also suggests that there will be a literal fulfillment of the Abrahamic, Davidic, and new covenants in ethnic Israel, but it also claims there is a present inaugural fulfillment of these covenants in the church.

There are a number of problems with this view. First, those who approach prophecy in such an allegorical way are inconsistent, for they approach the rest of Scripture in a literal fashion. Second, no objective criteria exist by which one can determine the alleged correct allegorical truth. Third, it goes against the precedent set by prophecies of Christ's first coming, all of which were fulfilled literally—including Christ being born of a virgin (Isaiah 7:14), in Bethlehem (Micah 5:2), from the line of Abraham (Genesis 15:1-6) and David (2 Samuel 7:12ff.).

What is your opinion on theological systems of interpretation?

I resonate most with the revised dispensational viewpoint. However, my goal is not to be a "faithful revised dispensationalist." My goal is to be a faithful *biblicist*. My allegiance is to the Scriptures, not to some man-made system of theology. To be fair, theological systems can be helpful in organizing the teachings of Scripture in a cohesive way. But we must always be about the business of testing our theological systems against Scripture. *Scripture alone* has authority, for it came to us from God.

6

The Distinction Between the Church and Israel

What is the universal church?

The universal church consists of born-again believers who comprise the ever-enlarging universal body of Christ over whom He reigns as Lord. Although the members of the church may differ in age, sex, race, wealth, social status, and ability, they are all joined together as one people (Galatians 3:28). All of them share in one Spirit and worship one Lord (Ephesians 4:3-6). This body is comprised of only believers in Christ. The way one becomes a member of this universal body is to simply place faith in Christ (Acts 16:31; Ephesians 2:8-9). If you believe in Jesus, you're in.

The word "church" is translated from the Greek word *ekklesia*, which comes from two smaller words. The first is *ek*, which means "out from among." The second is *klesia*, which means "to call." Combining the two words, *ekklesia* means "to call out from among." The church consists of those God has called out from among the world. And those God has called come from all walks of life. All are welcome in Christ's church.

Did the church exist in Old Testament times?

No. In Matthew 16:18 Jesus specifically says that He "will build" His church (future tense). This indicates that at the moment He spoke these words, the church did not yet exist. Further, there is not a single reference to the church anywhere in the Old Testament. The church is portrayed as a new entity in the New Testament (see Ephesians 2:15).

In what ways are Israel and the church similar?

Both Israel and the church are part of the people of God. Both are part of God's spiritual kingdom. And both participate in the spiritual blessings of the Abrahamic and new covenants. Without minimizing the importance of such similarities, however, Israel and the church are also quite distinct in the New Testament.

How are Israel and the church distinct from each other?

Israel and the church are distinct in at least four notable ways:

1. While the roots of Israel predate Moses, the church began on the day of Pentecost (Acts 1:5; 1 Corinthians 12:13).

2. While Israel is an earthly political entity (Exodus 19:5-6), the universal church is the invisible spiritual body of Christ (Ephesians 1:3).

3. While Israel was composed of Jews, the church is composed of both Jews and Gentiles (see Ephesians 2:15). Although God has a distinct plan for national Israel, if an individual Jew places faith in Christ in the current church age, he or she is absorbed into the body of Christ, becoming part of the church (see Romans 10:12-13; Galatians 3:28).

4. One becomes a Jew by physical birth, whereas one becomes a member of the church via a spiritual birth through faith in Christ (John 3:3,16).

Why is it wrong to consider the New Testament church as spiritual Israel—a continuation of Old Testament ethnic Israel?

There are a number of good reasons that such a view is wrong:

1. In New Testament times, the church is clearly portrayed as distinct from Israel (see 1 Corinthians 10:32, Romans 9:6, and Hebrews 12:22-24). Thus, the church is not a continuation of Old Testament Israel.

2. A consistent use of the historical-grammatical method demands that the unconditional land and throne promises

of the Abrahamic and Davidic covenants be literally fulfilled in Israel (Genesis 13:1-7; 2 Samuel 7:12ff.).

3. From the perspective of Jesus Christ Himself, the church was in no sense a continuation of Old Testament Israel; rather the church was yet future from the time He spoke (Matthew 16:18; see also Ephesians 3:1-10). The advent of the Holy Spirit on the day of Pentecost inaugurated the church (Acts 2:1-12; 1 Corinthians 12:13).

4. Since every single believer in the church age is baptized into the body of Christ (1 Corinthians 12:13), the church age must have begun on the day of Pentecost, for this is the day when this phenomenon first occurred (Acts 2; see also 11:15-16).

5. The church is called a "mystery" that was not revealed to past generations, but was revealed for the first time in the New Testament era. This mystery involved the idea of uniting Jewish and Gentile believers in one spiritual body (see Ephesians 3:3-5,9; Colossians 1:26-27). This lends support to the idea that the church age began on the day of Pentecost. (While individual Jews may become members of the church by faith in Christ in the present age, God still has a future purpose for national Israel. This will become increasingly clear throughout the rest of the book.)

6. We are told in Ephesians 1:19-20 that the church is built on the foundation of Christ's resurrection, meaning that the church could not have existed in Old Testament times.

7. The church is called a "new man" in Ephesians 2:15, meaning it could not have existed in Old Testament times.

8. The apostle Paul was clear that national Israel will be restored before Christ returns in the end times (Romans 11:1-2,29).

When will the church age end?

The genesis of the church was clearly on the day of Pentecost, and ever since then, we've been living in the church age. This church age will last up till the time the church is raptured off the earth, with the dead in Christ being resurrected and all living believers on the earth being instantly translated into their resurrection bodies (1 Thessalonians 4:13-17; 1 Corinthians 15:50-58). I will provide evidence in this book that the rapture takes place prior to the seven-year tribulation period. During the tribulation, God will resume His special dealings with Israel (Daniel 9:26-27).

What is replacement theology?

Replacement theology asserts that the church is the new or true Israel that has permanently replaced or superseded Israel as the people of God. It claims that God has already fulfilled all His promises to ancient Israel and that the church is the only people of God today. This means that the rebirth of Israel in 1948 has virtually no prophetic significance. Of course, the facts I have shared above argue against this view.

Does Joshua 21:43-45 support replacement theology?

When Israel finally took possession of the land of milk and honey, it was in direct fulfillment of God's promise to the nation. As we read in Joshua 21:43-45:

> Thus the LORD gave to Israel all the land that he swore to give to their fathers. And they took possession of it, and they settled there. And the LORD gave them rest on every side just as he had sworn to their fathers. Not one of all their enemies had withstood them, for the LORD had given all their enemies into their hands. Not one word of all the good promises that the LORD had made to the house of Israel had failed; all came to pass.

Proponents of replacement theology argue that because God is said to have given the Israelites the land, God's land promises to Israel are completely fulfilled. After all, the text tells us that "not one word of all the good promises that the LORD had made to the house of Israel had failed; all came to pass." Such individuals thus believe that the modern state of Israel has no legitimate biblical basis. They claim it is not a fulfillment of biblical prophecy. All of God's land promises to Israel were fulfilled in the past.

Several pertinent points can be made in response to this theology. As Joshua 21:43-45 tells us, God did fulfill His part in giving the Israelites the promised land. Israel, however, *failed to take full possession* of what God had promised to the nation, and they *failed to dispossess* all the Canaanites, despite the fact that the gift of land had been made. It was there for the taking. God had faithfully done for Israel what He promised. Israel, by contrast, was not completely faithful. The Lord had not failed to keep His promise even though Israel had failed to fully conquer and enter into *all* the land.

The idea that there are no further land promises to be fulfilled for Israel is proven to be false by the many prophecies written far after the time of Joshua that speak of Israel possessing the land in the future (see, for example, Isaiah 60:18,21; Jeremiah 23:6; 24:5-6; 30:18; 31:31-34; 32:37-40; 33:6-9; Ezekiel 28:25-26; 34:11-12; 36:24-26; 37; 39:28; Hosea 3:4-5; Joel 2:18-29; Amos 9:14-15; Micah 2:12; 4:6-7; Zephaniah 3:19-20; Zechariah 8:7-8; 13:8-9). In fact, every Old Testament prophet except Jonah speaks of a permanent return to the land of Israel by the Jews. Also, although Israel possessed the land at the time of Joshua, it was later dispossessed, whereas the Abrahamic covenant promised Israel that she would possess the land *forever* (Genesis 17:8). Hence, the replacement interpretation of Joshua 21:43-45 is simply faulty.

Is replacement theology contrary to the teachings of the New Testament?

I believe so. As noted previously, the church and Israel are still seen to be distinct in the New Testament. For example, we are instructed in 1 Corinthians 10:32, "Do not cause anyone to stumble, whether Jews, Greeks [Gentiles] or the church of God" (insert added). The Jews and the church are distinct from each other. Moreover, Israel and the church are seen as distinct throughout the book of Acts, with the word "Israel" being used 20 times and the word "church" 19 times. Further,

Paul argues in Romans 9–11 that God is not finished with Israel; He still has a future for her. So any claim that the church replaces Israel is in error.

Does replacement theology go against a literal interpretation of biblical prophecy?

Yes, and that is an important point. After all, the prophecies that have already been fulfilled in Scripture—such as the Old Testament prophecies about the first coming of Jesus Christ—have been fulfilled literally. From the book of Genesis to the book of Malachi, the Old Testament abounds with anticipation of the coming Messiah. Multiple prophecies relate to His birth, life, ministry, death, resurrection, and glory (for example, Isaiah 7:14; Micah 5:2; Zechariah 12:10). That these prophecies of the first coming have been fulfilled literally gives us strong confidence to expect that the prophecies not yet fulfilled will also be fulfilled literally.

Eventually, Israel will finally (and wonderfully) come to recognize Jesus as the divine Messiah and come into full possession of the promised land. The fullness of this possession will be in the future millennial kingdom. At present, however, Israel's regathering to the land is only partial and Israel is yet in unbelief. This partial regathering in unbelief is setting the stage for Israel to eventually go through the tribulation period—the "time of Jacob's trouble" (Jeremiah 30:7)—during which a remnant of Israel will be saved (see Romans 9–11). Israel will then come into full possession of her promised land in the millennial kingdom.

7

Israel's Rebirth and Rising Anti-Semitism

Did God make prophetic land promises to Israel?

Yes. It all began with Abraham. Abraham's name means "father of a multitude." He lived around 2000 BC, originating from the city of Ur, in Mesopotamia, on the river Euphrates. He was apparently a very wealthy and powerful man.

God called Abraham to leave Ur and go to a new land—the land of Canaan, which God was giving to Abraham and his descendants (Genesis 11:31). Abraham left with his wife, Sarah, and his nephew, Lot. Upon arriving in Canaan, his first act was to construct an altar and worship God. This was typical of Abraham—God was of first importance to him.

God made a pivotal covenant with Abraham around 2100 BC. In this covenant, God made specific land promises to Abraham. We read in Genesis 15:18-21: "On that day the LORD made a covenant with Abram, saying, 'To your offspring I give this land, from the river of Egypt to the great river, the river Euphrates, the land of the Kenites, the Kenizzites, the Kadmonites, the Hittites, the Perizzites, the Rephaim, the Amorites, the Canaanites, the Girgashites and the Jebusites.'" These are very specific territories.

Were the land promises repeated after Abraham's time?

Yes. The land promises originally made to Abraham were then passed down through Isaac's line. In Genesis 26:3-4 the Lord said to Isaac: "Sojourn in this land, and I will be with you and will bless you, for to you and to your offspring I will give all these lands, and I will

establish the oath that I swore to Abraham your father. I will multiply your offspring as the stars of heaven and will give to your offspring
all these lands. And in your offspring all the nations of the earth shall
be blessed."

The land promises then passed from Isaac to Jacob. The Lord said to
Jacob, "I am the LORD, the God of Abraham your father and the God
of Isaac. The land on which you lie I will give to you and to your offspring. Your offspring shall be like the dust of the earth, and you shall
spread abroad to the west and to the east and to the north and to the
south, and in you and your offspring shall all the families of the earth
be blessed" (Genesis 28:13-14).

God's covenant land promises are affirmed still later in the Bible.
For example, in Psalm 105:8-11 we read that God "remembers his covenant forever, the word that he commanded, for a thousand generations, the covenant that he made with Abraham, his sworn promise
to Isaac, which he confirmed to Jacob as a statute, to Israel as an everlasting covenant, saying, 'To you I will give the land of Canaan as your
portion for an inheritance.'"

The fact that God regularly repeated these land promises to the
Jews indicates they are a sure thing! God's covenant with Abraham is
an "everlasting covenant."

What does Bible prophecy specifically say about the rebirth of Israel in the end times?

When the modern state of Israel was born in 1948 as a self-
governing nation, it represented the beginnings of an actual fulfillment
of specific Bible prophecies about an international regathering of the
Jews in unbelief before the judgments of the tribulation period. This
regathering was to take place after centuries of exile in various nations
around the world.

In Ezekiel 36:10 God promised, "I will multiply people on you,
the whole house of Israel, all of it. The cities shall be inhabited and the
waste places rebuilt." God promised, "I will take you from the nations
and gather you from all the countries and bring you into your own
land" (36:24). In biblical times, Israel had been in bondage to single

nations, such as the Egyptians and the Babylonians, and in these cases, God delivered them after a time. But never in biblical history have the Israelites been delivered "from the nations" and "all the countries." This event did not find fulfillment until 1948 when Israel finally became a national entity again.

In the vision of dry bones in Ezekiel 37, the Lord is portrayed as miraculously bringing the bones back together into a skeleton, and the skeleton becomes wrapped in muscles and tendons and flesh, and God then breathes life into the body. There is no doubt that this chapter in Ezekiel is metaphorically speaking about Israel, for we read: "Son of man, these bones are the whole house of Israel" (verse 11). Hence, this chapter portrays Israel as becoming a living, breathing nation brought back from the dead, as it were.

In AD 70, Titus and his Roman warriors destroyed Jerusalem, definitively and thoroughly ending Israel as a political entity (see Luke 21:20). Since then, the Jews had been dispersed worldwide for many centuries. No one could have guessed that Israel would become a nation again. And yet it happened. Israel achieved statehood in 1948.

Have Jews continued streaming back to the holy land since 1948?

Yes. Joel Rosenberg explains:

> When Israel declared her independence on May 14, 1948, the country's population stood at only 806,000. Yet by the end of 2005, nearly 7 million people lived in Israel, 5.6 million of whom were Jewish. Thousands more arrive every year. In 2005 alone, some 19,000 Jews immigrated to Israel. Today more Jews live in the greater Tel Aviv area than in New York City, and as many Jews live in Israel as in the United States. It will not be long before the number of Jews who live in Israel will surpass the number of Jews who do not.[1]

It appears that the divine program of restoring Israel is in progress. Key elements in recent history include the following:

- *1881–1900:* About 30,000 Jews who had been persecuted in Russia moved to Palestine.

- *1897:* The goal of establishing a home in Palestine for Jewish people received great impetus when the First Zionist Congress convened in Basel, Switzerland, and adopted Zionism as a program.

- *1904–1914:* 32,000 more Jews who had been persecuted in Russia moved to Palestine.

- *1924–1932:* 78,000 Polish Jews moved to Palestine.

- *1933–1939:* 230,000 Jews who had been persecuted in Germany and central Europe moved to Palestine.

- *1940–1948:* 95,000 Jews who had been persecuted in central Europe moved to Palestine. Meanwhile, more than 6 million Jews were murdered by Adolf Hitler and Nazi Germany.

- *1948:* The new state of Israel was born.

- *1967:* Israel captured Jerusalem and the West Bank during the Six-Day War, which was precipitated by an Arab invasion.

In view of such facts, it would seem that since the late nineteenth century, God has been bringing gradual fulfillment to what He promised in Scripture. All eyes are on Israel and the Middle East at this time.

Though Israel is regathering to the holy land, aren't the Jews still in unbelief at this time?

Yes, and that's a very important point. Israel remains in unbelief—that is, the Jews do not believe in Jesus as their Messiah. But there is a day in the future, according to Joel 2:28-29, in which there will be a spiritual awakening in Israel. It would seem that Armageddon, at the very end of the tribulation period, will be the historical context in which Israel finally becomes converted (Zechariah 12:2–13:1). The restoration of Israel will include the confession of Israel's national sin (Leviticus

26:40-42; Jeremiah 3:11-18; Hosea 5:15), following which Israel will be saved, thereby fulfilling Paul's prophecy in Romans 11:25-27. In dire threat at Armageddon, Israel will plead for their newly found Messiah to return and deliver them ("they shall mourn for him, as one mourns for an only child"—Zechariah 12:10; Matthew 23:37-39; see also Isaiah 53:1-9), at which point their deliverance will surely come (see Romans 10:13-14). Israel's leaders will have finally realized the reason the tribulation has fallen upon them, perhaps due to the Holy Spirit's enlightenment of their understanding of Scripture (see 1 Corinthians 2:9–3:2). Later, in the millennial kingdom, Israel will experience a full possession of the promised land and the reestablishment of the Davidic throne (2 Samuel 7:5-17). It will be a time of physical and spiritual blessing based on the new covenant (Jeremiah 31:31-34).

Why do most Jews today continue to reject Jesus Christ as their Messiah?

Since the time of the Jewish rejection of Christ in the first century, Israel has experienced a judicial blindness and hardening as a judgment from God. The apostle Paul put it this way: "I do not want you to be unaware of this mystery, brothers: a partial hardening has come upon Israel, until the fullness of the Gentiles has come in [that is, until the full number of Gentiles who will be saved have become saved]" (Romans 11:25, insert added for clarification).

The backdrop is that the Jews in Israel had sought a relationship with God not by faith but by works (see Galatians 2:16; 3:2,5,10). Of course, attaining righteousness by observing the law requires that the law be kept perfectly (James 2:10), which no person is capable of doing. The Jews stumbled over the "stumbling stone," who is Jesus Christ (Romans 9:31-33). Jesus did not fit their preconceived ideas about the Messiah (Matthew 12:14,24), so they rejected Him. The result of this rejection is that a partial blindness and hardness has come upon Israel. Israel thus lost her favored position before God, and the gospel was then preached to the Gentiles, with a view to causing the Jews to become jealous and then become saved (Romans 11:11).

Since then, Gentiles who place faith in Jesus become a member of

God's church. Believing Jews also become members of God's church in the current age (see Ephesians 3:3-5,9; Colossians 1:26-27).

The good news is that Israel's hardening and casting off is only temporary. In dire threat at Armageddon, at the end of the tribulation period, the hardening will be removed, and Israel will finally recognize its Messiah and turn to Him for rescue from the invading forces of the antichrist (Zechariah 12:10; see also Romans 10:13-14). A remnant of Israel will be saved (Romans 11:25). Good news!

What does "prophetic postponement" mean?

The term "prophetic postponement" refers to the delay of the messianic program of redemption for the nation of Israel. Between the first and second comings of Jesus Christ, national Israel is subject to a judicial hardening (see Matthew 13:13-15; Mark 4:11-12; Luke 8:10; John 12:40; Acts 28:26-27; Romans 11:8-10). This prophetic postponement served to interrupt Israel's restoration as stipulated under the new covenant (Jeremiah 31:31-37). This postponement is illustrated in the interruption between the first 69 weeks of Daniel and the seventieth week, which is the future seven-year tribulation period (Daniel 9:26-27). However, at the end of the tribulation period, Israel will confess her sins and call out to her Messiah for deliverance at Armageddon. The Jewish remnant will be converted and restored. Israel will then experience the ultimate fulfillment of the land promises of the Abrahamic covenant and the throne promises of the Davidic covenant in Christ's 1000-year millennial kingdom, which follows the second coming of Christ (see Romans 9–11).

Is Israel's rebirth as a nation a "supersign" of the end times?

I believe that it is. After all, God's prophetic plan for the future hinges largely on Israel. Many of the other biblical prophecies of the end times relate in some way to Israel, and hence Israel must exist in order for these other prophecies to come to pass. Put another way, many of these other prophecies do not have meaning *until and unless* Israel is a nation. Hence, the year 1948 is extremely significant from a prophetic standpoint, for it was that year that Israel became a nation again.

To illustrate, one can ask: How can the antichrist sign a covenant with Israel, as prophesied in Daniel 9:26-27, unless Israel first exists as a nation again? How can the Jewish temple be rebuilt in the tribulation period unless Israel first exists as a nation again (Matthew 24:15)? (We could ask many similar questions.) Clearly, the rebirth of Israel is a super-sign, preparing the way for other prophecies to be fulfilled.

Why do Muslims today claim that God (Allah) gave the promised land to them?

Muslims claim that while the original Bible was the Word of God (the Word of Allah), and still retained its doctrinal purity by the time of Muhammad in the seventh century, it soon thereafter became corrupted by Jews and Christians. Since the time of Muhammad, the Bible has allegedly been infused with many "untruths." Hence, in today's Bible, the original and the fictitious, the divine and the human, are so intermingled that the grain cannot be separated from the chaff.

Muslims claim the Jews inserted many things into the Old Testament that served to benefit them. More specifically, Muslims claim that while they are the true and rightful heirs of the promises made to Abraham through Ishmael (who, they claim, gave rise to the Arab nations), the Jews, for personal gain, concocted a story that Isaac became Abraham's heir of the holy land promises and inserted it into the manuscript copies of the Old Testament. In this "falsified" Jewish version, Ishmael and his descendants became outcasts and thus have no right to the land. The original Old Testament, they say, did not have this concocted story. The land, by divine right, belongs to the Muslims.

Aside from Allah's alleged promise, modern Arabs claim a long and continuous residency in the land. Besides, the British MacMahon-Hussein Agreement promised the land to the Arabs back in the early 1900s. In view of such facts, modern "Palestinian authorities" say the existence of the "Zionist state" is the entire cause of the current Middle East conflict. The land belongs to the Arabs, they assert, and Israel cannot continue to exist.

What's the problem with this Muslim claim?

It is both inaccurate and unreasonable to claim that the Bible became corrupted soon after Muhammad's time. By the seventh century countless thousands of manuscript copies of the Bible were dispersed over a large part of the world. To successfully corrupt the Bible, all these copies would have to be meticulously gathered and then the changes made. Moreover, hundreds of years before Muhammad was even born, the Bible had already been translated into numerous languages. It is impossible to fathom that these various translations were identically altered all over the world so they would have a uniform corruption. While Muslims may not like to admit it, God's land promises to Abraham, Isaac, Jacob, and Israel have the support of countless thousands of reliable manuscript copies, many of which predate the time of Muhammad by centuries, some as early as the second century AD.

What are some of the key components in today's Middle East conflict?

While the Jews view Israel as the land of Jewish people, Arabs believe Palestine belongs to the Arabs. While Jews believe Israel includes both sides of the Jordan, including Transjordan (as stipulated in the Balfour Declaration of 1917 that recognized the Jewish people's right to a national home in the land of Israel), the Arabs have never accepted this.

Jews today seek to grant Jewish immigration and repatriation to all Jews who wish to repatriate. This is based on an important piece of legislation adopted by the new state of Israel called the "Law of Return"— a law that provides all Jews the legal right to immigrate to Israel and immediately become citizens if they so choose. The Arabs, by contrast, say Jewish immigration to Palestine must stop.

As a result of the ongoing conflict between the Israelis and Arabs, many Palestinians have been displaced and have taken up residence in refugee camps in Jordan, the West Bank, and Gaza. Today there are millions of Palestinian refugees. While Jews from anywhere in the world are welcomed as Israeli citizens in Israel, Palestinian refugees are prevented from becoming citizens in neighboring Arab countries— except for Jordan.

The Israelis are willing to participate in a limited way in solving the refugee problem, but they do not want to allow millions of unhappy Palestinians into the Jewish state who could later become allies with Arab nations seeking to attack Israel. The most they have been willing to do in the past is to allow a limited number of Palestinians to live outside of Israel proper, segregate the Jews and Palestinians by a perimeter wall, and demilitarize the Palestinian area.

Palestinians, by contrast, want permission to return to their former homes or be given compensation for choosing not to return. They claim Israel is not honoring the UN Security Council Resolutions 194 and 242, which grant repatriation and war reparations to the ousted Palestinians.

Resentment among Arabs and Muslims is very high today. The extremist Muslims want to "wipe Israel off the map." They want to destroy this "lesser Satan," along with the "greater Satan" that supports Israel—that is, the United States. The Middle East conflict continues to escalate, with no ultimate solution.

What is the Islamic Fatah, and how does it relate to Israel's rebirth as a nation?

Islamists view the entire existence of Israel as an aggression. The initial settlement in the land was illegitimate to start with, they say, for the Jews had no right to return or come back to a land under Islamic authority. Following the Islamic logic of the Fatah and of jihad, any territory that was at some time opened by a legitimate Islamic authority cannot revert to a non-Islamic authority. This means Israel cannot reemerge on Muslim land. It constitutes a grievous offense to Allah. Therefore the land must go back to the Muslims, and the Muslims won't rest until this becomes a reality.

What are some of the conflicting ideologies in the Middle East conflict?

Three conflicting ideologies are notable:

Zionism. Zionism gets its name from Mount Zion, the hill in ancient Jerusalem where King David's palace once stood. Zion became a symbol for Jerusalem during David's reign (see 2 Samuel 5:7). Zionism is another name for a type of Jewish nationalism that has the goal of reestablishing the Jewish ancestral homeland. It involves not just the idea that the Jews have returned to the land, but also the return of Jewish sovereignty to the ancestral homeland. Zionism, then, is essentially a national liberation movement of the Jewish people. Christians who uphold the right of the Jewish people to return to the land and establish an independent state are often referred to as Christian Zionists.

Arab Nationalism. Arab Nationalism emerged as a movement that seeks to unify Arabs as one people by appealing to a sense of their common history, culture, and language. This movement is secular, and seeks to gain and maintain Arab power in the Arab lands of the Middle East. Arab nationalists seek to end, or at least minimize, direct Western influence in the Arab world. As well, Israel is viewed as a cancerous tumor that must be removed.

Islamic Fundamentalism. Islamic fundamentalism is a radical and extremist religious philosophy that seeks to establish Islamic dominance in the Middle East and eventually the rest of the world. Israel, a symbol of Jewish power, is viewed as a grievous insult to Allah and cannot be allowed to exist in the Islamic world. Israel must therefore be pushed into the sea. The United States, Israel's ally, must also be destroyed.

Here, then, is a powder-keg formula: Zionism plus Arab nationalism plus Islamic fundamentalism equals hostile conflict.

Does the Bible prophesy that Israel will continue to be a sore spot in the world in the end times?

I believe so. In Zechariah 12:2 God affirms: "Behold, I am about to make Jerusalem a cup of staggering to all the surrounding peoples." The nations that surround Israel are Islamic. There's a lot of staggering in the Middle East these days. And most of those who stagger are anti-Semitic.

8

The Signs of the Times

Can we guesstimate dates for end time events?

It is unwise to even attempt it! Scripture reveals that no one can know the day or the hour of specific end-time events. In Matthew 24:36, Jesus Himself tells us, "Concerning that day and hour no one knows, not even the angels of heaven, nor the Son, but the Father only." Likewise, Jesus affirms in Acts 1:7: "It is not for you to know times or seasons that the Father has fixed by his own authority."

While date-setting is prohibited, the Lord Jesus did indicate that we can deduce that His coming is not far off: "From the fig tree learn its lesson: as soon as its branch becomes tender and puts out its leaves, you know that summer is near. So also, when you see all these things, you know that he is near, at the very gates" (Matthew 24:32-33).

The Lord lets us know we are in the end times via the "signs of the times."

What is meant by "signs of the times"?

The phrase "signs of the times" refers to specific characteristics or conditions that will exist in the end times, and when people on earth witness these, they can deduce that they are living in the end times. In a way, such signs might be considered God's "intel in advance." By the signs of the times, God gives us an intelligence report regarding what the world will look like as we enter into the end times.

Aren't certain signs of the times limited to the seven-year tribulation period?

Yes. Scripture reveals that certain signs will take place during the seven-year tribulation period. In Matthew 24:3, the disciples asked Jesus: "When will these things be, and what will be the sign of your coming and of the end of the age." In verses 4 and following, Jesus proceeds to speak of a number of signs of the times that will predominate in the years prior to the second coming, and these years unfold during the tribulation period.

Some might be tempted to think that the tribulation signs of the times are not relevant for us today since the rapture will apparently precede the tribulation. However, we are witnessing many events in the world that are setting the stage for the fulfillment of prophecies during the future tribulation period. Hence, any stage-setting that indicates the tribulation period may be drawing near is also an indication that the rapture of the church is even nearer.

Dr. John F. Walvoord, one of my former mentors at Dallas Theological Seminary, gave an illustration that helps us to understand all this. Walvoord compared the rapture to Thanksgiving and the second coming to Christmas. There are all kinds of signs—TV, radio, newspaper ads, manger scenes, lights, and decorations—that indicate Christmas is drawing near. The signs are everywhere. But Thanksgiving can sneak up on us. We really don't see obvious signs that Thanksgiving is approaching, but if Thanksgiving has not yet taken place, and we're seeing clear signs for the soon arrival of Christmas, we know that Thanksgiving is all the nearer. By analogy, as we witness the stage being set today for events that will transpire during the tribulation period in anticipation of the second coming of Christ, we can know that the rapture is indeed drawing near.

I believe that just as minor tremors (or foreshocks) often occur before major earthquakes, so preliminary manifestations of some of these signs are emerging prior to the tribulation period. Someone said that prophecies cast their shadows before them. I think this is true. Prophecies that relate specifically to the tribulation period are presently casting their shadows before them. The stage is now being set for their fulfillment.

Are there different kinds of "signs of the times"?

I believe so. To make the signs of the times more accessible to students of prophecy, I have come up with six categories: the rebirth of Israel sign, moral signs, religious signs, national alignment signs, earth-and-sky signs, and technological signs.

How is the rebirth of Israel a sign of the times?

In the previous chapter, I noted that Israel's rebirth is a *super*sign. This particular sign far precedes the tribulation period, but also sets the stage for it.

Scripture reveals that the Jews will be regathered from the "four corners of the earth" in the end times (Isaiah 11:12) after the nation is reestablished (Isaiah 66:7-8). God promised: "I will take you from the nations and gather you from all the countries and bring you into your own land" (Ezekiel 36:24). Notice that these verses do not say the Jews would be regathered from a single nation, as was the case in the Babylonian captivity. Rather, the Jews would be regathered from "the nations" and "all the countries" and be brought back to their own land.

This is what makes the year 1948 so significant, for it was this year that Israel achieved statehood. Then, in 1967, Israel captured Jerusalem and the West Bank during the Six-Day War. Jews have been returning to their homeland ever since. While we might call the present regathering of the Jews a "regathering in unbelief," a day is coming—I believe in immediate proximity to the second coming—where the Jews will finally recognize Jesus as the divine Messiah and call upon Him for deliverance from the armies gathered for Armageddon (Zechariah 12:10; Matthew 23:37-39; see also Isaiah 53:1-9), at which point their deliverance will surely come (see Romans 10:13-14).

Is the Middle East conflict also an indicator of the end times?

The entire Middle East has been an arena of conflict for over 60 years. Wars in the region include the War of Independence, which brought Israel's statehood (1947–1948), the Suez War/Sinai Campaign (1956), the Six-Day War (1967), the War of Attrition (1968–1970), the Yom Kippur/October War (1973), the Lebanese Civil War (1975–1976), the Iran-Iraq War (1980–1988), the Lebanon War (1982–1985), the Persian Gulf War (1991), the War with Iraq (1991–2003), and the War on Terror (2001 to present). Many wonder whether there will ever be peace in the Middle East.

Today many are crying out for a leader who can take control of world crises and solve the Middle East problem. This yearning for a solution to the Middle East problem is setting the stage for what is to come. For Scripture prophesies that the antichrist—the leader of a revived Roman Empire, a "United States of Europe"—will one day sign a covenant with Israel (Daniel 9:27). To the amazement of everyone, he will have solved the Middle East dilemma. Seen in this light, the Middle East conflict is an indicator of the end times.

What are some moral signs of the times?

Scripture speaks of moral signs that will emerge during the end times (Matthew 23:3). In 2 Timothy 3:1-5 we read:

> Understand this, that in the last days there will come times of difficulty. For people will be lovers of self, lovers of money, proud, arrogant, abusive, disobedient to their parents, ungrateful, unholy, heartless, unappeasable, slanderous, without self-control, brutal, not loving good, treacherous, reckless, swollen with conceit, lovers of pleasure rather than lovers of God, having the appearance of godliness, but denying its power. Avoid such people.

Notice that in the last days there will be *lovers of self* (we might call this humanism), *lovers of money* (we might call this materialism), and *lovers of pleasure* (we might call this hedonism). Humanism, materialism, and hedonism are three of the most prominent philosophies in our world today, and they often go together in a complementary fashion.

Related to this, Jesus Himself warned about the end times: "Because lawlessness will be increased, the love of many will grow cold...For as were the days of Noah, so will be the coming of the Son of Man. For as in those days before the flood they were eating and drinking, marrying and giving in marriage, until the day when Noah entered the ark, and they were unaware until the flood came and swept them all away, so will be the coming of the Son of Man" (Matthew 24:12,37-39). While this passage refers to the future tribulation period, we cannot help but see even in our own day the attitude Jesus described. People are merrily going about their way, seemingly without concern for the things of God.

What are some religious signs of the times?

Prophetic Scripture refers to many religious signs that will find fulfillment in the tribulation period and before. These include:

False Christs. In Matthew 24:24 Jesus Himself warned about the end times: "False christs and false prophets will arise and perform great signs and wonders, so as to lead astray, if possible, even the elect" (see also Mark 13:22). The apostle Paul also warned of a different Jesus (2 Corinthians 11:4). The danger, of course, is that a counterfeit Jesus who preaches a counterfeit gospel yields a counterfeit salvation (see Galatians 1:8). There are no exceptions to this maxim.

Even in our own day, we witness an unprecedented rise in false Christs and self-constituted messiahs affiliated with the kingdom of the cults and the occult. This will no doubt continue to escalate as we move further into the end times.

False prophets and teachers. Scripture contains many warnings against false prophets and false teachers for the simple reason that God's own people can be deceived (see Ezekiel 34:1-7; Matthew 7:15-16; Acts 20:28-30; 2 Corinthians 11:2-3). In view of this, the Bible exhorts believers to test those who claim to be prophets (see 1 John 4:1ff.).

False apostles. The apostle Paul warned of false apostles who are "deceitful workmen, disguising themselves as apostles of Christ" (2 Corinthians 11:13). The two key characteristics we see here are that these individuals (1) deceive people doctrinally, and (2) they pretend to be true apostles of Jesus Christ. Christ commends those who take a stand against false apostles (Revelation 2:2).

Increasing apostasy. Scripture prophesies a great end-times apostasy involving a massive defection from the truth (2 Thessalonians 2:3; see also Matthew 24:10-12). First Timothy 4:1-2 warns: "The

Spirit expressly says that in later times some will depart from the faith by devoting themselves to deceitful spirits and teachings of demons, through the insincerity of liars whose consciences are seared." Likewise, 2 Timothy 4:3-4 warns: "The time is coming when people will not endure sound teaching, but having itching ears they will accumulate for themselves teachers to suit their own passions, and will turn away from listening to the truth and wander off into myths." Can anyone doubt that we are witnessing such things in our day?

What are some examples of national alignment signs of the times?

Scripture reveals that in the end times a United States of Europe will emerge—a ten-nation confederacy that will constitute a revived Roman Empire (see Daniel 2:41-44; 7:7,23-24; Revelation 17:12-13). There will also be an end-times military coalition that arises against Israel that includes Russia, Iran, Sudan, Turkey, Libya, and other Muslim nations (Ezekiel 38–39).

When this northern military coalition moves against Israel, no other nation on earth will stand with Israel—not even the United States. It may be that America will weaken in the end times. This could be due to any number of possible factors, including a nuclear attack, an electromagnetic pulse (EMP) attack, implosion due to moral degeneracy, or perhaps even the rapture. It also seems likely that in the end times, America may become an ally with the revived Roman Empire.

In any event, we seem to be witnessing the setting of the stage for such alignments in our day. For example, the military coalition of Ezekiel 38–39 seems to be forming before our very eyes. And the present European Union (EU) may be the forerunner of a revived Roman Empire.

What are some earth-and-sky signs of the times?

Scripture reveals that in the future tribulation period (Matthew 23:3) there will be a great increase in frequency and intensity of earthquakes and signs in the heavens (Matthew 24:7). In Luke 21:11 we read: "There will be great earthquakes, and in various places famines and pestilences. And there will be terrors and great signs from heaven."

Such things are said to be "the beginning of the birth pains" (Matthew 24:8). Just as birth pangs increase in frequency and intensity, so these signs will do the same.

Signs in the heavens could include any number of things, including strange weather patterns, falling stars, a darkening of the moon and other celestial bodies (specifically during the tribulation period), and large bodies striking the earth. For example, in the context of the future tribulation period, we find reference to "wormwood" in Revelation 8:10-12:

> The third angel blew his trumpet, and a great star fell from heaven, blazing like a torch, and it fell on a third of the rivers and on the springs of water. The name of the star is Wormwood. A third of the waters became wormwood, and many people died from the water, because it had been made bitter. The fourth angel blew his trumpet, and a third of the sun was struck, and a third of the moon, and a third of the stars, so that a third of their light might be darkened, and a third of the day might be kept from shining, and likewise a third of the night.

Many believe this "star" will, in fact, be a case of near-extinction-level deep impact of a large meteor or an asteroid striking the earth. It has the appearance of a star because it bursts into flames—burning like a torch—as it plummets through earth's atmosphere. It turns a third of the waters bitter so that people who drink it die. This large volume of water may be contaminated by the residue from the disintegrating meteor as it blasts through earth's atmosphere. Or it may be that the meteor plummets into the headwaters from which some of the world's major rivers and underground water sources flow, thereby spreading the poisonous water to many people.

Some scholars have speculated that it may be this deep impact that ultimately causes a reduction in sunlight and other celestial bodies. Following this impact, a catastrophic level of earth-dust will be kicked up into the atmosphere for a significant time, thereby blocking light (see Revelation 8:12).

What are some technological signs of the times?

Certain technological advances must occur in order for some of the things prophesied in Scripture for the tribulation period to be possible. We might call these technological signs. Many prophecy scholars believe that the technology is now in place for these things to occur.

For example, Matthew 24:14 tells us that prior to the second coming of Christ, the gospel must be preached to every nation. With today's technology—satellites, the Internet, global media, translation technologies, publishing technologies, rapid transportation, and the like—this has never been more possible.

Another example relates to the mark of the beast. We do not know specifically what form this mark will take, but we do know that the false prophet will control who will be able to buy and sell, depending on whether they submit to worshipping the antichrist (Revelation 13:16-17). With today's satellites, the Internet, supercomputers, biometric identification procedures (hand scanners, retina scanners, facial recognition scanners), radio frequency identification (RFID) chips, and smart card technology, it would be easy for every selling establishment and every buyer to have a separate account number that would enable such control by the false prophet. This technology exists today!

Still further, there may be some evidence in Scripture that there will be nuclear detonations in the end times. Revelation 8:7 tells us that "a third of the earth was burned up, and a third of the trees were burned up, and all the green grass was burned up." Moreover, Revelation 16:2 tells us that people around the world will break out with loathsome and malignant sores. Could this be a result of radiation poisoning following the detonation of nuclear weapons?

Some believe Jesus may have been alluding to nuclear weaponry when He spoke of "people fainting with fear and with foreboding of what is coming on the world. For the powers of the heavens will be shaken" (Luke 21:26). Whether or not this is so, it is clear that the technology now exists for a third of the earth to be burned up and for mass casualties.

Is the modern movement toward globalism also an indicator of the end times?

I believe so. We see globalist policies emerging in economics, banking, commerce and trade, business, management, manufacturing, environmentalism, population control, education, religion, agriculture, information technologies, the entertainment industry, the publishing industry, science and medicine, and even government. The book of Revelation tells us that the antichrist will ultimately lead a global union—an anti-God union (see Revelation 13:3-18). It will be a political union, an economic union, and a religious union.

When one considers the multiple cascading problems now facing humanity—including the Middle East conflict, terrorism, overpopulation, starvation, pollution, national and international crime, cyber warfare, and economic instability—it is entirely feasible that increasing numbers of people will come to believe that such problems can be solved only on a global level. They may think that the only hope for human survival is a strong and effective world government.

Even now, as the danger continues to mount, people worldwide seem to be yearning for a leader who can take control and fix everything. The global economy is reeling, people are suffering, and there is a sense of urgency for a powerful leader who can once-for-all chart a clear global course toward stability. Such a leader is coming, and he may already be alive in the world. Scripture identifies him as the antichrist.

Of great significance is the fact that the technology that makes possible a world government is now in place. Technology has greased the skids for the emergence of globalism in our day.

Is ever-increasing anti-Semitism another possible indicator of the end times?

I believe so. It seems clear from prophetic Scripture that Satan-inspired anti-Semitism will escalate in the end times, especially during the tribulation period. Revelation 12:13 tells us, "When the dragon saw that he had been thrown down to the earth, he pursued the woman who had given birth to the male child." This verse indicates that when Satan is definitively cast out of heaven during the future tribulation, he will engage in great persecution against the woman (Israel) who gave birth to the male child (Jesus Christ).

Much of Satan's persecution against Israel will take place through the antichrist, whom he energizes (see 2 Thessalonians 2:9). This European leader seems to be the friend of Israel at the beginning of the tribulation period, but it becomes clear by the middle of the tribulation that he is her worst enemy! He will break his peace treaty with Israel at the midpoint of the seven-year agreement. Following the double cross, the antichrist will slaughter the Jews mercilessly (see Daniel 7:25; 8:24; 11:44). He will attempt to finish what Hitler started. He will attempt genocide. Zechariah 13:8 reveals that while two-thirds of the people of Israel will die, one-third will be left in the land. This persecution of Israel will be inspired by the devil himself.

Does God desire that we be aware of these signs of the times?

Yes, I believe so. In the New Testament, Jesus urged His followers to be thoughtful observers of the times. One day when He was speaking to the Sadducees and Pharisees, who rejected Him as the divine Messiah, He said: "When it is evening, you say, 'It will be fair weather, for the sky is red.' And in the morning, 'It will be stormy today, for the sky is red and threatening.' You know how to interpret the appearance of the sky, but you cannot interpret the signs of the times" (Matthew 16:1-3).

These Jewish leaders were supposed to be experts in interpreting the Old Testament Scriptures. In messianic passages like Isaiah 11 and Isaiah 35, we are told that when the Messiah came, the lame would walk, the deaf would hear, and the blind would see. When Jesus came on the scene, this is precisely what happened. These Jewish leaders should have been able to read the "signs of the times" and recognize that Jesus indeed was the promised Messiah. But they were blind to this reality.

You and I are called by Jesus to be thoughtful observers of the times. Properly discerning the times involves measuring current events against what the Bible reveals in order to consider whether there is a legitimate correlation. If we conclude there is, we can rejoice in God's sovereign control of human history while at the same time we resist the temptation to set dates, recognizing that this is something God forbids (Acts 1:7). All the while, we avoid sensationalism, recognizing that Christ calls His followers to live soberly and alertly as they await His coming (Mark 13:32-37).

What does Scripture say about end-time scoffers?

Christians are warned in 2 Peter 3:3-4 of the unbelief that will predominate on planet Earth in the end times. We are told that "scoffers will come in the last days with scoffing, following their own sinful desires" (verse 3). They will scoff by saying, "Where is the promise of his coming? For ever since the fathers fell asleep, all things are continuing as they were from the beginning of creation" (verse 4; see John 14:1-3; Acts 1:11; 1 Corinthians 15:23; 2 Corinthians 1:14; Philippians 1:6; 1 Thessalonians 3:13; 4:14-18; 2 Thessalonians 1:10; 2:1; 1 Timothy 6:14; 2 Timothy 4:8; Titus 2:13; Hebrews 9:28; James 5:7). Jude 18 likewise affirms, "In the last time there will be scoffers, following their own ungodly passions."

Christians who believe in the "signs of the times" will be increasingly mocked and ridiculed for their beliefs. Such is already occurring among a new, more vitriolic breed of atheists and humanists.

Christian, be prepared!

9

America in Prophecy

Is there a consensus among Christians about America in Bible prophecy?

No. Far from it. Christians have two broad viewpoints on this issue. Some believe that though America is not explicitly mentioned in Bible prophecy, perhaps America is indirectly referred to. Other Christians believe America is not mentioned in Bible prophecy at all.

What is an example of an indirect mention of America in Bible prophecy?

There are a number of general prophetic references to "the nations" and "the peoples" in the tribulation period that may include the United States. For example, it is predicted that events in Israel will become a cause of stumbling for "all the peoples" of the earth (Zechariah 12:2-3). God will in the future "shake all nations" (Haggai 2:6-7). God will be glorified among the nations (Isaiah 66:18-20). Such general passages, however, do not tell us anything specific about the role of the United States in the end times.

Is it possible that the land divided by rivers in Isaiah 18:1-7 is an indirect prophetic reference to America?

Some think so, since the United States is divided by rivers, such as the Mississippi River. Isaiah 18:7 also notes that this nation is "mighty and conquering," perhaps referring to the military might of the United States. The obvious problem with this view is that the nation is explicitly identified in Isaiah 18:1-2 as ancient Cush, which is modern Sudan.

Is it possible that the land of Tarshish in Ezekiel 38:13 is an indirect prophetic reference to America?

Some think so. Ezekiel 38:13 informs us that when a great northern military coalition composed of Russia and a number of Muslim nations invades Israel, a small group of nations will lamely protest the invasion: "Sheba and Dedan and the merchants of Tarshish and all its leaders will say to you, 'Have you come to seize spoil? Have you assembled your hosts to carry off plunder, to carry away silver and gold, to take away livestock and goods, to seize great spoil?'"

This is a highly debated passage. Some Bible expositors believe ancient Tarshish may refer to modern Spain. Others say it may be Great Britain. Others say it may refer to the colonies of Western Europe and the nations that have subsequently arisen from them, including the United States. Still others say Tarshish might represent virtually all the Western nations of the end times, which would include the United States. It is thus reasoned, based on Ezekiel 38:13, that the United States might be among the nations that lodge a protest against the massive invasion into Israel. But the protest is a feeble one, with no military action to back the words.

My personal assessment is that ancient Tarshish does not refer to the United States.

Is it possible that the Babylon of Revelation 17 and 18 is an indirect prophetic reference to the United States?

Some interpreters have seen parallels between Babylon the Great in the book of Revelation and the United States—or, more narrowly, New York City. After all, it is reasoned, both Babylon and the United States are dominant, both are immoral, both are excessively rich, and both think they are invulnerable. This scenario is not given much credence by most serious Bible interpreters. Such a view involves more eisegesis (reading a meaning into the text of Scripture) than exegesis (drawing the meaning out of the text of Scripture). I'll address Babylon in greater detail later in the book.

If America is not mentioned in Bible prophecy, why not?

The United States is the world's single remaining superpower that also happens to be Israel's principal ally. One therefore might expect at least a passing reference to the United States in Bible prophecy. If America is not mentioned in Bible prophecy, could the reason be that America may weaken in the end times? It is entirely possible that this is indeed the case. We know that the balance of power will shift toward the United States of Europe—a revived Roman Empire headed by the antichrist—in the end times (see Daniel 2, 7). This in itself suggests a possible weakening of the United States.

Is it possible that the United States might decline due to a nuclear attack?

It is possible. Government advisors say that a nuclear attack on U.S. soil within the next ten years is "more likely than not."

Granted, it seems unlikely that the entire United States could be destroyed by a nuclear attack. But if one major city—such as New York City, Los Angeles, Chicago, or Dallas—were destroyed, this would have a devastating effect on the already-fragile, debt-ridden U.S. economy.

One problem faced by the United States is that it has so many easy entrances across its borders. It would not be difficult for a terrorist to smuggle a nuclear bomb into the country. A bomb could also be shipped into the United States. Of the 50,000 cargo containers that are shipped into the United States each day, only 5 percent get screened. A bomb could easily make its way into the country in one of the 95 percent that remain unscreened.

It is also possible, experts say, that a terrorist group could launch a nuclear weapon from a commercial ship off the coast of the United States. About 75 percent of the U.S. population is within 200 miles of an ocean coast. With so many registered merchant ships sailing off U.S. coastal waters (over 130,000 from 195 countries), the nuclear danger is obvious.

How does all of this relate to Islamic jihad?

"Jihad" comes from the Arabic word *jahada*, which principally means "to struggle" or "to strive in the path of Allah." Muslims today often use the term in reference to armed fighting and warfare in defending Islam and standing against what they perceive to be evil. For most Muslims today, any war that is viewed as a defense of one's own country, home, or community is called a jihad.

Radical Islamic fundamentalists are well known for their use of arms and explosives in defending their version of Islam. Jihad, in their thinking, has the goal of terrorizing perceived enemies of Islam into submission and retreat. Many Muslims believe Muhammad's mission was to conquer the world for Allah. The goal of jihad for them is to establish Islamic authority over the whole world. In their view, Islam teaches that Allah is the only authority, and all political systems must be based on Allah's teaching.

Many Shiite Muslims believe that at the apocalyptic end of days, a great, armed jihad will result in the subjugation of the entire world to Islam. Many such Shiites have long believed in the eventual return of the Twelfth Imam, believed to be a direct (bloodline) descendant of Muhammad's son-in-law, Ali, whose family, it is believed, constitutes the only legitimate successors to Muhammad. The Twelfth Imam, who allegedly disappeared as a child in AD 941, will supposedly return in the future as the Mahdi ("the rightly guided One") and create a messianic-like era of global order and justice for Shiites in which Islam will be triumphant.

In this line of thought, the appearance of the Twelfth Imam can be hastened through apocalyptic chaos and violence—that is, by unleashing an apocalyptic holy war against Christians and Jews. It is thus believed that it is within the power of modern Muslims to bring about the end of days. It is within their power to influence the divine timetable. The radical Muslim goal is to attain a world without America and Zionism. Once this goal is reached, the Twelfth Imam can be expected to return. Extremist Muslim leaders now say that humanity will soon know what it is like to live in a Jew-free and USA-free world. "Death to America" is a common slogan among such radical Muslims.

Of course, a religious motivation for many Muslims to participate in jihad is that any Muslim who loses his or her life in service to Allah is guaranteed entrance into paradise (Hadith 9:459). According to Muslim tradition, Muhammad said: "The person who participates in (Holy battles) in Allah's cause and nothing compels him to do so except belief in Allah and His Apostles, will be recompensed by Allah either with a reward, or booty (if he survives) or will be admitted to Paradise (if he is killed in the battle as a martyr)" (Hadith 1:35). This is highly significant to Muslims, for there is virtually no other way a Muslim can have eternal security—that is, be assured of going to paradise.

Why do extremist Muslims hate America so much?

There are a number of reasons. Among them is America's support of Israel, with over $800 million given in aid annually, as well as support for Israel's military buildup. Muslims hate Israel because in 1948 the Israeli state was reborn on land that Muslims believe Allah gave to them. Because the United States supports Israel, both Israel and the United States are targeted by Muslim extremists. The United States and Israel are allegedly the "great Satan" and the "lesser Satan."

Further resentment of Americans is rooted in America's alleged meddling in Middle Eastern affairs, such as positioning U.S. troops ("infidels") on Muslim soil—in Saudi Arabia, Iraq, and elsewhere. Still further, it is claimed that Americans are arrogant and imperialistic, trying to muscle their way around throughout the Middle East, with their eyes on the Arabic oil fields.

Is it possible that the United States might decline due to an electromagnetic pulse (EMP) attack?

Yes. This possibility is documented in a report issued in 2004 by a blue-ribbon commission created by Congress. It is called: "Commission to Assess the Threat to the United States from Electromagnetic Pulse Attack." Based on this report, a number of highly respected government officials lament that the technology is now here to bring America's way of life to an end.

The commission found that a single nuclear weapon, delivered by a missile to an altitude of a few hundred miles over the United States, would yield catastrophic damage to the nation. Such a missile could be launched from a freighter off the coast of the United States. The commission explained that the higher the altitude of the weapon's detonation, the larger the affected geographic area would be. At a height of 300 miles, the entire continental United States would be exposed, along with parts of Canada and Mexico.

The commission warned that the electromagnetic pulse produced by such a weapon would have a high likelihood of severely damaging electrical power systems, electronics, and information systems. At high risk would be electronic control, the infrastructures for handling electric power, sensors and protective systems of all kinds, computers, cell phones, telecommunications, cars, boats, airplanes, trains, transportation, fuel and energy, banking and finance, emergency services, and even food and water. Anything electrical is at risk.

The consequences of an EMP attack would be especially harmful to American society today since our infrastructure—civilian *and* military—runs on electricity and electronic components. The commission estimated that it could take "months to years" to fully recover from such an attack.

Is it possible that moral implosion may bring down the United States?

Yes, America may experience an ever-escalating moral and spiritual degeneration, thereby causing its downfall. Lots of statistics show the trouble this country is in morally and spiritually. For example, George Barna's organization recently released a report titled, "The End of Absolutes: America's New Moral Code." The report—based on statistics—convincingly argues that "Christian morality is being ushered out of American social structures and off the cultural main stage, leaving a vacuum in its place—and the broader culture is attempting to fill the void." The report indicates that for a majority of Americans, experience—*whatever is right for you*—has now become the basis of morality. The report further notes that "a sizable number of Americans see morality as a matter of cultural consensus."[2] One thing is certain. If the moral fiber of this country continues to erode, and people continue to ignore the Bible, then the demise of this country is only a matter of time.

Because of the high level of immorality in this country, it is entirely possible that God may bring judgment upon it. Christian leaders have been warning about this possibility for decades, and their warnings are typically met with deaf ears, much like prophets were often ignored during Old Testament times.

Can God really bring down a country in judgment?

Yes, indeed. Scripture reveals that God is absolutely sovereign (Psalm 50:1; 66:7; 93:1; Proverbs 19:21; Isaiah 14:24; 46:10), and in His sovereignty He blesses nations that submit to Him and brings down nations that rebel against Him. In the book of Job we read, "He makes nations great, and he destroys them; he enlarges nations, and leads them away" (Job 12:23). Daniel 2:20-21 tells us that God "removes kings and sets up kings." Because America is now in a moral and spiritual free fall, with no repentance in sight, it is legitimate to ask: *Might God sovereignly judge America in the end times for turning away from Him?*

Is it possible that Romans 1:18-28 might apply to the United States in its rebellion against God?

I hate to say it, but I think it is a real possibility. If this passage tells us anything, it is that when a nation willfully rejects God and His Word, turning its back on His moral requirements, God eventually reveals His wrath against that nation. God has a long track record of wrath against ungodly nations. This passage reveals that one way God reveals His wrath is by allowing the people of that nation to experience the full brunt of the ravaging consequences of their sin.

If America turns its back on Israel in the end times, might that be a contributing factor to God's judgment?

Yes. In Genesis 12:3 God promised Abraham and his descendants: "I will bless those who bless you, and him who dishonors you I will curse." This ancient promise from God has never been revoked or repealed. Should the day ever come when the United States turns against Israel, woe unto this country! It is good for us to remember that God is a promise keeper, and He will bless those who bless Israel and stand against those who stand against Israel.

Is it possible that the rapture of the church could cause the United States to decline?

Yes. It seems fair to say that because there is such a high concentration of Christians in the United States, it will be negatively affected by the rapture more than most other nations.

Following the rapture, many workers of all kinds will no longer show up for work. Many bills and mortgages will go unpaid. Many college tuition bills and loans will go unpaid. Many business leaders will no longer show up to lead their companies. Many law enforcement personnel will no longer be here to keep the peace, and fears will rise. The stock market will crash like never before because of the panic over millions of people suddenly vanishing. This and much more will follow the rapture.

Is it possible that the United States will be in league with the antichrist in the end times?

It is possible. It may be that following the rapture of the church, the United States will be in general cooperation with the revived Roman Empire headed by the antichrist. Since many U.S. citizens have come from Europe, it would be natural for the U.S. to become an ally of this Roman power.

In this theory, the United States will eventually be subsumed into the globalism that will emerge and prevail during the tribulation. Even in our day, our government seems to be moving us away from American national sovereignty and is open to handling more and more problems globally.

When Armageddon breaks out at the end of the tribulation period, troops from the United States may be there, standing against Israel. I hate to say that, but Zechariah 12:3 seems clear on the matter: "On that day I will make Jerusalem a heavy stone for all the peoples. All who lift it will surely hurt themselves. And *all the nations of the earth will gather against it.*" The phrase, "all the nations of the earth," would seem to include the United States.

Likewise, in Zechariah 14:2 we read: "For I will gather *all the nations* against Jerusalem to battle, and the city shall be taken and the houses plundered and the women raped. Half of the city shall go out into exile, but the rest of the people shall not be cut off from the city." Again, "all the nations" would appear to include the United States.

Further, we read in Revelation 16:14 that "the kings of the whole world" will be gathered together "for battle on the great day of God the Almighty." The "kings of the whole world" would certainly include the president of the United States.

Keep in mind that following the rapture of the church, there will not be any Christians on the earth, including in the United States. This means that many of the people in the United States who have long supported Israel have just vanished and gone to be with the Lord in heaven. It is easy to see how a Christian-less United States could ally with the revived Roman Empire and then find itself in league with the antichrist against Israel.

It is a sobering thing to ponder.

10

The Ezekiel Invasion

What is the Ezekiel invasion?

Some 2600 years ago, the prophet Ezekiel prophesied that the Jews would be regathered from "many nations" to the land of Israel in the end times (Ezekiel 36–37). He then prophesied that, sometime later, there would be an all-out invasion into Israel by a massive northern assault force, with Russia heading up a coalition of Muslim nations, including modern Iran, Sudan, Turkey, Libya, and other Islamic nations (38–39). Their goal will be to utterly obliterate the Jews.

How do we know that "Rosh" in Ezekiel 38:2 refers to Russia (NASB, ASV, NKJV, MEV)?

There are a number of reasons for making this identification. Not only have many highly respected Hebrew scholars come to this conclusion, but there also is considerable historical evidence that a place known as Rosh—sometimes using alternate spellings such as Rus, Ros, and Rox—was very familiar in the ancient world, and was located in the territory now occupied by modern Russia. There is evidence of a people named Rosh/Rashu in the ninth through seventh centuries BC in Assyrian sources that predate the book of Ezekiel. Hence, quite early, we find evidence of a "Ros" people that was geographically located in today's Russia. Rosh also appears as a place name in Egyptian inscriptions as Rash, dating as early as 2600 BC. One inscription that dates to 1500 BC refers to a land called Reshu that was located to the north of Egypt (as is the case with modern Russia). Finally, in Ezekiel 39:2 Rosh is said to be in "the uttermost parts of the north." The term "north" is to be understood in relation to Israel. If one draws a line from Israel and goes straight north, one ends up in Russia.

Why does the term "Rosh" not appear in the ESV, NIV, NET, HCSB, and NLT translations except as a marginal reading?

The Hebrew word in this verse can be taken as either a proper noun (a geographical place called Rosh) or as an adjective (meaning "chief"). If it's an adjective, it qualifies the meaning of the word *prince*, so that it is translated "chief prince."

Hebrew scholars debate the correct translation. I believe Hebrew scholars C.F. Keil and Wilhelm Gesenius are correct in saying Rosh refers to a geographical place. The evidence suggests that the errant translation of Rosh as an adjective ("*chief* prince") can be traced to the Latin Vulgate, translated by Jerome—who himself admitted that he did not base his translation on grammatical considerations. He resisted translating Rosh as a proper noun simply because He could not find it mentioned as a geographical place anywhere else in Scripture. A number of English translations followed Jerome on this verse.

Taking Rosh as a geographical place is the most natural rendering of the original Hebrew (as reflected in the NASB translation). I see no legitimate linguistic reason for taking it as an adjective.

Does modern Russia have a track record of aggression against Israel?

There's no question about it. During the 1967 Six-Day War, the Russians were poised to attack Israel, but backed down after President Johnson ordered the U.S. Sixth Fleet to steam toward Israel. When Egypt, Syria, and some other Arab/Islamic countries launched an attack against Israel in 1973, it soon became clear that Russia was providing the military muscle behind the attack, including weaponry, ammunition, intelligence, and military training. In 1982, then-Israeli Prime Minister Menachem Begin revealed that a secret but massive cache of Russian weaponry had been discovered in deep underground cellars in Lebanon, apparently pre-positioned for later use in a future ground invasion into Israel. In recent years, we have witnessed the emergence of Russian alliances with Iran and other Muslim countries. This is understandably of great concern to Israel.

What geographical region is Magog in this northern military coalition?

Magog, one of the nations in the anti-Israel coalition (Ezekiel 38:2), probably constitutes the geographical area in the southern portion of the former Soviet Union. Many scholars take Magog to generally refer to the mountainous area near the Black and Caspian Seas, the former domain of the Scythians. More specifically, it likely refers to the area that is today occupied by the former Soviet republics of Kazakhstan, Kyrgyzstan, Uzbekistan, Turkmenistan, Tajikistan, and possibly even northern parts of modern Afghanistan. Significantly, this entire area is Muslim dominated, with more than enough religious motivation to move against Israel.

What geographical regions are Meshech and Tubal in this northern military coalition?

Meshech and Tubal—often mentioned together in Scripture (for example, Ezekiel 38:2)—refers to the geographical territory to the south of the Black and Caspian Seas of Ezekiel's day, which is today modern Turkey, though there may be some overlap with some neighboring countries. This is evident in that Meshech and Tubal are apparently the same as the Mushki and Tabal of the Assyrians, and the Moschi and Tibareni of the Greeks, who inhabited the territory that constitutes modern Turkey. This is confirmed by the ancient historian Herodotus.

Is modern-day Iran the same as ancient Persia (Ezekiel 38:5)?

Yes, indeed. Persia occupies the exact same territory as is presently occupied by modern Iran. Persia became Iran in 1935. Then, during the Iranian Revolution in 1979, the name changed to the Islamic Republic of Iran.

In view of what biblical prophecy reveals about the alliance between Rosh and Persia (Russia and Iran) as well as other Muslim nations, it is highly revealing that Iran has now become the third largest recipient of Russian arms, with an estimated annual trade of $500 million. The Iranian government is involved in a massive, 25-year military modernization program—one entailing upgrades to its air defense, naval warfare, and land combat capabilities, and built almost entirely around Russian technology and weaponry. Russia has also been assisting Iran in its nuclear program. Through Russia's assistance, Iran seems destined to become a dominant nation in the Middle East—far more dominant than Westerners (and, obviously, Israelis) are comfortable with.

What geographical territory is Cush (also called Ethiopia) in this northern military coalition?

This territory is just south of Egypt on the Nile River—what is today known as Sudan (see Ezekiel 38:5). Sudan is a hardline Islamic nation that is a kindred spirit with Iran in its venomous hatred of Israel. These nations are already such close allies that a mutual stand against Israel would not be unexpected. This nation is infamous for its ties to terrorism and its harboring of Osama bin Laden from 1991 to 1996.

What geographical territory is Put in this northern military coalition?

Put, a land to the west of Egypt, is modern-day Libya (Ezekiel 38:5). However, ancient Libya is larger than the Libya that exists today, and hence the boundaries of Put refer to in Ezekiel 38–39 may extend beyond modern Libya, perhaps including portions of Algeria and Tunisia.

What is the land of Gomer in this northern military coalition?

Gomer is likely modern-day Turkey (see Ezekiel 38:6). In support of this view, the ancient historian Josephus said Gomer founded those whom the Greeks called the Galatians. The Galatians of New Testament times lived in the region of central Turkey. Hence, there is a direct connection of ancient Gomer to modern Turkey. Moreover, many claim Gomer may be a reference to the ancient Cimmerians or

Kimmerioi. History reveals that from around 700 BC, the Cimmerians occupied the geographical territory that is modern Turkey.

What geographical region is Beth-togarmah in this northern military coalition?

Beth-togarmah is a compound word. In Hebrew, "beth" means "house." Hence, Beth-togarmah is a Hebrew term that literally means "the house of Togarmah." Ezekiel 38:6 makes reference to Beth-togarmah as being from the remote parts of the north. Hence, Beth-togarmah must be located to the north of Israel. Some expositors believe Beth-togarmah is another reference to modern-day Turkey, which is to the far north of Israel. (Keep in mind that Turkey used to be broken down into several smaller territories.) This view is in keeping with the geography of Ezekiel's time, for in that day there was a city in Cappadocia (modern Turkey) known as Tegarma, Tagarma, Tilgarimmu, and Takarama. If this identification is correct, this means that Turkey will be one of the nations in the northern military coalition that will invade Israel in the end times (Ezekiel 38:1-6).

Will Iraq be a part of the invading force in the Ezekiel invasion?

It's hard to say. We know from Ezekiel 38:1-6 that the northern coalition of nations will include Russia, Iran, Sudan, Turkey, Libya, Kazakhstan, Kyrgyzstan, Uzbekistan, Turkmenistan, Tajikistan, Armenia, and possibly northern Afghanistan. But Iraq is not specifically mentioned. One wonders why not.

There are several possible answers. First, it is possible that Iraq will be a part of this invading coalition. In addition to the specific nations mentioned in Ezekiel 38, we find the phrase "and many peoples with you" (verse 15). It may be that Iraq is among the "many peoples."

Another possibility—perhaps the better option—is that Iraq will not be a part of this invading coalition because a rebuilt Babylon (capital of Iraq) will eventually become the headquarters of the antichrist during the tribulation period (Revelation 17–18). Scripture reveals that the antichrist will first emerge as a leader in the United States of Europe (a revived Roman Empire) and will sign a seven-year peace pact with Israel (Daniel 9:27). This will constitute the beginning of the tribulation period. The antichrist will then eventually relocate to Babylon. One can therefore infer that if the Ezekiel invasion takes place in the first half of the tribulation, antichrist-controlled Iraq will likely not be a part of the invading force. There's a good possibility that the nations of Ezekiel 38:1-6 launch an invasion into Israel in defiance of the antichrist. In any event, God utterly destroys the invaders (Ezekiel 38:19–39:6). Babylon remains as a headquarters for the antichrist (see Isaiah 13:19).

Who is the "Gog" who heads up this northern military coalition against Israel?

The word "Gog" is a reference to the powerful leader of the end-times northern military coalition that will launch an invasion against Israel (Ezekiel 38). Gog is referred to as "the chief prince of Meshech and Tubal" (verse 2). This term appears eleven times in Ezekiel 38–39, thereby indicating that he plays a significant role in this end-times invasion.

Gog may or may not be a proper name. There is reference to an altogether different Gog in 1 Chronicles 5:4, where we read that among the sons of Joel were "Shemaiah his son, Gog his son, Shimei his son," and others. This verse at least indicates that the term can be used as a proper name. It would seem, however, that the term is not intended as a proper name in the context of Ezekiel 38–39.

The term may refer to a king-like role—such as pharaoh, caesar, czar, or president. The term literally means "high," "supreme," "a height," or "a high mountain." Apparently, then, this leader—this czar-like military leader—will be a man of great stature who commands tremendous respect.

It is critical to understand that Gog is not just another name for the antichrist. We will end up in prophetic chaos if we try to make this identification. The antichrist heads up a revived Roman Empire (Daniel 2, 7), while Gog heads up an invasion force made up of Russia and a number of Muslim nations (Ezekiel 38:1-6). Moreover, Gog's invasion into Israel constitutes a direct challenge to the antichrist's covenant with Israel (Daniel 9:27). Further, Gog's moment in the limelight is short-lived (it's all over when God destroys the invading force—Ezekiel 39), whereas the antichrist is in power over the span of a significant part of the tribulation period.

Has an alliance between the nations in the Ezekiel coalition ever occurred in history?

No. But it is occurring in modern days, which lends credence to the possibility that Christians today are living in the end times.

Here's something else to think about. An alliance between many of the nations mentioned in Ezekiel 38–39 likely wouldn't have made good sense in Ezekiel's day since some are not even located near each other. But it makes great sense in our day because the nations that make up the coalition are predominantly Muslim. That in itself is more than enough reason for them to unify in attacking Israel—especially given current Islamic hatred for Israel.

We can also observe that while Ezekiel wrote his book some 2600 years ago, Islam did not come into being until the seventh century AD. This means that at the time Ezekiel wrote his book, the conditions for the unification of these nations did not yet exist. Nevertheless, as a prophet of God, he set forth his divinely inspired prophecies, and in our day—with the existence of Islam—the prophecies make perfect sense, especially when measured against current events.

What about those who claim that the Ezekiel invasion probably took place back in Bible days?

Such a view is untenable. Here are some factors to consider:

1. There has never been an invasion into Israel on the multination scale described in Ezekiel 38–39. Nor has there ever been an invasion into Israel involving the specific nations mentioned in the passage. Since the prophecy has not been fulfilled yet, its fulfillment must yet be future.

2. Ezekiel said the invasion would take place "in the latter years" (Ezekiel 38:8) and "in the last days" (38:16) from the standpoint of his day. Such phrases point to the prophetic end times.

3. Ezekiel said the invasion would occur sometime after Israel had

been regathered from all around the earth—"gathered from many peoples" (Ezekiel 38:8,12)—to a land that had been a wasteland. Certainly there were occasions in Israel's history where the Jews were held in bondage. For example, they were held in bondage in Egypt. They went into captivity in Babylon. But in each of these cases, their deliverance involved being set free from a single nation, not many nations around the world. The only regathering of Jews from "many peoples" around the world is occurring in modern days—especially since 1948, when Israel achieved statehood.

4. Since chapters 36–37 are being literally fulfilled (a regathering from "many peoples"), it is reasonable and consistent to assume that chapters 38–39 will likewise be literally fulfilled. This is in keeping with the well-established precedent of biblical prophecies throughout the Old Testament being literally fulfilled.

What does Scripture mean when it says Israel will be dwelling securely—at peace—when the Ezekiel invasion takes place (Ezekiel 38:8,11)?

There's quite a bit of debate on this issue. Some prophecy experts believe that Israel is already in a state of relative security. Among the factors leading to this security are Israel's well-equipped army, first-rate air force, effective missile-defense system, strong economy, and strong relationship with the United States. Such factors are said to account for Israel being "at peace."

Other interpreters relate this state of security and peace to the covenant that the antichrist will sign with Israel—the covenant that marks the beginning of the tribulation period (Daniel 9:27). The backdrop is that since Israel became a nation in 1948, she has had to stay on high alert because of the danger she is in from all her Arab and Muslim neighbors. There has never been a time when Israel has been able to let her guard down. Because of the constant conflict and tension in the Middle East, one Western leader after another has tried to broker a peace deal for the region. After all, stability in the Middle East and the Persian Gulf is a high priority for the entire world, especially pertaining to the uninterrupted flow of oil to world markets.

In view of this, some believe that Israel will experience true security only when the leader of a revived Roman Empire—a European superstate—signs a peace pact or covenant with Israel, an event that will officially begin the tribulation period (Daniel 9:27). This leader—the antichrist—will seemingly accomplish the impossible, solving the Middle East peace puzzle. From the moment of the signing of the covenant on through the next three and a half years, Israel will enjoy a heightened sense of security, and this security will be backed by the military might of the most powerful political leader in the world.

How does Israel's state of security and peace relate to the actual timing of the Ezekiel invasion?

If one holds to the view that Israel is presently in a state of security, the invasion of the northern military coalition could take place at any time, even before the tribulation period begins. If one holds that Israel's state of security depends on the antichrist's signing of the covenant with Israel, then the invasion cannot take place until the tribulation period begins.

What is the case for the Ezekiel invasion taking place after the rapture but before the beginning of the tribulation period?

I believe there are five key considerations:

1. The world will likely be in a state of chaos following the rapture. Since the United States has such a heavy population of Christians, the rapture will have a devastating effect on the U.S. Russia and her Muslim allies may well seize the moment, considering this the ideal time to launch a massive attack against Israel, which, up until this time, had been protected by the United States.

2. Once God destroys Russia and the Muslim invaders prior to the tribulation period, this may open the door for an easier rise of the antichrist as the leader of a revived Roman Empire—a European superstate.

3. With the Muslim invaders having already been destroyed prior to the beginning of the tribulation period, this might make it easier for the antichrist to sign a peace pact with Israel (Daniel 9:27), guaranteeing that Israel will be protected (especially from Muslim attacks).

4. This scenario may account for Israel's ability to construct the Jewish temple on the temple mount in Jerusalem. With Muslim forces decimated, Muslim resistance will be greatly minimized.

5. If the invasion takes place after the rapture, and the rapture takes place at least three and a half years prior to the beginning of the tribulation period, then this scenario would allow for the weapons used in the invasion to be completely burned for seven years (Ezekiel 39:9-10) prior to the midpoint of the tribulation, when Israel is forced to take flight from Jerusalem (Matthew 24:15-21). It may well be, then, that a significant time lapse exists between the rapture and the beginning of the tribulation.

What will motivate this invasion into Israel?

Not only do Muslims hate the Jews because they believe the land of Israel belongs to them by divine right (Allah allegedly gave it to them), they also want Israel's wealth (see Ezekiel 38:11-12). Ezekiel states that the invaders want Israel's "silver and gold" and "cattle and goods" and "great spoil" (38:13).

This "great spoil" might actually take a number of forms. A number of wealthy people live in Israel—over 6600 millionaires with total assets exceeding $24 billion. Moreover, the mineral resources of the Dead Sea, including 45 billion tons of sodium, chlorine, sulfur, potassium, calcium, magnesium, and bromide, are worth trillions of dollars. There is also the possibility that gas and oil discoveries in Israel will be part of the spoil. All in all, whoever controls the land of Israel can look forward to an incalculably large economic boost.

Will any nations come to Israel's defense when she is invaded by this vast force?

Not a one! Israel will stand alone when attacked by the massive northern military coalition. Some nations—"Sheba, Dedan, the merchants of Tarshish" (apparently Saudi Arabia and some Western nations)—diplomatically ask, "Have you come to seize spoil?" (Ezekiel 38:13). But all they offer is *words* with *no action*. Israel will stand utterly alone.

How does God destroy this massive invading force?

Ezekiel 38:17–39:8 describes God's fourfold judgment of the invaders:

1. There will be a massive earthquake (Ezekiel 38:19-20). The result is that transportation will be disrupted, and apparently the armies of the multinational forces will be thrown into utter chaos (verse 20).

2. Infighting will break out among the invading troops (Ezekiel 38:21). God sovereignly induces the various armies of the invading force to turn on each other and kill each other. It is possible that this may be at least partially due to the confusion and chaos following the massive earthquake. Fear and panic will sweep through the forces so each army will shoot indiscriminately at the others. Adding to the confusion is the fact that the armies of the various nations speak different languages, including Russian, Farsi, Arabic, and Turkic, and communication will be difficult at best. It may also be that the Russians and Muslim nations turn on each other. Perhaps in the midst of the chaos, they mutually suspect that the other is double-crossing them, and they respond by opening fire on each other. In any event, there will be countless casualties.

3. There will be a massive outbreak of disease (Ezekiel 38:22a). Following the earthquake, and following the infighting of the invading troops, countless dead bodies will be lying around everywhere. Transportation will be disrupted so it will be difficult if not impossible to transfer the wounded or bring in food and medicine. Meanwhile, myriad birds and other predatory animals will feast on this unburied flesh. All this is a recipe for the outbreak of pandemic disease—disease which, according to Ezekiel, will take many more lives.

4. There will be torrential rain, hailstones, fire, and burning sulfur

(Ezekiel 38:22b). It is possible that the powerful earthquake may set off volcanic deposits in the region, thrusting into the atmosphere a hail of molten rock and burning sulfur (volcanic ash) which then falls upon the enemy troops, thereby utterly destroying them.

Will nuclear weapons be detonated at any point?

It's hard to say. It is interesting to observe that after God destroys the invaders, He says: "I will rain down fire on Magog and on all your allies who live safely on the coasts" (Ezekiel 39:6). "Magog" seems to refer to the geographical area in the southern part of the former Soviet Union—perhaps including the former Soviet republics of Kazakhstan, Kyrgyzstan, Uzbekistan, Turkmenistan, Tajikistan, and possibly even northern parts of modern Afghanistan. We are told in this prophetic verse that God will rain fire down upon this area of the world, as well as Magog's "allies who live safely on the coasts." Destruction may include not only military targets such as missile silos, military bases, radar installations, and the like, but also religious centers, mosques, madrassas, Islamic schools and universities, and other facilities that preach hatred against the Jews. This may be a direct infliction of fire by God Himself, or God could cause this fire through Israel's (or some other nation's) nuclear weaponry.

How does God's protection of Israel relate to the Abrahamic covenant?

As the Protector of Israel, God's primary purpose in destroying the coalition will be to deliver Israel from harm. Ultimately, this is an outworking of the ancient covenant God made with His friend Abraham. In Genesis 12:3, God promised Abraham: "I will bless those who bless you, and him who dishonors you I will curse." Surely the Muslims—those who comprise this vast invading force—dishonor Israel by seeking her destruction, and hence God's curse falls upon the invaders in the form of an annihilating judgment.

Are there any indications that the Ezekiel invasion is drawing near?

The very nations prophesied to join this alliance in the end times are already coming together in our day. The fact that this alliance is beginning to emerge after Israel became a nation again in 1948—with Jews continuing to stream into their homeland ever since, so that today there are more Jews in Israel than anywhere else on earth—is considered by many to be highly significant.

It appears that the stage may be being set for this prophesied future invasion into Israel.

11

The Rapture of the Church

What is the rapture?

The rapture is that glorious event in which Christ will descend from heaven, the dead in Christ will be resurrected, and living Christians will be instantly translated into their resurrection bodies. Both groups will be caught up to meet Christ in the air and taken back to heaven (1 Thessalonians 4:13-17; John 14:1-3; 1 Corinthians 15:51-54). This means one generation of Christians will never pass through death's door. They will be alive on earth one moment; the next moment they will be with Christ in the air.

Why is the rapture called a "mystery"?

A mystery, in the biblical sense, is a truth that cannot be discerned simply by human investigation but requires special revelation from God. Generally, this word refers to a truth that was unknown to people living in Old Testament times but is now revealed to humankind by God (Matthew 13:17; Colossians 1:26). This is illustrated in a key passage about the rapture of the church—1 Corinthians 15:51-55:

> Behold! I tell you a mystery. We shall not all sleep, but we shall all be changed, in a moment, in the twinkling of an eye, at the last trumpet. For the trumpet will sound, and the dead will be raised imperishable, and we shall be changed. For this perishable body must put on the imperishable, and this mortal body must put on immortality. When the perishable puts on the imperishable, and the mortal puts on immortality, then shall come to pass the saying that is written: "Death is swallowed up in victory."

What is the biblical basis for a pretribulational rapture of the church?

Scripture affirms that the church is not appointed to wrath (Romans 5:9; 1 Thessalonians 1:9-10; 5:9). This means the church cannot go through the "great day of wrath"—the tribulation period (Revelation 6:17). This view is known as pretribulationism (meaning *before the tribulation*). This is my personal view.

First Thessalonians 1:10 explicitly states that Jesus "*delivers us* from the wrath to come." "Delivers" in the original Greek means "to draw or snatch out to oneself, to rescue, to save, to preserve." The verb literally means "to draw to one's self" in order to deliver one from danger. This verse clearly seems to refer to the rapture of the church prior to the beginning of the tribulation period.

The "snatching up" in 1 Thessalonians 1:10 sounds amazingly similar to the description of the rapture in 1 Thessalonians 4:16-17: "For the Lord himself will descend from heaven with a cry of command, with the voice of an archangel, and with the sound of the trumpet of God. And the dead in Christ will rise first. Then we who are alive, who are left, will be *caught up* together with them in the clouds to meet the Lord in the air, and so we will always be with the Lord." "Caught up" here literally means "snatch up or take away."

Does God typically deliver His people before judgment falls?

God is often seen protecting His people before His judgment falls (see 2 Peter 2:5-9). Enoch was transferred to heaven before the judgment of the flood. Noah and his family were in the ark before the judgment of the flood. Lot was taken out of Sodom before judgment was poured out on Sodom and Gomorrah. The firstborn among the Hebrews in Egypt were sheltered by the blood of the Paschal lamb before judgment fell. The spies were safely out of Jericho and Rahab was secured before judgment fell on Jericho. So, too, will the church be secured safely (via the rapture) before judgment falls in the tribulation.

How fast will the rapture occur?

In 1 Corinthians 15:51-52 the apostle Paul describes the rapture as occurring "in the twinkling of an eye." This phrase is Paul's way of demonstrating how brief the moment of the rapture will be. The fluttering of an eyelid—the blinking of an eye—is exceedingly fast. This means the bodily transformation that living believers will experience at the rapture will be near instantaneous. One moment they will be on earth in mortal bodies, the next moment they will meet Christ in the clouds, instantly transformed into their glorified resurrection bodies.

Will the angels be present at the rapture?

I believe so. The apostle Paul tells us that the rapture of the church will follow "a cry of command, with the voice of an archangel" (1 Thessalonians 4:16). Scholars debate what is meant by the phrase, "with the voice of an archangel." Some suggest that perhaps Jesus will issue the shout with an archangel-like voice. However, it seems more natural to the text to interpret this shout as actually coming from the archangel himself. Scripture reveals that at the second coming, the Lord Jesus shall be "revealed from heaven with his mighty angels" (2 Thessalonians 1:7). If the angels accompany Christ at the second coming, then surely this includes the archangel Michael. And if the angels accompany Jesus at the second coming, there is no reason to assume they will not also accompany Him seven years earlier at the rapture. After all, angels are often portrayed as being heavily involved in end-time events (see Revelation 5:11; 7:1-2,11; 8:2,4,6,13; 9:14-15; 10:10; 12:7,9; 14:10; 15:1,6-8; 16:1; 17:1; 21:9,12).

Does God promise to deliver the church from the actual time period of the tribulation?

I believe so. In Revelation 3:10, Jesus speaks the following words to the church at Philadelphia: "Because you have kept my word about patient endurance, I will keep you from the *hour of trial* that is coming on the whole world, to try those who dwell on the earth." Posttribulationists interpret this verse as saying that believers will be "kept through" Satan's wrath (unscathed) during the tribulation. Pretribulationists respond, however, that the Greek text does not say believers will be kept *through* the tribulation (which would require use of the Greek word *dia*, meaning "through"). Rather, the verse indicates believers will be saved "out of" or "from" (Greek, *ek*) the actual time (or hour) of the tribulation. Pretribulationism is consistent with God's promise to deliver the church from the "wrath to come" (1 Thessalonians 1:10; 5:9).

We know that Jesus' words about keeping Christians out of the "hour of trial" is meant for more than just the church of Philadelphia. After all, Jesus immediately goes on to say: "He who has an ear, let him hear what the Spirit says *to the churches*" (Revelation 3:13).

Are there any Bible verses that portray the church as being in the tribulation period?

Not a one. No Old Testament passage on the tribulation mentions the church (Deuteronomy 4:29-30; Jeremiah 30:4-11; Daniel 8:24-27; 12:1-2). Likewise, no New Testament passage on the tribulation mentions the church (Matthew 13:30,39-42,48-50; 24:15-31; 1 Thessalonians 1:9-10; 5:4-9; 2 Thessalonians 2:1-11; Revelation 4–18). The church's complete absence would seem to indicate that it is not on earth during the tribulation.

Do Scripture passages about the rapture agree with each other?

I believe so. Consider the direct parallels that exist between 1 Thessalonians 4:13-18 (a key rapture passage) and Jesus' description of the rapture in John 14:1-3:

- John 14:3 depicts Jesus as coming again to earth, which obviously involves a descent from the heavenly realm. Likewise, 1 Thessalonians 4:16 says Christ "will descend from heaven."

- In John 14:3, Jesus says to believers that He "will take you to myself." First Thessalonians 4:17 reveals the believers will be "caught up" to Christ.

- John 14:3 also reveals that believers will be with Christ

("where I am"). First Thessalonians 4:17 affirms that believers "will always be with the Lord."

- John 14:1 reveals that the purpose of this revelation about the rapture is that the hearts of Christ's followers will not be troubled. Likewise, 1 Thessalonians 4:13,18 reveals that the purpose of this revelation about the rapture is to minimize grief and bring encouragement.

How does the rapture relate to the bride and bridegroom metaphor often used in the New Testament for Christ and the church?

In Scripture, Christ is portrayed as the Bridegroom (John 3:29) while the church is portrayed as the Bride of Christ (Revelation 19:7). The backdrop to this imagery is rooted in Hebrew weddings. There were three phases: (1) the marriage was legally consummated by the parents of the bride and groom, after which the groom went to prepare a place to live in his father's house; (2) the bridegroom came to claim his bride; and (3) there was a marriage supper, a feast lasting several days. All three of these phases are seen in Christ's relationship to the church or bride of Christ:

1. As individuals living during the church age come to salvation, under the Father's loving and sovereign hand, they become a part of the Bride of Christ (the church). Meanwhile Christ the Bridegroom is in heaven, preparing a place for the Bride of Christ to live in His Father's house.

2. The Bridegroom comes to claim His bride at the rapture, at which time He takes His bride to heaven, where He has prepared a place (John 14:1-3). The actual marriage takes place in heaven prior to the second coming (Revelation 19:11-16).

3. The marriage supper of the Lamb will follow the second coming, apparently taking place during a 75-day interim period between the second coming of Christ and the beginning of the millennial kingdom (see Daniel 12:11; compare with Matthew 22:1-14; 25:1-13). (More on this interim period later in the book.)

There are other parallels as well:

- Just as ancient Jewish grooms would pay a purchase price to establish the marriage covenant, so Jesus paid a purchase price for the church (1 Corinthians 6:19-20).

- Just as a Jewish bride was declared sanctified or set apart in waiting for her groom, so the church is declared sanctified and set apart for Christ the Bridegroom (Ephesians 5:25-27; 1 Corinthians 1:2; 6:11; Hebrews 10:10; 13:12).

- Just as a Jewish bride was unaware of the exact time her groom would come for her, so the church is unaware of the exact time that Jesus the Bridegroom will come at the rapture, though it is an imminent event.

Does the doctrine of the rapture relate to the removal of "he who now restrains" the antichrist (2 Thessalonians 2:7-8)?

Yes, I believe so. This passage reads: "The mystery of lawlessness is already at work. Only he who now restrains it will do so until he is out of the way. And then the lawless one will be revealed, whom the Lord Jesus will kill with the breath of his mouth and bring to nothing by the appearance of his coming." I believe that "he who now restrains" is the Holy Spirit.

Here's my reasoning: When the rapture occurs, it will be the church—the universal body of believers in Christ from the day of Pentecost right up to the present (Ephesians 1:3; 2:5; see also Acts 1:5; 1 Corinthians 12:13)—that will be raptured or caught up to be with Christ in the air. This church is indwelt by the Holy Spirit. We know this because 1 Corinthians 3:16 tells us, "Do you not know that you are God's temple and that God's Spirit dwells in you?" First Corinthians 6:19 tells us, "Do you not know that your body is a temple of the Holy Spirit within you, whom you have from God?" So, when the church is taken off planet Earth at the rapture (John 14:1-3; 1 Corinthians 15:51-54; 1 Thessalonians 4:13-17), the Holy Spirit will be "taken out of the way." This removal of the Holy Spirit's restraint allows the antichrist, as energized by Satan (the *un*-holy spirit), to come into power during the tribulation period.

Will the Holy Spirit still be active during the tribulation?

I'm convinced of it. Following the rapture of the church, the Holy Spirit will no longer be restraining the antichrist, but He *will* continue His work in bringing people to salvation. A multitude of people will become believers in Jesus during the tribulation period (see Matthew 24:14; Revelation 7:9-14).

How is the rapture different from the second coming?

Every eye will see Jesus at the second coming (Revelation 1:7), but the rapture is never described as being visible to the whole world. At the rapture, Jesus will come *for* His church (John 14:1-3; 1 Thessalonians 4:13-17); at the second coming, Jesus will come *with* His church (Colossians 3:4; Jude 14; Revelation 19:14). At the rapture, Christians meet Jesus in the air (1 Thessalonians 4:13-17); at the second coming, Jesus' feet touch the Mount of Olives (Zechariah 14:4). At the rapture, Christians are taken and unbelievers are left behind (1 Thessalonians 4:13-17); at the second coming, unbelievers are taken away in judgment (Luke 17:34-36) and mortal believers remain to enter into Christ's millennial kingdom (Matthew 25:31-46). At the rapture, Jesus will receive His bride; at the second coming, He will execute judgment (Matthew 25:31-46). The rapture will take place in the blink of an eye (1 Corinthians 15:52); the second coming will be more drawn out, and every eye will see Him (Matthew 24:30; Revelation 1:7).

What are some good Bible verses on the rapture and the second coming?

Key verses on the rapture: John 14:1-3; Romans 8:19; 1 Corinthians 1:7-8; 15:51-53; 16:22; Philippians 3:20-21; 4:5; Colossians 3:4; 1 Thessalonians 1:10; 2:19; 4:13-18; 5:9,23; 2 Thessalonians 2:1,3; 1 Timothy 6:14; 2 Timothy 4:1,8; Titus 2:13; Hebrews 9:28; James 5:7-9; 1 Peter 1:7,13; 5:4; 1 John 2:28–3:2; Jude 21; Revelation 2:25; 3:10.

Key verses on the second coming: Daniel 2:44-45; 7:9-14; 12:1-3; Zechariah 12:10; 14:1-15; Matthew 13:41; 24:15-31; 26:64; Mark 13:14-27; 14:62; Luke 21:25-28; Acts 1:9-11; 3:19-21; 1 Thessalonians

3:13; 2 Thessalonians 1:6-10; 2:8; 1 Peter 4:12-13; 2 Peter 3:1-14; Jude 14-15; Revelation 1:7; 19:11–20:6; 22:7,12,20.

Does Christ's second coming "with" His saints support a pretribulational rapture?

I believe it does. Pretribulationists believe the rapture involves Christ coming *for* His saints in the air prior to the tribulation, whereas at the second coming He will come *with* His saints to the earth to reign for a thousand years (Revelation 19; 20:1-6). The fact that Christ comes "with" His "holy ones" (redeemed believers) at the second coming presumes they've been previously raptured. He cannot come *with* them until He has first come *for* them.

Why is the rapture called the "blessed hope" (Titus 2:13)?

The rapture is blessed in the sense that it brings *blessedness* to believers. The term carries the idea of joyous anticipation. Believers can hardly wait for it to happen. At this momentous event, the dead in Christ will be resurrected while believers still alive on earth will be instantly translated into their resurrection bodies (see Romans 8:22-23; 1 Corinthians 15:51-58; Philippians 3:20-21; 1 Thessalonians 4:13-18; 1 John 3:2-3). These bodies will never again be subject to sickness, pain, and death. While we live in this fallen world as pilgrims, we are empowered by this magnificent blessed hope.

Will babies and young children be raptured before the tribulation along with all Christians or will they be left behind to encounter the antichrist and the judgments of the tribulation?

Though scholars have different views on this, I believe the scriptural evidence supports the idea that infants and young children will be raptured along with all Christians. I say this because of my firm belief that babies and young children who die before the age of accountability are saved. For me, the same biblical principles that render them "savable" also render them "rapture-able." Following are the biblical principles:

There comes a time when each child becomes morally responsible before God. Christians have often debated what age constitutes the age of accountability. Actually, it is not the same for everyone. Some children mature faster than others. Some come into an awareness of personal evil and righteousness before others do.

We read in James 4:17, "Whoever knows the right thing to do and fails to do it, for him it is sin." Hence, it would seem that when a child truly comes into a full awareness and moral understanding of "oughts" and "shoulds," he or she at that point has reached the age of accountability.

I believe that at the moment the child dies—and not before—the benefits of Jesus' atoning death on the cross are applied to him or her. At that moment, the child becomes saved and is immediately issued into the presence of God in heaven. Consider…

- In all the descriptions of hell in the Bible, we never read of infants or little children there. Not once. Only adults capable of making decisions are seen there.

- Nor do we read of infants and little children standing before the great white throne judgment, which is the judgment of the wicked dead and the precursor to the lake of fire (Revelation 20:11-15). The complete silence of Scripture regarding the presence of infants in eternal torment militates against their being there.

- The basis of the judgment of the lost involves deeds done while on earth (Revelation 20:11-13). Hence, infants and young children cannot possibly be the objects of this judgment because they are not responsible for their deeds. Such a judgment against infants would be a travesty.

- Jesus indicated that children have a special place in His kingdom (Matthew 18:1-14). In fact, He said that adults must become like little children to enter into His kingdom.

- King David in the Old Testament certainly believed he would again be with his son who died. In 2 Samuel 12:22-23, David said, "While the child was still alive, I fasted and wept, for I said, 'Who knows whether the LORD will be gracious to me, that the child may live?' But now he is dead. Why should I fast? Can I bring him back again? I shall go to him, but he will not return to me." David displayed complete confidence that his little one was with God in heaven, and that he would one day join his son in heaven.

For these and other reasons, I am convinced that infants and young children who die before the age of accountability are saved. I believe we can theologically infer that God will apply this same kind of saving grace to infants and young children at the rapture, thereby sparing them of any encounter with the antichrist or the horrific judgments of the tribulation period.

What does it mean to say that the rapture is imminent?

The term "imminent" literally means "ready to take place" or "impending." The New Testament teaches that the rapture is imminent—that is, nothing must be fulfilled before the rapture occurs (see 1 Corinthians 1:7; 16:22; Philippians 3:20; 4:5; 1 Thessalonians 1:10; Titus 2:13; Hebrews 9:28; James 5:7-9; 1 Peter 1:13; Jude 21). The rapture is a signless event that can occur at any moment. This is in contrast to the second coming of Christ, which is preceded by many events in the seven-year tribulation period (see Revelation 4–18).

Imminency is certainly implied in the apostle Paul's words in Romans 13:11-12: "You know the time, that the hour has come for you to wake from sleep. For salvation is *nearer to us now than when we first believed.* The night is far gone; the *day is at hand.* So then let us cast off the works of darkness and put on the armor of light." The word "salvation" in this context must be eschatological, referring to the rapture, for this "salvation" is a specific future event referenced by Paul. At the end of each day, the Christian is that much closer to the time when the rapture may occur.

Imminency is also implied in James 5:7-9:

> Be patient, therefore, brothers, until the coming of the Lord. See how the farmer waits for the precious fruit of the

earth, being patient about it, until it receives the early and the late rains. You also, be patient. Establish your hearts, for *the coming of the Lord is at hand.* Do not grumble against one another, brothers, so that you may not be judged; behold, the Judge is *standing at the door.*

Of course, imminency makes sense only within the theology of pretribulationism. In midtribulationism, the rapture is at least three and a half years into the tribulation. In posttribulationism, the rapture follows the tribulation. Hence, imminency is impossible in these systems. The doctrine of imminency is a supportive evidence for pretribulationism.

The fact that the rapture is a signless event that could occur at any moment ought to spur the Christian to live in purity and righteousness (see Titus 2:13-14). How blessed it will be for the Christian to be living in righteousness at that moment. How embarrassing it will be for the Christian to be engaged in sin at that moment.

Following the rapture, will our resurrection bodies last forever?

Yes! In an instant—in the twinkling of an eye—dead believers will be raised from the dead. Even better, at that same rapture, the bodies of living Christians will be instantly transformed into resurrection bodies, and we will all meet the Lord in the air (1 Thessalonians 4:13-17). Never again will we be subject to the frailties of our weak, mortal bodies.

In 1 Corinthians 15:42-43 the apostle Paul says of the resurrection body: "The body that is sown is perishable, it is raised imperishable; it is sown in dishonor, it is raised in glory; it is sown in weakness, it is raised in power." What a forceful statement this is of the nature of our future resurrection bodies.

Paul here graphically illustrates the contrasts between our present earthly bodies and our future resurrection bodies. The reference to *sowing* ("the body that is sown") is probably a metaphorical reference to burial. Just as one sows a seed in the ground, so a dead body is sown in the sense that it is buried in the ground. When our bodies are placed in the grave, they decompose and return to dust.

The exciting thing is what is raised out of the ground—the

resurrection body. Paul notes that our present bodies are *perishable*. The seeds of disease and death are ever upon them. It is a constant struggle to fight off dangerous infections. We often get sick. And all of us eventually die. It is just a question of time. Our new resurrection bodies, however, will be raised *imperishable*. All liability to disease and death will be forever gone. Never again will we have to worry about infections or passing away. Glorious!

Will our new resurrection bodies be strong?

Paul notes that our present bodies are characterized by weakness. From the moment we are born, the "outward man is decaying" (2 Corinthians 4:16; see also 1:8-9). Vitality decreases, illness comes, and old age follows with its wrinkles and weakness. Eventually, we may become incapacitated, not able to move around and do the simplest of tasks.

By contrast, our resurrection body will be one of great power (1 Corinthians 15:42-43). Never again will we tire or become weak or incapacitated. Words truly seem inadequate to describe the incredible differences between our present bodies (those that will be sown in the earth) and our future resurrection bodies.

Why does Paul compare our present bodies to a tent, and our future resurrection bodies to a building (2 Corinthians 5:1-4)?

Paul was speaking in terms his listeners would have readily understood. After all, the temporary tabernacle of Israel's wanderings in the wilderness (a giant tentlike structure) was eventually replaced with a permanent building (temple) when Israel entered the promised land. In like manner, the temporary tent (or body) in which believers now dwell will be replaced on the day of the rapture with an eternal, immortal, imperishable body (see 1 Corinthians 15:42,53-54).

Prior to the rapture, do believers who die go to heaven in a disembodied state?

Yes. This relates to Paul's statement in 1 Corinthians 5:4: "For while

we are in this tent [of our present mortal body], we groan and are bur-
dened, because we do not wish to be unclothed [without a body] but
to be clothed with our heavenly dwelling [resurrection body], so that
what is mortal [our earthly body] may be swallowed up by life [res-
urrection]" (inserts added for clarification). Paul here indicates that
being "unclothed"—that is, being without a physical body as a result of
death—is a state of incompletion, and for him carries a sense of naked-
ness. Even though departing to be with Christ in a disembodied state
is far better than life on earth (Philippians 1:21), Paul's true yearning
was to be clothed with a physically resurrected body (see 2 Corinthians
5:6-8). And that yearning will be fully satisfied on that future day of
resurrection at the rapture.

What is the posttribulational view of the rapture?

Posttribulationism is the view that Christ will rapture the church
after the tribulation at the second coming of Christ. This means the
church will go through the time of judgment prophesied in the book
of Revelation, but believers will allegedly be "kept through" the wrath
of the tribulation (Revelation 3:10).

What biblical evidence do posttribulationists
cite in favor of their view?

A primary argument relates to Revelation 20:4-6, which allegedly
proves that *all* believers will be resurrected at the end of the tribulation,
and hence posttribulationism must be correct. Pretribulationists argue
that, in context, only those believers who die during the tribulation will
be resurrected at this time (Revelation 20:4). Pretribulationists affirm
that believers who live prior to the tribulation will be resurrected earlier at the rapture (1 Thessalonians 4:13-17).

Does the fact that there will be saints on earth during
the tribulation period support posttribulationism?

At first glance, you might think so. But I believe another expla-
nation makes better sense. Pretribulationists grant that there will be
saints who live during the tribulation (for example, Revelation 6:9-11).

However, these people apparently become Christians *sometime after* the rapture. Perhaps they become believers as a result of the 144,000 Jewish evangelists mentioned in Revelation 7 and 14. Or perhaps they become believers as a result of the ministry of God's two prophetic witnesses in Revelation 11. Seen in this light, the presence of saints in the tribulation period is perfectly compatible with pretribulationism.

Doesn't Matthew 24:37-40 support posttribulationism?

Posttribulationists often cite Matthew 24:37-40, a passage that relates to the second coming: "Two men will be in the field; one will be taken and the other left." This may sound like it supports a post-tribulational rapture. However, those who are taken are taken not in the rapture but are *taken away in judgment, to be punished.* A key cross reference, Luke 17:35-37, makes this clear: "There will be two women grinding together. One will be taken and the other left. And they said to him, 'Where, Lord?' He said to them, 'Where the corpse is, there the vultures will gather.'" Those who are "taken" become corpses that feed the vultures. Hence, the passage does not refer to the rapture.

Does the fact that pretribulationism emerged late in church history argue against its validity?

Posttribulationists often claim that pretribulationism emerged late in church history, finding its origin in John Nelson Darby (1800–1882), who allegedly got it from Edward Irving (1792–1834). Thus, the majority of church history knew nothing of this novel view.

Pretribulationists assert that this argument from church history is fallacious, wrongly supposing that truth is somehow determined by time. They observe that some in the first five centuries of church history held to false doctrines, such as baptismal regeneration. Just because a doctrine appeared early does not mean it is correct. Conversely, just because a doctrine emerged late does not mean it is incorrect.

Pretribulationists believe that with the process of doctrinal development through the centuries, it makes sense that eschatology would become a focus later in church history. Besides, many throughout church history—as early as the first century—have held to the doctrine of the imminent return of Christ, a key feature of pretribulationism but not of posttribulationism.

Moreover, the key consideration is, "Is the doctrine biblical?" rather than, "When in church history did the doctrine emerge?" Pretribulationalists argue that their position makes the best sense of the scriptural data.

Are there any theological problems with posttribulationism?

Yes. A big one relates to the question of who will populate Christ's thousand-year millennial kingdom in their mortal bodies, as Scripture clearly teaches. Scripture says that the believers who enter the millennial kingdom will still be married, bear children, grow old, and die (see Isaiah 65:20; Matthew 25:31-46). If all believers are raptured (with resurrection bodies) at the second coming, there are no believers left to enter the millennial kingdom in their mortal bodies. This is no problem for pretribulationism, which teaches that after the rapture, many will become believers during the tribulation period. It is these who enter the millennial kingdom in their mortal bodies.

What is the midtribulational view of the rapture?

Midtribulationism claims that Christ will rapture the church in the *middle* of the tribulation period. In this view, the last half of the seventieth week of Daniel (Daniel 9:24-27) is much more severe than the first half. (The seventieth week of Daniel is a reference to the seven-year period of tribulation.) It is this last half of the tribulation that the church will be delivered from.

Why do midtribulationists believe the church will be caught up to the Lord in the middle of the tribulation?

Midtribulationists argue that the two prophetic witnesses of Revelation 11, who are caught up to heaven in the middle of the tribulation period, are representative of the church. This is in contrast to pretribulationists, who argue that there is no indication in the context that these prophetic witnesses represent the church. Pretribulationists believe this is an example of eisegesis—reading a meaning into the text that is not there.

How do midtribulationists deal with God's deliverance of the church from His wrath?

Proponents of midtribulationism argue that the church will be delivered from God's wrath (1 Thessalonians 5:9), which, they say, is *only* in the second half of the tribulation. However, the church will not be delivered from the general tribulation in the first half of the tribulation.

This is in contrast to pretribulationists, who argue that since the entire tribulation period is characterized by wrath (Zephaniah 1:15,18; 1 Thessalonians 1:10; Revelation 6:17; 14:7,10; 19:2), it makes more sense to say the church is delivered from the entire seven-year period (1 Thessalonians 1:9-10; 5:9; Revelation 3:10).

What is the "trumpet" argument offered by midtribulationists?

Proponents of midtribulationism argue that because the rapture occurs at the last trumpet (1 Corinthians 15:52), and because the seventh trumpet sounds in the middle of the tribulation (Revelation 11:15-19), then the rapture must occur at the midpoint of the tribulation. Pretribulationists respond, however, that the seventh trumpet in Revelation 11 is unrelated to the rapture but rather deals with the unleashing of judgment. This is different from the trumpet in 1 Corinthians 15, which relates to the rapture and glorification. These are two entirely different contexts, and hence the trumpets are unrelated to each other.

What is the partial rapture theory?

The partial rapture theory is based on the parable of the ten virgins, which depicts five virgins being prepared and five unprepared (Matthew 25:1-13). This is interpreted to mean that only faithful, watchful, and praying Christians will be raptured. Only Christians who have "loved his appearing" (2 Timothy 4:8) and those "who are eagerly waiting for him" (Hebrews 9:28) will be caught up to meet the Lord in the air. Unfaithful Christians, or professed Christians who are not really Christians at all, will be left behind to suffer through the tribulation. In this view, multitudes who expect to be raptured will not be raptured. Unfaithful and unprepared Christians will be sifted and refined by the fiery trials of the tribulation, so that they will be made ready to meet the Lord at the second coming.

What's the problem with the partial rapture theory?

Pretribulationists respond that Matthew 25:1-13 has nothing to do with the rapture. Those virgins who are unprepared represent people living during the tribulation period who are unprepared for Christ's second coming (seven years after the rapture). Some claim the partial rapture theory amounts to a Protestant version of purgatory in which Christians get purged into readiness to meet the Lord at the second coming. This implies that trusting in the atonement of Christ alone (2 Corinthians 5:21) is not sufficient to bring one to heaven (see also Romans 5:1; Colossians 2:13). Scripture reveals that if one is a believer, one is "saved" (John 3:16-17; Acts 16:31) and that alone qualifies one to participate in the rapture (1 Corinthians 15:51-52).

Moreover, the Spirit's baptism places *all* believers into Christ's body (1 Corinthians 12:13) and therefore all believers will be raptured (1 Thessalonians 4:16-17). The partial rapture theory denies the perfect unity in the body of Christ (1 Corinthians 12:12-13). First Corinthians 15:51 settles the issue, for it specifically tells us that "we shall *all* be changed." "We" includes even the carnal believers in the Corinthian church, to whom Paul was writing. "All" will participate in the rapture.

What is the pre-wrath theory of the rapture?

The pre-wrath theory argues that the rapture will occur toward the end of the tribulation period before "the great wrath of God" falls. Proponents say the Bible indicates that the church will go through the first part of the seventieth week of Daniel (the tribulation, Daniel 9:24-27), but not experience the wrath of God (2 Thessalonians 1:5-10). Since the word "wrath" does not appear in Revelation until after the sixth seal, this must mean God's wrath will not be poured out until the seventh seal (Revelation 6:12–8:1). Hence, the rapture must take place between the sixth and seventh seals in the latter part of the tribulation, and not before.

What's the problem with the prewrath theory of the rapture?

The claim that God's wrath is not poured out on the earth prior to the seventh seal is simply false (Zephaniah 1:15,18; 1 Thessalonians 1:10; Revelation 6:17; 14:7,10; 19:2). Scripture pictures the seven seals as a sequence, all coming from the same ultimate source—God (Revelation 6; 8). This sequence features divine judgments that increase in intensity with each new seal. Both human beings and warfare are seen to be instruments of God's wrath during the first six seals. Even the unsaved who experience this wrath recognize it specifically as the "wrath of the Lamb" (Revelation 6:15-16), who Himself opens each seal that causes each respective judgment (see Revelation 6:1-12; 8:1).

How should Christians with differing views on the timing of the rapture relate to each other?

Despite the differences Christians may have on the timing of the rapture, we can point to many agreements that ought to serve as a basis for unity even in the midst of our diversity on the issue. For example, all agree that God is sovereignly in charge of the precise timing of endtime events. All agree there will be a rapture. All agree there will be a physical second coming of Christ. All agree there will be a future resurrection from the dead. All agree there will be a future judgment. All agree there will be an eternal state in which resurrected believers will live eternally with God. All agree that one beneficial aspect of studying biblical prophecy is that it motivates one to holiness in life. The best policy is therefore to *agree to disagree in an agreeable way* on the timing of the rapture!

12

The Judgment Seat of Christ

Will Christians face judgment?

Yes. All believers will one day stand before the judgment seat of Christ (Romans 14:8-10; 1 Corinthians 3:11-15; 9:24-27). At that time each believer's life will be thoroughly examined by Christ, the divine Judge.

What is a "judgment seat"?

The idea of a judgment seat goes back to the athletic games of Paul's day. After the games concluded, a dignitary took his seat on an elevated throne in the arena. One by one the winning athletes came up to the throne to receive a reward—usually a wreath of leaves, a victor's crown. In the case of Christians, each of us will stand before Christ the Judge and receive (or possibly *lose*) rewards.

Can we lose our salvation at the judgment seat of Christ?

No. Those who have placed faith in Christ are permanently saved, and nothing threatens that. Believers are eternally secure in their salvation (see John 10:28-30; Romans 8:29-39; Ephesians 1:13; 4:30; Hebrews 7:25). This judgment has to do with the reception or loss of rewards, depending upon whether the Christian has lived faithfully or unfaithfully during his or her earthly life (see 1 Corinthians 3:12-15).

Will Christians be held accountable for all their actions on earth?

Yes. The Christian's judgment will focus on his or her personal stewardship of the gifts, talents, opportunities, and responsibilities given to him or her in this life. The very character of each Christian's life and service will be utterly laid bare under the unerring and omniscient vision of Christ, whose eyes are "like a flame of fire" (Revelation 1:14).

Numerous Scripture verses reveal that each of our actions will be judged before the Lord. For example, the psalmist affirmed to the Lord: "You will render to a man according to his work" (Psalm 62:12; see also Matthew 16:27). In Ephesians 6:7-8 we read that "whatever good anyone does, this he will receive back from the Lord."

What about our thoughts? Will they be judged too?

Though it might seem a bit unnerving, the answer is yes. In Jeremiah 17:10 God said, "I the LORD search the heart and test the mind, to give every man according to his ways, according to the fruit of his deeds." The Lord "will bring to light the things now hidden in darkness and will disclose the purposes of the heart" (1 Corinthians 4:5). The Lord is the One "who searches mind and heart" (Revelation 2:23). So—all our motives will be laid bare.

Will the words we spoke on earth come up at the judgment seat of Christ?

Again, it's a bit unnerving to think about, but the answer is yes. Christ once promised: "I tell you, on the day of judgment people will give account for every careless word they speak, for by your words you will be justified, and by your words you will be condemned" (Matthew 12:36-37). Think about that a minute. If even our careless words are carefully recorded, how much more will our calculated boastful claims, our cutting criticisms of others, our off-color jokes, and our unkind comments be taken into account. This is an important aspect of judgment, for tremendous damage can be done through the human tongue (see James 3:1-12).

Will we be judged on anything else?

The judgment will be comprehensive. Our accountability to God embraces all of life. We will be held accountable for how we use our God-given talents and abilities (Matthew 25:14-29; Luke 19:11-26;

1 Corinthians 12:4-7; 2 Timothy 1:6; 1 Peter 4:10) and for how we spend our time (Psalm 90:9-12; Ephesians 5:15-16; Colossians 4:5; 1 Peter 1:17). We will be held accountable for how we treat others (Matthew 10:41-42; Hebrews 6:10), our hospitality to strangers (Matthew 25:35-36; Luke 14:12-14), responding in a godly way to mistreatment (Matthew 5:11-12; Mark 10:29-30; Luke 6:27-28,35; Romans 8:18; 2 Corinthians 4:17; 1 Peter 4:12-13), and making efforts toward winning souls for Christ (Proverbs 11:30; Daniel 12:3; 1 Thessalonians 2:19-20). We will also be held accountable for our attitude toward money (Matthew 6:1-4; 1 Timothy 6:17-19). All this is a powerful motivation to submit to Christ in all areas of our lives.

Is 1 Corinthians 3:12-15 referring to the judgment of Christ?

Yes. This passage metaphorically refers to the possibility of building our lives using bad materials (such as hay, straw, or wood) or good materials (such as precious metals and stones). Notice that these materials are combustible in increasing degrees. Obviously the hay and straw are the most combustible. Then comes wood. Precious metals and stones are not combustible.

Some of these materials are useful for building while others are not. If you construct a house made of hay or straw, it surely will not stand long. It can burn to the ground very easily. But a house constructed with solid materials such as stones and metals will last a long time. Christ says we should build our lives with good materials.

What do the various materials in 1 Corinthians 3:12-15 represent?

Scripture doesn't specify. But I think it likely that gold, silver, and costly stones refer to things we accomplish by the power of the Holy Spirit—things we do with Christ-honoring motives and godly obedience. Wood, hay, and straw, on the other hand, likely represent carnal attitudes, sinful motives, pride-filled actions, and selfish ambition.

What are we to make of the fire mentioned in 1 Corinthians 3:12-15?

Fire in Scripture often symbolizes the holiness of God (Leviticus 1:8; Hebrews 12:29). There are clear cases in the Bible in which fire portrays God's judgment upon what His holiness has condemned (Genesis 19:24; Mark 9:43-48). We surmise, then, that God will examine our works, and they will be tested against the fire of His holiness. If our works are built with good materials—with Christ-honoring motives and godly obedience—our works will stand. But if our works are built with bad materials—carnal attitudes, sinful motives, pride-filled actions, and selfish ambition—they will burn up.

What kinds of rewards will believers receive at the judgment seat of Christ?

Scripture often speaks of the rewards Christians receive at the judgment as crowns that they wear. A number of different crowns symbolize the various spheres of achievement and award in the Christian life. These include:

- *The crown of life*—given to those who persevere under trial, and especially to those who suffer to the point of death (James 1:12; Revelation 2:10)
- *The crown of glory*—given to those who faithfully and sacrificially minister God's Word to the flock (1 Peter 5:4)
- *The crown incorruptible*—given to those who win the race of temperance and self-control (1 Corinthians 9:25)
- *The crown of righteousness*—given to those who long for the second coming of Christ (2 Timothy 4:8)

Are our crowns intended to bring us glory in heaven?

Revelation 4:10 portrays believers casting all their crowns before the throne of God in an act of worship and adoration. This communicates something very important to us. The crowns—as rewards—are bestowed on us not for our own glory but ultimately for the glory of

God. We are told elsewhere in Scripture that believers are redeemed in order to bring glory to God (1 Corinthians 6:20). The act of placing our crowns before the throne of God is an illustration of this.

Here's something else to think about. The greater the reward or crown we have received, the greater our capacity to bring glory to the Creator in the afterlife. The lesser reward or crown we have received, the lesser our capacity to bring glory to the Creator in the afterlife. Because of the different rewards handed out at the judgment seat of Christ, believers will have differing capacities to glorify God.

When will the judgment seat of Christ take place?

Apparently, this judgment will take place immediately after the rapture, after believers enter into heaven (John 14:1-3; 1 Corinthians 15:51-54; 1 Thessalonians 4:13-17). This is a theological inference based on several scriptural facts. First, many Bible expositors believe that the 24 elders in heaven represent believers (see Revelation 4:1,10). After all, these elders are portrayed as having crowns on their heads at the very start of the tribulation period. It seems logical to surmise that if the elders represent believers, and if they already have crowns early in the tribulation period, then they must have faced judgment right after the rapture.

In keeping with this, Scripture reveals that at the second coming of Christ, which follows the tribulation period, the Bride of Christ (the corporate body of Christians) will return with Him. They will be adorned in "fine linen, bright and pure" (Revelation 19:8). Such apparel seems to indicate that believers have already passed through judgment.

Is the judgment seat of Christ intended as an encouragement or a warning?

Perhaps this judgment is intended to be both an encouragement *and* a warning. It is an encouragement to those who are consistently serving Christ with good motives. It is a warning to those who have fallen into carnal living. God will render perfect justice in the end.

Is it possible that some Christians may be ashamed at the judgment seat of Christ?

It is entirely possible. One of the more sobering realities to ponder is that Christians who live a carnal lifestyle may subsequently experience a sense of shame and embarrassment at the judgment seat of Christ. Such Christians will forfeit rewards that could have been theirs had they been faithful. This seems to be implied in 2 John 8, where John urges: "Watch yourselves, so that you may not lose what we have worked for, but may win a full reward" (see also 1 John 2:28). A loss of rewards is here presented as a genuine possibility for the believer.

How can we be happy throughout eternity if we don't fare well at the judgment seat of Christ?

While some will not fare as well as others at the judgment seat of Christ (2 John 8), we must keep all this in perspective. Christ's coming for us at the rapture and the prospect of living eternally with Him is something that should give each of us joy. And our joy will last for all eternity. An analogy is that some high school students may receive better grades than others, but they're all thrilled to graduate. All are thankful for the future that lies ahead.

I once heard it said that in heaven all of our cups will be running over, but some cups will be larger than others. Perhaps the most important thing to ponder is that each one of us will be able to perpetually and forever "proclaim the excellencies of him who called you out of darkness into his marvelous light" (1 Peter 2:9).

What should be our attitude toward the judgment seat of Christ?

I am firmly convinced that Jesus delights to reward His people. He *yearns* to do it. It will bring a smile to His face to be able to hand you a reward at the judgment seat. That fact—in addition to the wondrous salvation He has provided us—should motivate us all to serve and obey Him with joy and a sense of thrill for the future.

13

The Tribulation Period

How does general tribulation compare with the future tribulation period?

The Greek word for "tribulation" (*thlipsis*) literally means "to press" (as grapes), "to press together," "to press hard upon," and often refers to times of oppression, affliction, and distress. It is translated variously as "tribulation," "affliction," "anguish," "persecution," "trouble," and "burden." The word has been used in relation to...

- those "hard pressed" by the calamities of war (Matthew 24:21)

- a woman giving birth to a child (John 16:21)

- the afflictions of Christ (Colossians 1:24)

- those "pressed" by poverty and lack (Philippians 4:14)

- great anxiety and burden of heart (2 Corinthians 2:4)

- a period in the end times that will have unparalleled suffering (Revelation 7:14)

All Christians can expect a certain amount of general tribulation in their lives. Jesus said to the disciples, "In the world you will have tribulation" (John 16:33). Paul and Barnabas likewise warned that "through many tribulations we must enter the kingdom of God" (Acts 14:22).

Such general tribulation is to be distinguished from the tribulation period of the end times, based on the following six facts:

- Scripture refers to a definite period of tribulation at the end of the age (Matthew 24:29-35; Revelation 3:10).

- It will be of such severity that no period in history—past or future—will equal it (Matthew 24:21).

- It is called the time of Jacob's trouble, for it is a judgment on Messiah-rejecting Israel (Jeremiah 30:7; Daniel 12:1-4). ("Jacob" refers to Israel.)

- The unbelieving nations will also be judged for their sin and rejection of Christ during this period of tribulation (Isaiah 26:21; Revelation 6:15-17).

- This tribulation period is precisely seven years in length (Daniel 9:24,27; compare with Revelation 11:2,14; 12:6).

- This period will be so bad that people will want to hide and even die (Revelation 6:16).

How bad will the future tribulation period be?

Scripture reveals that the tribulation period will be characterized by wrath (Zephaniah 1:15,18), judgment (Revelation 14:7), indignation (Isaiah 26:20-21), trial (Revelation 3:10), trouble (Jeremiah 30:7), destruction (Joel 1:15), darkness (Amos 5:18), desolation (Daniel 9:27), overturning (Isaiah 24:1-4), and punishment (Isaiah 24:20-21). Simply put, no passage of Scripture can be found to alleviate to any degree whatsoever the severity of this time that shall come upon the earth.

Will the tribulation period encompass the entire earth?

Yes. Revelation 3:10 describes the tribulation period as "the hour of trial that is coming on the whole world, to try those who dwell on the earth." Isaiah likewise speaks of this period: "Behold, the Lord will empty the earth and make it desolate, and he will twist its surface and scatter its inhabitants...Terror and the pit and the snare are upon you, O inhabitant of the earth" (Isaiah 24:1,17). The tribulation period thus involves *global* tribulation.

What is the purpose of the tribulation period?

Scripture reveals several purposes of the tribulation period. First, the tribulation will bring to conclusion "the times of the Gentiles," which refers to the time of Gentile domination over Jerusalem. This period began with the Babylonian captivity that started in 606 BC. The "times of the Gentiles" was well entrenched by AD 70 when Titus and his Roman warriors overran Jerusalem and destroyed the Jewish temple. This "time" will last into the seven-year tribulation period (Revelation 11:2) and will not end until the second coming of Jesus Christ (see Luke 21:24).

Beyond this, the tribulation will bring judgment against the Christ-rejecting nations of the world (Isaiah 26:21; Revelation 6:15-17). It also will purge Christ-rejecting Israel and prepare for her restoration and regathering in the millennial kingdom of Christ following the second coming (Jeremiah 30:7; Daniel 12:1-4).

It is critical to recognize that the purpose of the tribulation has nothing to do with the church, for the church has been promised deliverance from the wrath to come (1 Thessalonians 1:10; 5:9).

What is the source of the tribulation period?

The tribulation period is a time of both divine wrath and satanic wrath—but especially divine wrath. We are told that the tribulation is "the day of the wrath of the LORD" (Zephaniah 1:18). The earth will experience "the wrath of the Lamb" (Revelation 6:16-17). "The LORD will empty the earth, and make it desolate" (Isaiah 24:1), and "the LORD is coming out from his place to punish the inhabitants of the earth for their iniquity" (Isaiah 26:21). Satan's wrath is evident in Revelation 12:4,13,17.

What does the book of Revelation say about God's judgments during the tribulation period?

Human suffering will steadily escalate throughout the tribulation period. First come God's seal judgments, involving bloodshed, famine, death, economic upheaval, a great earthquake, and cosmic disturbances (Revelation 6). Then come His trumpet judgments, involving hail and fire mixed with blood, the sea turning to blood, water turning bitter, further cosmic disturbances, affliction by demonic scorpions, and the death of a third of humankind (Revelation 8:6–9:21).

Finally come His increasingly worse bowl judgments, involving horribly painful sores on human beings, more bodies of water turning to blood, the death of all sea creatures, people being scorched by the sun, rivers drying up, total darkness engulfing the land, a devastating earthquake, widespread destruction, and much more (Revelation 16). Such is the judgment of God on a Christ-rejecting world.

What kinds of cosmic disturbances will occur during the tribulation period?

Some cosmic disturbances are associated with God's seal judgments: "When he opened the sixth seal, I looked, and behold, there was a great earthquake, and the sun became black as sackcloth, the full moon became like blood" (Revelation 6:12). The same will be true of the trumpet judgments: "The fourth angel blew his trumpet, and a third of the sun was struck, and a third of the moon, and a third of the stars, so that a third of their light might be darkened, and a third of the day might be kept from shining, and likewise a third of the night" (8:12).

Cosmic disturbances will also occur just prior to the second coming of Christ. Matthew 24:29-30 tells us: "Immediately after the tribulation of those days the sun will be darkened, and the moon will not give its light, and the stars will fall from heaven, and the powers of the heavens will be shaken. Then will appear in heaven the sign of the Son of Man, and then all the tribes of the earth will mourn, and they will see the Son of Man coming on the clouds of heaven with power and great glory" (see also Isaiah 13:10; 24:23; Ezekiel 32:7; Joel 2:10,31; 3:15; Amos 5:20; 8:9; Zephaniah 1:15; Acts 2:20).

What is the meaning of the first horseman of the apocalypse?

The four horsemen of the apocalypse relate to the seal judgments that are poured out on humankind during the tribulation (see Revelation 6). We first find reference to a person riding a white horse (6:2). Some have speculated that perhaps the rider is Jesus Christ, since He is later seen riding a white horse (19:11). However, the contexts are entirely different. In Revelation 19 Christ returns to the earth as a conqueror on a horse at the end of the tribulation period. By contrast, Revelation 6 describes a rider on a horse at the beginning of the tribulation, in association with three other horses and their riders, all associated with the seal judgments. Most scholars believe the rider of the white horse in Revelation 6:2 is none other than the antichrist (Daniel 9:26). The crown suggests that this individual is a ruler. It may be that the mention of the bow without an arrow is symbolic of the idea that the antichrist's initial world government will be accomplished without warfare. It would seem that his government begins with a time of peace, but it is short-lived, for destruction will surely follow (see 1 Thessalonians 5:3).

What is the meaning of the second horseman of the apocalypse?

A second horse is mentioned in Revelation 6:3-4, and it is red—a color that represents bloodshed, killing with the sword, and war (see also Matthew 24:6-7). The rider himself carries a large sword. These verses symbolize that this man's efforts at bringing about peace will be utterly frustrated, for peace will be taken from the entire earth. As bad as this will be, however, it will represent only the initial "birth pangs" of what is yet to come upon the earth (see Matthew 24:8; Mark 13:7-8; Luke 21:9). Of course, history tells us that whenever there is war, there is also economic instability and food shortages.

What is the meaning of the third horseman of the apocalypse?

A third horse mentioned in Revelation 6:5-6 is black. The rider is carrying a pair of scales in his hand. This apparently symbolizes famine (with subsequent death), as the prices for wheat and barley are extravagantly high, requiring a full day's wages just to buy a few meals. Such a famine would not be unexpected following global war.

Runaway inflation will emerge during this time. The buying power of money will drop dramatically. The cost of any available food will be exorbitantly high.

Black is an appropriate color here for it points to the lamentation and sorrow that naturally accompanies extreme deprivation. That black can represent hunger is illustrated for us in Lamentations 4:8-9: "Now their face is blacker than soot; they are not recognized in the streets; their skin has shriveled on their bones; it has become as dry as wood. Happier were the victims of the sword than the victims of hunger, who wasted away, pierced by lack of the fruits of the field."

Such famine is in keeping with Jesus' own words regarding the end times. He affirmed that the first three birth pangs will be false messiahs, war, and famine (Matthew 24:5-7). While some of this famine will be due to the outbreak of war (second horse), some famine may also relate to the fact that believers in God who refuse to take the mark of the beast will not be permitted to buy or sell, which means they will have much less food than everyone else. As economic outcasts, believers during the tribulation will experience much hunger. By contrast, those who reject God will be motivated to receive the mark of the beast so they can eat. These will be black days indeed.

What is the meaning of the fourth horseman of the apocalypse?

A fourth horse mentioned in Revelation 6:7-8 is pale—literally, "yellowish-green," the color of a corpse. The rider of this horse is appropriately named Death. It would seem that the death symbolized here is the natural consequence of the previous judgments (war and famine). The death toll will be catastrophic—a fourth of earth's population.

Woe to those who dwell on the earth during this time!

Are there parallels between the book of Revelation and Jesus' prophetic Olivet Discourse regarding the tribulation period?

Yes, I believe so. Consider the following parallels:

- Jesus speaks of the rise of false Christs (Matthew 24:4-5), just as the first seal speaks of the rise of the antichrist (Revelation 6:1-2).

- Jesus speaks of wars and rumors of wars (Matthew 24:6),

just as the second seal is said to involve warfare in which nations rise up against each other (Revelation 6:3-4).

- Jesus speaks of famines (Matthew 24:7), just as the third seal involves famine (Revelation 6:5-6).

- Jesus speaks of earthquakes (Matthew 24:7), just as the sixth seal involves an earthquake (Revelation 6:12-14).

What are Daniel's 70 weeks, and how do these weeks relate to the tribulation period (Daniel 1:25-27)?

In Daniel 9 God provides a prophetic timetable for the nation of Israel. The prophetic clock began ticking when the command went out to restore and rebuild Jerusalem following its destruction by Babylon (Daniel 9:25). According to this verse, Israel's timetable was divided into 70 groups of 7 years, totaling 490 years.

The first 69 groups of 7 years—or 483 years—counted the years "from the going out of the word to restore and build Jerusalem to the coming of an anointed one, a prince" (Daniel 9:25). The "anointed one," of course, is Jesus Christ. "Anointed one" literally means "Messiah." The day that Jesus rode into Jerusalem to proclaim Himself Israel's Messiah was exactly 483 years to the day after the command to restore and rebuild Jerusalem had been given.

At that point God's prophetic clock stopped. Daniel describes a gap between these 483 years and the final 7 years of Israel's prophetic timetable. Several events were to take place during this gap, according to Daniel 9:26:

- The Messiah would be killed.

- The city of Jerusalem and its temple would be destroyed (which occurred in AD 70).

- The Jews would encounter difficulty and hardship from that time on.

The final "week" of seven years will begin for Israel when the antichrist confirms a "strong covenant" for seven years (Daniel 9:27). When this peace pact is signed, this will signal the beginning of the tribulation period. That signature marks the beginning of the seven-year countdown to the second coming of Christ, which follows the tribulation period.

Why is the second half of the tribulation period called the "great tribulation"?

There are a number of reasons for distinguishing the two halves of the tribulation period. First, the foundational prophecy in Daniel 9:27 makes a distinction between the two halves. This verse speaks of the antichrist during the tribulation period: "He shall make a strong covenant with many for one week, and for half of the week he shall put an end to sacrifice and offering." The "week" refers to a week of years—the seven years of the tribulation period. For half of that week—that is, the last three and a half years—the antichrist will put an end to animal sacrifices in the rebuilt Jewish temple. The antichrist will do this because of his desire to be worshipped as God. He will take his seat in the Jewish temple, announce that he is God, and demand that his subjects worship him alone (see Daniel 7:8,11,20,25; 11:36-37; 2 Thessalonians 2:3-4; Revelation 13:4-8,11-17; 19:20; 20:4).

In this context, the latter part of Daniel 9:27 takes on great significance: "He shall make a strong covenant with many for one week, and for half of the week he shall put an end to sacrifice and offering. *And on the wing of abominations shall come one who makes desolate, until the decreed end is poured out on the desolator.*" Once the antichrist puts an end to the animal sacrifices in the Jewish temple, he will apparently desecrate the temple at the midpoint of the tribulation period. Jesus tells us what happens next: "Then there will be *great tribulation*, such as has not been from the beginning of the world until now, no, and never will be" (Matthew 24:21).

What is the day of the Lord, and how does it relate to the tribulation period?

"Day of the Lord" is used in several senses in Scripture. The Old Testament prophets sometimes used the term to describe an event to be fulfilled in the near future. At other times, they used the term of an event in the distant eschatological future—the future tribulation period. The immediate context generally indicates which sense is intended.

In both cases, the day of the Lord is characterized by God intervening supernaturally in order to bring judgment against sin in the world. The day of the Lord is a time in which God controls and dominates history in a direct way, instead of working through secondary causes.

Among the New Testament writers, the term is generally used of the judgment that will climax in the end-times seven-year tribulation period (see 2 Thessalonians 2:2; Revelation 16–18), as well as the judgment that will usher in the new earth (2 Peter 3:10-13; Revelation 20:7–21:1; see also Isaiah 65:17-19; 66:22; Revelation 21:1). This theme of judgment against sin runs like a thread through the many references to the day of the Lord.

Are there scriptural evidences that the church will escape the tribulation period?

Yes. I address this is in detail in chapter 11, "The Rapture of the Church." Briefly:

- The tribulation relates to Israel and Gentiles, not the church.

- No Old or New Testament passage on the tribulation mentions the church.

- The church is promised deliverance from the wrath to come (1 Thessalonians 1:10; 5:9).

- The church is promised deliverance from the actual *time period* of the tribulation (Revelation 3:10).

- It is characteristic of God to deliver believers before divine wrath and judgment fall (for example, Noah and Lot).

- Pretribulationism does not confuse terms like "believers" (general) with terms like "church" (specific). So, the presence of "believers" in the tribulation does not prove the church is in the tribulation. These people become believers during the tribulation.

- Pretribulationism distinguishes between general tribulation and the tribulation period.

- Pretribulationism is the only view that uses a consistently literal interpretation of all Old Testament and New Testament passages on the tribulation.

- If the church is raptured at the end of the tribulation, as posttribulationists hold, there will be no believers left on earth to populate the millennial kingdom *in their mortal bodies* (see Matthew 25:31-46).

- At the rapture, the church goes to the Father's house (John 14:3), not back to earth again as posttribulationists hold.

- Since the first 69 weeks of Daniel were subject to literal fulfillment, the final (seventieth) week will have a similar literal fulfillment. All 70 weeks of Daniel relate to Israel and her relation to Gentile powers and the rejection of Israel's Messiah. There is no reference to the church.

See chapter 11 for more on all this.

Will the balance of power shift to Europe during the tribulation period?

I believe so. The Bible is clear that in the end times, a political and economic powerhouse will be a revived Roman Empire—what we might call the United States of Europe. God's Word prophetically addresses this in the book of Daniel (see Daniel 7:3-8). The antichrist will eventually come into absolute power and dominance over this revived Roman Empire (see 2 Thessalonians 2:3-10; Revelation 13:1-10).

Will this be a united empire during the tribulation period?

Apparently not. In Daniel 2 we read of a prophetic dream that Nebuchadnezzar had. In this dream, this end-times Roman Empire was pictured as a mixture of iron and clay (see verses 41-43). Daniel, the great dream-interpreter, saw this as meaning that just as iron is strong, so this latter-day Roman Empire will be strong. But just as iron and clay do not naturally mix with each other, so this latter-day Roman Empire will have some divisions. The component parts of this empire will not be completely integrated with each other.

Is it possible that today's European Union is a good prospect for the ultimate fulfillment of this prophecy?

I believe that may be the case. The goal of the European Union is to unite all of Europe into a single union that will promote peace, harmony, and prosperity among its constituent parts. Such a union would eliminate national rivalries and conflicts within Europe.

Does the clay and iron metaphor in Daniel 2 fit today's European Union?

It very well may. The clay and iron referenced in Daniel 2 indicate weakness and strength at the same time. Today the European Union possesses great economic and political strength, but the nations that comprise this union are quite diverse in culture, language, and politics, and hence are not perfectly united. At present, the European Union has its own parliament, a rotating presidency, a supreme court, a common currency used in many member nations, allows for unrestricted travel of citizens among member nations, and is working toward a unified military. Perhaps the stage is now being set for the ultimate fulfillment of Daniel 2. What is taking place in Europe today may be a prelude to the eventual revived Roman Empire of Daniel's prophecy.

Does the rise of a revived Roman Empire mean that the United States will weaken in the end times?

It's not just possible, it's highly likely. The United States may decline due to a moral implosion, an economic collapse, a nuclear attack, an electromagnetic pulse (EMP) attack, the rapture of the church, or a combination of these. See chapter 9, "America in Prophecy."

14

The Antichrist and the False Prophet

Who is the antichrist?

The apostle Paul warned of a "man of lawlessness"—the antichrist (2 Thessalonians 2:3,8-9). The apostle John described this anti-God individual as "the beast" (Revelation 13:1-10). This Satan-energized individual will rise to prominence in the tribulation period. He'll head up a revived Roman Empire, and will initially enact a peace treaty with Israel (Daniel 9:27). He'll then seek to dominate the world, double-cross and seek to destroy the Jews, persecute believers, and set up his own kingdom (Revelation 13). He will speak arrogant and boastful words in glorifying himself (2 Thessalonians 2:4). His character will be one of perpetual self-exaltation.

Why is the antichrist called a beast?

"Beast" is the most frequently used title of the antichrist in the book of Revelation, being used there 32 times (see Revelation 13:1-3). The Greek word for "beast" (*therion*) indicates a wild and rapacious animal. The symbol of the beast was apparently chosen by God to designate the beastly or animal nature of the antichrist.

We read of another beast in Revelation 13:11 who will serve as the antichrist's first lieutenant. This second beast—the false prophet—will seek to bring about the worship of the antichrist through performing great and miraculous signs, such as bringing fire down from heaven (verse 13). Those who refuse to worship the antichrist bring a death sentence upon themselves (verse 15). In those days no one will be able to buy or sell without having received the mark of the beast (verses 16-17).

These three—Satan, the antichrist, and the false prophet—will form a counterfeit trinity.

How does the antichrist, as a "beast," contrast with Jesus Christ?

Just as the term "beast" is often used of the antichrist in Revelation, so in this same book "the Lamb" is often used of Jesus Christ:

- The "Lamb" is the Savior of sinners; the "beast" is the persecutor and slayer of the saints.

- "Lamb" calls attention to the gentleness of Christ; "beast" tells of the ferocity of the antichrist.

- "Lamb" reveals Christ as the "harmless" one (Hebrews 7:26); "beast" points to the antichrist as the cruel and heartless one.

- The Holy Spirit came upon the Lamb in the form of a dove at Jesus' baptism; the one who comes upon the antichrist as "the beast" is Satan (see 2 Thessalonians 2:9; Revelation 12:9).

What is the mark of the beast?

The book of Revelation reveals that the false prophet will seek to force humans to worship the antichrist, the man of sin. He "causes all, both small and great, both rich and poor, both free and slave, to be marked on the right hand or the forehead, so that no one can buy or sell unless he has the mark, that is, the name of the beast or the number of its name" (Revelation 13:16-17). This squeeze play—demanding the mark of the beast—will effectively force people to make a choice: either worship the antichrist or starve (with no ability to buy or sell).

What is the mark that will be placed on people? Apparently people will somehow be branded, just as animals today are branded and as slaves were once branded by their slave owners. The mark of the beast will thus indicate ownership and submission, religious commitment, and "religious orthodoxy" in submitting to the antichrist, who positions himself as God.

The mark of the beast is separate and distinct from the technology that enables him to enforce his economic system. The mark may well be something like a barcode tattoo. Modern technology such as chip implants, scan technology, and biometrics will likely be used to enforce this mark globally.

Receiving the mark of the beast is apparently an unpardonable sin (Revelation 14:9-10). It reveals an implicit approval of the antichrist as a leader and an implicit agreement with his purpose. No one takes this mark as an accident. One must volitionally choose to do so, with all the facts on the table. It will be a deliberate choice with eternal consequences. Those who choose to receive the mark will do so with the full knowledge of what they have done.

The choice will cause a radical polarization. There is no possible middle ground. One chooses either for or against the antichrist. One chooses either for or against God. While people in our day think they can avoid God and His demands upon their lives by feigning neutrality, no neutrality will be possible during the tribulation, for one's very survival will be determined by a decision for or against God. One must choose to either receive the mark and live (being able to buy and sell) or reject the mark and face suffering and possible death. One must choose to follow antichrist and eat well or reject the antichrist and possibly starve.

What is the significance of the number 666 in relation to the antichrist?

In Revelation 13:18, the number 666 is used in reference to the antichrist: "Let the one who has understanding calculate the number of the beast, for it is the number of a man, and his number is 666." Bible interpreters through the centuries have offered many suggestions as to the meaning of 666. A popular theory is that inasmuch as 7 is a number of perfection, and 777 is a number reflecting the perfect Trinity, perhaps 666 points to a being who aspires to perfect deity (like the Trinity), but never attains it. In reality, the antichrist is ultimately just a man, though energized by Satan. Others have suggested that perhaps the number refers to a specific man, such as the Roman emperor Nero.

It is suggested that if Nero's name is translated into the Hebrew language, the numerical value of its letters is 666.

Of course, all this is highly speculative. The truth is, Scripture doesn't clearly define what is meant by 666. Hence, interpreting this verse involves some guesswork.

In what ways will the antichrist mimic Christ?

The antichrist will mimic the true Christ in a number of ways:

- Just as Christ performed miracles, signs, and wonders (Matthew 9:32-33; Mark 6:2), so the antichrist will engage in counterfeit miracles, signs, and wonders (Matthew 24:24; 2 Thessalonians 2:9).

- Christ will appear in the millennial temple (Ezekiel 43:6-7); the antichrist will sit in the tribulation temple (2 Thessalonians 2:4).

- Jesus is God (John 1:1-2; 10:36); the antichrist will claim to be God (2 Thessalonians 2:4).

- Jesus is the lion from Judah (Revelation 5:5); the antichrist will have a mouth like a lion (Revelation 13:2).

- Jesus causes human beings to worship God (Revelation 1:6); the antichrist will cause human beings to worship both Satan and himself (Revelation 13:3-4).

- Jesus' 144,000 Jewish followers are sealed on their foreheads (Revelation 7:4; 14:1); followers of the antichrist will be sealed on their forehead or right hand (Revelation 13:16-18).

- Jesus has a worthy name (Revelation 19:16); the antichrist will have blasphemous names (Revelation 13:1).

- Jesus will be married to a virtuous bride—the church (Revelation 19:7-9); the antichrist will be affiliated with a vile prostitute—a false religion (Revelation 17:3-5).

- Jesus will be crowned with many crowns (Revelation

19:12); the antichrist will be crowned with ten crowns (Revelation 13:1).

- Jesus is the King of kings (Revelation 19:16); the antichrist will be called "the king" (Daniel 11:36).

- Jesus was resurrected (Matthew 28:6); the antichrist will experience an apparent resurrection (Revelation 13:3,14).

- Jesus will have a 1000-year worldwide kingdom (Revelation 20:1-6); the antichrist will have a three-and-a-half-year worldwide kingdom (Revelation 13:5-8).

- Jesus is part of the Holy Trinity—Father, Son, and Holy Spirit (2 Corinthians 13:14); the antichrist is part of an *un*holy trinity—Satan, the antichrist, and the false prophet (Revelation 13).

What are some notable dissimilarities between Christ and the antichrist?

One is called the Christ (Matthew 16:16); the other the antichrist (1 John 4:3). One is called the man of sorrows (Isaiah 53:3); the other the man of sin (2 Thessalonians 2:3). One is called the Son of God (John 1:34); the other the son of perdition (2 Thessalonians 2:3). One is called the Lamb (Isaiah 53:7); the other the beast (Revelation 11:7). One is called the Holy One (Mark 1:24); the other the wicked one (2 Thessalonians 2:8).

Christ came to do the Father's will (John 6:38); the antichrist will do his own will (Daniel 11:36). Christ was energized by the Holy Spirit (Luke 4:14); the antichrist will be energized by Satan, the *un*holy spirit (Revelation 13:4). Christ submitted Himself to God (John 5:30); the antichrist defies God (2 Thessalonians 2:4). Christ humbled Himself (Philippians 2:8); the antichrist exalts himself (Daniel 11:37).

Christ cleansed the temple (John 2:14,16); the antichrist defiles the temple (Matthew 24:15). Christ was rejected of men (Isaiah 53:7); the antichrist will—by force—be accepted by men (Revelation 13:4). Christ was slain for the people (John 11:51); the antichrist slays the people (Isaiah 14:20). Christ was received up into heaven (Luke 24:51); the antichrist goes down into the lake of fire (Revelation 19:20).

Is the antichrist the "Gog" of the Ezekiel invasion?

No. The Bible interpreter will end up in prophetic chaos if he or she tries to make this identification. The antichrist heads up a revived Roman Empire (Daniel 2, 7), while Gog heads up an invasion force made up of Russia and a number of Muslim nations (Ezekiel 38:1-6). Moreover, Gog's invasion into Israel constitutes a direct challenge to the antichrist's covenant with Israel (Daniel 9:27). Further, Gog's moment in the limelight is short-lived—it's all over when God destroys the invading force (Ezekiel 39). By contrast, the antichrist is in power during a significant part of the seven-year tribulation (see Revelation 4–18).

Will the antichrist experience a supernatural birth?

There is no indication in Scripture of a supernatural birth. Scripture consistently portrays the antichrist as just a human being who will be heavily influenced—perhaps indwelt—by Satan. He is called "the man of lawlessness" in 2 Thessalonians 2:3. We are told that "the coming of the lawless one is by the activity of Satan with all power and false signs and wonders" (verse 9). So even though the antichrist is a man, he will be empowered by Satan to do seemingly supernatural things.

We likewise read in Revelation 13:4 that the dragon (Satan) "had given his authority to the beast." The beast is portrayed as a man who will be born from the people who destroyed Jerusalem—that is, he will be a Roman (Daniel 9:26)—but he will be given the power and authority of the unholy spirit, Satan.

Will the antichrist know that he is the antichrist as he is growing up as a child?

I don't know of a single verse in Scripture that even remotely addresses this. Based on my general knowledge of biblical prophecy, however, my answer is no.

Because Satan is not omniscient as God is, he does not know God's sovereign timing of end-time events with pinpoint precision. He has to guess about the timing, including the timing of the initial emergence of a full-grown adult antichrist.

Satan's inability to pinpoint prophetic events even a few decades down the road would seem to make impossible the idea of a child growing up who knows that he is the antichrist. It is difficult to fathom how a child could know he is the antichrist, and then three or four decades later emerge as an adult political leader in perfect synchronization with God's overall prophetic plan—a plan requiring the rapture first (1 Thessalonians 4:13-17), followed by the emergence of a revived Roman Empire (Daniel 2, 7), with its leader (the antichrist) signing a covenant with Israel (Daniel 9:26-27). This is a highly speculative issue.

How old will the antichrist be when he comes into power?

Jesus was apparently around 30 years of age when He began His public ministry. Some might argue that if the antichrist is a true counterfeit to Jesus, then perhaps he too will be at least 30 when he rises to power. But this is purely speculation. The truth is, Scripture reveals nothing about this.

We might note, however, that most world leaders are a bit older—from the mid-forties and up. It seems reasonable to assume that the antichrist will emerge on the world scene around this general age.

Is it possible the antichrist could emerge from the United States?

I don't think so. Keep in mind the explicit statement in Daniel 9:26: "The people of the prince who is to come shall destroy the city and the sanctuary." The nation that destroyed Jerusalem and its temple in AD 70 was the Roman Empire. This means that the "prince who is to come" (the antichrist) will emerge from a revived Roman Empire, not the United States.

Will the antichrist be able to read other peoples' minds?

I do not think so. Scripture says of God: "You, *you only*, know the hearts of all the children of mankind" (1 Kings 8:39). God is portrayed in Scripture as being omniscient (Matthew 11:21), and He certainly knows our thoughts: "Even before a word is on my tongue, behold, O Lord, you know it altogether" (Psalm 139:4).

The antichrist, by contrast, is just a man. It is true that he will be energized by Satan, but no Scripture indicates that Satan has the ability to read people's minds. Satan is portrayed in Scripture as a creature with creaturely limitations. Nevertheless, Satan is a highly intelligent being (Ezekiel 28:12) who has had thousands of years of experience in dealing with human beings, and thus may give the appearance of knowing people's thoughts. Satan is also the head of a vast network of demonic spirits who answer to him (Revelation 12:7), and this too may give the appearance of Satan being omniscient. But there is no indication anywhere in Scripture that he is capable of reading people's minds. Hence, he cannot energize the antichrist to do what he himself cannot do.

Will the antichrist be a homosexual?

Some Bible expositors suggest that the antichrist may be a homosexual. Daniel 11:37 says of him: "He shall pay no attention to the gods of his fathers, or to the one beloved by women." The King James Version (KJV) of this verse says he will show no "regard" for "the desire of women." Largely based on the KJV rendering, some conclude that the antichrist will be a homosexual. It is suggested that this would be in keeping with his being energized by Satan, who is vile and depraved.

This verse could indicate that the antichrist will be a homosexual. However, because the correct meaning of this verse is widely disputed, it is not wise to be dogmatic and build one's theology upon it. The verse could actually mean that the antichrist will be so intoxicated by personal power and glory (see Daniel 11:38-39) that he—as a heterosexual—will have no interest in women.

Will the antichrist be a Jew?

Some think so. There was an early tradition that the antichrist would come from the tribe of Dan (in the twelve tribes of Israel). Some relate this to the fact that the tribe of Dan fell into deep apostasy and idolatry, setting up for themselves a graven image (Judges 18:30). In the noncanonical book the Testament of Dan (5:6), Satan is said to be the prince of the tribe. Irenaeus, writing in the latter part of the second century, noted that the omission of Dan from the tribes listed in

Revelation 7 was due to a tradition that the antichrist was to come from that tribe.

The problem with this view is that Revelation 13:1 and 17:15 picture the antichrist as rising up out of the sea, and the term "sea" in Scripture often refers to the Gentile nations. Antiochus Epiphanes, himself a Gentile, typifies the future antichrist in Daniel 11. Hence, it is unlikely the antichrist will be a Jew. This is especially so since he is pictured as being the great persecutor of Jews in the tribulation period (Jeremiah 30:7; Matthew 24:15-21; Revelation 12:6,13-14). Why would a Jew persecute Jews?

Why do some Christians believe the antichrist will be a Muslim?

Advocates of this position draw support for it by noting alleged similarities between the biblical antichrist and the coming Muslim Mahdi, whom Muslims believe will emerge in the end times and subject the entire world to Islam. It is suggested:

- Both the antichrist and the Mahdi will be an unparalleled political, military, and religious leader who will emerge in the last days.

- Just as the Bible reveals that the antichrist will seek to subdue the earth by a powerful army, so Muslim eschatology reveals that the Mahdi will seek to subdue the earth by a powerful army.

- Just as the Bible reveals that the antichrist will establish a new world order, so Muslim eschatology reveals that the Mahdi will establish a new world order—an Islamic world order.

- Just as the Bible reveals that the antichrist will institute new laws for the whole earth, so Muslim eschatology reveals that the Mahdi will institute Sharia law all over the earth.

- Just as the Bible reveals that the antichrist will institute a world religion, so Muslim eschatology reveals that the Mahdi will institute a world religion—Islam.

- Just as the Bible reveals that the antichrist will behead those who refuse to submit (Revelation 20:4), so Muslim eschatology reveals that the Mahdi will behead those who refuse to submit to Islam.

- Just as the Bible reveals that the antichrist will seek to kill Jews, so Muslim eschatology reveals that the Mahdi will seek to kill Jews.

- Just as the Bible reveals that the antichrist will seek to conquer and seize Jerusalem, so Muslim eschatology reveals that the Mahdi will seek to conquer and seize Jerusalem for Islam.

- Just as the Bible reveals that the antichrist will ride on a white horse, so Muslim eschatology reveals that the Mahdi will ride on a white horse.

- Just as the Bible reveals that the antichrist will make a peace treaty with Israel for seven years, so Muslim eschatology reveals that the Mahdi will make a peace treaty through a Jew (specifically a Levite) for seven years.

- Just as the Bible says the spirit of antichrist denies key doctrines of Christianity (such as the Incarnation), so Islam denies key doctrines of Christianity (including the Incarnation).

In view of these similarities, it is reasoned that the antichrist must be a Muslim—more specifically, the Muslim Mahdi.

Does all Islamic Scripture and tradition reflect the view described above?

By no means! Many of the passages in the hadith (Islamic tradition) that deal with the end times are contradictory. This makes it difficult to piece together a cohesive Islamic theology of the end times. Unfortunately, books and articles written by Christian proponents of the antichrist-Muslim hypothesis avoid addressing this reality. The reason is understandable: It would weaken their case!

Isn't Islamic eschatology largely dependent on Christian eschatology?

Yes. Muhammad obtained most of his ideas about the end times from discussions he had with Christians and Jews. These discussions took place when he was a businessman traveling in caravans, often encountering people of different faiths. These ideas were later embellished by Muhammad's followers who were even better acquainted with biblical prophecies of the end times. So, Islamic eschatology is a *borrowed* eschatology.

Academics who study Islam have often noted such theological dependency. An illustration of this may be found in some of the Islamic "signs of the times," which point to the end times. These signs include an increase in false prophets, apostasy, an increase in natural calamities, and an increase in wars—events all found in the Christian Scriptures, which far predate the time of Muhammad (see, for example, Matthew 24).

We might also note the role of Satan, the father of lies (John 8:44). Scripture is quite clear that Satan has the ability to inspire false religions and cults (see, for example, 1 Timothy 4:1; 1 John 4:1). Further, since Satan quotes from Scripture in seeking to tempt Christ (Matthew 4:1-11), we infer that he has knowledge of Scripture. It is thus quite feasible that Satan—who knows biblical prophecy—has sought to give credence to the false religion of Islam by inspiring similar prophecies (a one-world religion, riding on a white horse, a false prophet, and the like) in that religion. Satan is a great deceiver.

Do all Muslims agree on the nature of the Mahdi?

No. This is a primary area of doctrinal conflict between Shi'ite and Sunni Muslims. Shi'ite Muslims believe the Mahdi is now on earth but is in hiding and will soon emerge. Sunni Muslims believe that the Mahdi has yet to make his earthly appearance. As one historian put it, Shi'ite Muslims believe in a "coming out" of the Mahdi, whereas Sunni

Muslims believe in a "coming back" of the Mahdi. Christian proponents of the antichrist-Muslim hypothesis seem to ignore such conflicting views.

What is the case against the idea that the antichrist will be a Muslim?

First and foremost, Scripture reveals that the antichrist will be a Roman. How do we know this? Daniel 9:26, speaking of the 70 weeks of Daniel, tells us: "After the sixty-two weeks, an anointed one shall be cut off and shall have nothing. And *the people of the prince who is to come shall destroy the city and the sanctuary.* Its end shall come with a flood, and to the end there shall be war. Desolations are decreed." This passage tells us that Jerusalem and its temple would be destroyed by the "people of the prince who is to come." Who destroyed Jerusalem and its temple in AD 70? Titus and his Roman army. The Roman people are the people of "the prince who is to come," the antichrist. In view of this, it seems unlikely that the antichrist will be a Muslim.

Another factor that militates against the possibility of a Muslim antichrist is the covenant the antichrist will sign with Israel. This event marks the beginning of the tribulation period. In Daniel 9:27 we read that the antichrist "shall make a strong covenant with many for one week" (that is, one week of years—seven years). Why would a Muslim leader sign a covenant with Israel guaranteeing protection of Israel? After all, most Muslims today hate the Jewish people, and they want the land of Israel back. They want the Jews out of Israel and do not want to protect the Jewish people within Israel. It seems inconceivable that a Muslim antichrist would sign a covenant with Israel.

Not only does it stretch credulity to say that a Muslim leader would sign a covenant protecting Israel, it is positively inconceivable that Israel would trust its security to a Muslim leader. This is especially so given today's rhetoric about Muslims wanting to "wipe Israel off the face of the earth" and "push Israel into the sea."

Further, there is no way the people in various Muslim countries around the world would go along with any Muslim leader who made such a covenant with Israel. The antichrist-Muslim hypothesis assumes that Muslims will universally submit to such a covenant. I cannot believe it. Based on a long historical precedent, it seems clear that Muslims would strongly react against such a covenant made by a Muslim leader.

Still further, Daniel 11:36 tells us the antichrist "shall exalt himself and magnify himself above every god." We also read in 2 Thessalonians 2:4 that the antichrist ultimately "opposes and exalts himself against every so-called god or object of worship, so that he takes his seat in the temple of God, proclaiming himself to be God." A Muslim antichrist who claims to be God would represent an absolute and heinous trashing of the Muslim creed: "There is one God named Allah, and Muhammad is his prophet." I cannot imagine a true Muslim making any claim that he was God. Just as it is anathema to Muslims to call Jesus "God incarnate" or the "Son of God," so it would be anathema to Muslims for any human to claim he was God. A Muslim antichrist would be viewed as an infidel among Quran-believing Muslims.

In keeping with this is the Muslim teaching that "God can have no partners." Muslims generally say this as a means of arguing against the doctrine of the Trinity. But it is certainly applicable to human leaders on earth who claim to be God.

Further, Muslims teach that Allah is so radically unlike any earthly reality—so utterly transcendent and beyond anything in the finite realm—that he cannot be described using earthly terms. So how could a human Muslim (the antichrist) claim (*as* the antichrist) to be God...a God described in earthly terms? All things considered, this presents an insurmountable problem to the Muslim-antichrist theory.

Does Revelation 13:3,14 indicate that the antichrist will be resurrected from the dead?

The answer to this question is largely dependent on the answer to another question: *Does Satan have the power to resurrect a human being from the dead?* Although Satan has supernatural power, there is a gigantic difference between the devil and God. Satan does not possess attributes that belong to God alone, such as omnipresence and omniscience. Satan is a creature with creaturely limitations.

God is infinite in power; the devil is finite and limited. Moreover, only God can create life (Genesis 1:1,21; Deuteronomy 32:39); the devil cannot (see Exodus 8:19). We infer from such doctrinal facts that only God can truly raise the dead (John 10:18; Revelation 1:18).

Certainly the devil has great power to deceive people (Revelation 12:9). He is a master magician and a super-scientist. And with his vast knowledge of God, man, and the universe, he is able to perform "false signs and wonders" (2 Thessalonians 2:9; see also Revelation 13:13-14). But the devil's counterfeit miracles do not compete with God's major-league miracles (Acts 8:9-13).

"Grade A" miracles can be performed only by God. Only God can fully control and supersede the natural laws He Himself created, though on one occasion He did grant Satan the power to bring a whirl-wind on Job's family (Job 1:19). As the account of Job illustrates, all the power the devil has is granted him by God and is carefully limited and monitored (see Job 1:10-12). Satan is on a leash. His finite power is under the control of God's infinite power.

In view of this scriptural evidence, it seems reasonable to conclude that Satan will either engage in a limited "Grade B" miracle in healing the wounded antichrist (that is, wounded but not really dead), or he will engage in some kind of masterful deception—or perhaps a com-bination of both. In any event, the world will be amazed.

Is it possible that Christians might be able to know the identity of the antichrist before the rapture?

I don't think so. I say this because the single event that begins the tribulation period is the antichrist's signing of a covenant with Israel (see Daniel 9:27). Since the rapture of the church precedes the sign-ing of this covenant (as I argue elsewhere in this book), there is no way for Christians to know the precise identity of this individual. Speaking tongue in cheek, if you have clearly identified the antichrist, then you have been "left behind."

Was Antiochus Epiphanes a type of the antichrist?

A type may be defined as a figure or representation of something to come. It is an Old Testament institution, event, person, object, or ceremony that has reality and purpose in biblical history, but which also—by God's design—foreshadows something yet to be revealed. Types are therefore prophetic in nature.

Antiochus Epiphanes ruled the Seleucid Empire from 175 BC until his death in 164 BC. He was vile, vengeful, and cruel. That Antiochus Epiphanes was a type of the antichrist is clear from the following factors:

- Both persecute the Jewish people, even seeking to exterminate them.

- Both are self-exalting and demand worship.

- Both defile the Jewish temple, thereby causing an abomination of desolation. Antiochus Epiphanes sacrificed a pig upon the altar of burnt offering in the temple. The antichrist will set up an image of himself in the temple.

- Both are assisted by a religious leader. The priest Menelaus assisted Antiochus Epiphanes; the false prophet will assist the antichrist.

What is the "spirit of antichrist"?

Not only will there be a future person known as the antichrist who comes to power in the future seven-year tribulation period (2 Thessalonians 2:1-9; Revelation 13), there is also a "spirit of the antichrist" that is already at work today, promoting heretical and cultic doctrine (1 John 4:1-3). Based on John's writings, we can conclude that the spirit of antichrist involves deception (2 John 7), denies that Christ came in the flesh (1 John 4:2-3), denies the Father and the Son (1 John 2:22), is already in the world (1 John 4:3), was even prevalent in apostolic times (1 John 2:18), and is closely related to false prophets (1 John 4:1).

Many theologians believe that the "spirit of the antichrist" refers to demonic spirits who promulgate anti-Christian teachings (1 John 4:3). In keeping with this, 1 Timothy 4:1 warns, "The Spirit expressly says that in later times some will depart from the faith by devoting themselves to deceitful spirits and teachings of demons."

What is the ultimate fate of the antichrist, the false prophet, and Satan?

The diabolical trinity is destined for doom. In Revelation 19:20 we read that the antichrist and the false prophet will be "thrown alive into the lake of fire that burns with sulfur." This will take place before the beginning of Christ's millennial kingdom. Then, at the end of the millennial kingdom—1000 years after the antichrist and the false prophet were thrown into the lake of burning sulfur—the devil will be "thrown into the lake of fire and sulfur where the beast and the false prophet were, and they will be tormented day and night forever and ever" (Revelation 20:10).

Notice that the antichrist and false prophet are not burned up or annihilated at the time the devil is thrown into the lake of burning sulfur. They are still burning after 1000 years. These sinister beings, along with unbelievers of all ages, will be tormented day and night forever (Revelation 20:14-15).

The good news, for you and me, is that this diabolical trio will be eternally quarantined away from us as we live eternally—*face-to-face*—with our Savior, Jesus Christ.

15

God's Servants: The 144,000 Jews and the Two Prophetic Witnesses

What is the case for the 144,000 of Revelation 7 and 14 being the church and not Jews?

Some Bible expositors argue that the 144,000 of Revelation 7 and 14 are a symbolic description of the completed church composed of both Jews and Gentiles. It is not a reference to Israel.

Those who hold this position reason that the 144,000 could not be literal tribes of Israel because the tribe of Dan is omitted from the 12 tribes, and the tribe of Levi is included. Moreover, Galatians 3:29 tells us that "if you are Christ's, then you are Abraham's offspring, heirs according to promise." Followers of Christ are called "the circumcision" in Philippians 3:3. Followers of Christ are also called "the Israel of God" in Galatians 6:16. Such verses indicate that the church fulfills the role as the true Israel. This being so, the 144,000 in Revelation 7 and 14 must represent the church and not Israel.

What is the case against the 144,000 representing the church?

The context indicates the passage is referring to 144,000 Jewish men—12,000 from each tribe—who live during the future tribulation period (Revelation 7:1-8; 14:4). The very fact that 12 specific tribes are mentioned in this context, along with specific numbers for those tribes, removes all possibility that this is a figure of speech. Nowhere else in the Bible does a reference to 12 tribes of Israel mean anything but 12 tribes of Israel. Indeed, the word "tribe" is never used of anything but a literal ethnic group in Scripture. Why should Revelation 7 and 14 be an exception?

If Revelation 7 and 14 refer to literal Jewish tribes, why was the tribe of Dan omitted?

The Old Testament has some 20 variant lists of tribes. Hence, no list of the 12 tribes of Israel must be identical. Most scholars today agree that Dan's tribe was omitted because that tribe was guilty of idolatry on many occasions and, as a result, was largely obliterated (Leviticus 24:11; Judges 18:1,30; see also 1 Kings 12:28-29). To engage in unrepentant idolatry is to be cut off from God's blessing.

If Revelation 7 and 14 refer to literal Jewish tribes, why was the tribe of Levi included—a tribe not included in Old Testament tribal lists?

The priestly functions of the tribe of Levi ceased with the coming of Jesus Christ, the ultimate High Priest. Indeed, the Levitical priesthood was fulfilled in the person of Christ (see Hebrews 7–10). Because there was no further need for the services of the Levis as priests, there was no further reason for keeping this tribe distinct and separate from the others. Hence, they were properly included in the tribal listing in the book of Revelation.

Does Galatians 3:29 prove the 144,000 metaphorically refers to the church?

Galatians 3:29 tells us that "if you are Christ's, then you are Abraham's offspring, heirs according to promise." This does not mean that distinctions between the church and Israel are thereby obliterated. Those who become joined to Christ by faith become spiritual descendants of Abraham and consequently become beneficiaries of some of God's promises to him. To be more specific, God made some promises to *all the physical descendants of Abraham* (Genesis 12:1-3,7). He made other promises to the *believers among the physical descendants of Abraham* (Romans 9:6,8). And he made other promises to the *spiritual seed of Abraham who are not Jews*. This is what Galatians 3:29 refers to. Hence, though believers in Christ are indeed Abraham's spiritual offspring, they remain distinct from Israel. One must not forget the pivotal teaching of the apostle Paul in Romans 9–11 that God still has a plan for ethnic Israel, as distinct from the church.

Does Philippians 3:3 prove the 144,000 metaphorically refers to the church?

In Philippians 3:3 believers in Christ are called "the circumcision." However, Paul was referring not to physical circumcision (as practiced by the Jews) but to the circumcision *of the heart* that occurs the moment a person trusts in Jesus Christ for salvation. It is a huge leap in logic to say that this verse proves that the church becomes the new Israel.

Does Galatians 6:16 prove the 144,000 metaphorically refers to the church?

The apostle Paul refers to "the Israel of God" in Galatians 6:16. This does not mean the church is the new Israel. Rather, Paul is here referring to *saved Jews*—that is, Jews who have trusted in Jesus Christ for salvation. The term "Israel" refers to physical Jews everywhere else in the New Testament (some 65 times). There is no indication in Galatians 6:16 that the term is to be taken any differently. In Paul's writings, the church and Israel remain distinct (see 1 Corinthians 10:32; Romans 9–11).

Why would God call 144,000 Jews to evangelize during the tribulation period?

God had originally chosen the Jews to be His witnesses, their appointed task being to share the good news of God with all other people around the world (see Isaiah 42:6; 43:10). The Jews were to be God's representatives to the Gentile peoples. Biblical history reveals that the Jews failed at this task, especially since they did not even recognize Jesus as the divine Messiah, but nevertheless this was their calling. During the future tribulation, these 144,000 Jews—who become believers in Jesus the divine Messiah sometime following the rapture—will finally fulfill this mandate from God, as they will be His witnesses all around the world. And their work will yield a mighty harvest of souls (see Revelation 7:9-14).

Why are the 144,000 "sealed" by God?

These witnesses—God's faithful remnant—will be protectively

"sealed" by God. Seals in Bible times were signs of ownership and protection. These Jewish believers are "owned" by God and by His sovereign authority He protects them during their time of service during the tribulation period (Revelation 14:1-4; see also 13:16-18; 2 Corinthians 1:22; Ephesians 1:13; 4:30).

These sealed servants of God will apparently be preachers. They will fulfill Matthew 24:14: "This gospel of the kingdom will be proclaimed throughout the whole world as a testimony to all nations, and then the end will come."

When will the 144,000 Jewish evangelists carry out their ministry?

I believe the 144,000 will emerge on the scene in the early part of the tribulation period, sometime after the rapture. Some Bible expositors suggest that they must engage in their work of evangelism early in the tribulation, for the believers who are martyred in the fifth seal judgment (Revelation 6:9-11) are among the fruit of their labors, and the seal judgments are definitely in the first half of the tribulation period.

It is likely that these Jews become believers in Jesus in a way similar to that of the apostle Paul, himself a Jew, and his Damascus-road encounter with the risen Christ (see Acts 9:1-9). Interestingly, in 1 Corinthians 15:8, Paul refers to himself in his conversion to Christ as "one untimely born." Some Bible expositors believe Paul may have been alluding to his 144,000 Jewish tribulation brethren, who would be spiritually "born" in a way similar to his spiritual birth—only Paul was spiritually born long before they were.

Is there a connection between these 144,000 and the judgment of the nations, which follows the second coming (Matthew 25:31-46)?

Very possibly. The nations mentioned in Matthew 25:31-46 is composed of the sheep and the goats, representing the saved and the lost among the Gentiles. According to Matthew 25:32, they are intermingled and require separation by a special judgment. They are judged based upon how they treat Christ's "brothers." Who are these brothers? It is likely that they are the 144,000 Jews mentioned in Revelation 7, Christ's Jewish brothers who bear witness of Him during the tribulation.

These Jewish witnesses will find it difficult to buy food because they refused to receive the mark of the beast (Revelation 13:16-17). Only true believers in the Lord will be willing to jeopardize their lives by extending hospitality to the messengers. These sheep (believers) who treat the brothers (the 144,000) well will enter into Christ's millennial kingdom. The goats (unbelievers), by contrast, go into eternal punishment.

What does Scripture reveal about God's two prophetic witnesses who will emerge during the tribulation period?

During the tribulation period, God will raise up two mighty witnesses who will testify to the true God with astounding power. In fact, the power of these witnesses brings to mind Elijah (1 Kings 17; Malachi 4:5) and Moses (Exodus 7–11). It is significant that in the Old Testament two witnesses were required to confirm testimony (see Deuteronomy 17:6; 19:15; Matthew 18:16; John 8:17; Hebrews 10:28).

In Revelation 11:3-6 we read God's prophetic promise:

> I will grant authority to my two witnesses, and they will prophesy for 1,260 days, clothed in sackcloth. These are the two olive trees and the two lampstands that stand before the Lord of the earth. And if anyone would harm them, fire pours from their mouth and consumes their foes. If anyone would harm them, this is how he is doomed to be killed. They have the power to shut the sky, that no rain may fall during the days of their prophesying, and they have power over the waters to turn them into blood and to strike the earth with every kind of plague, as often as they desire.

Is it possible that these two witnesses are Moses and Elijah?

Some expositors believe so. Among their supportive evidences:

1. The tribulation—the seventieth week of Daniel—is a period in which God deals with the Jews, just as He did in the first

69 weeks of Daniel. Moses and Elijah are unquestionably the two most influential figures in Jewish history. It makes good sense that they would be on the scene during the tribulation period.

2. Both the Old Testament and Jewish tradition expected Moses (Deuteronomy 18:15,18) and Elijah (Malachi 4:5) to return in the future.

3. Moses and Elijah appeared on the Mount of Transfiguration with Jesus. This shows their centrality. Hence, it would be appropriate for them to be on the scene during the future tribulation period.

4. The miracles portrayed in Revelation 11 are very similar to those previously performed by Moses and Elijah in Old Testament times (see Exodus 7–11; 1 Kings 17; Malachi 4:5).

5. Both Moses and Elijah left the earth in unusual ways. Elijah never died, but was transported to heaven in a fiery chariot (2 Kings 2:11-12). God supernaturally buried Moses' body in a location unknown to man (Deuteronomy 34:5-6; Jude 9).

In view of such factors, some Bible expositors suggest that in the tribulation period, God will send two of His mightiest servants: Moses, the great deliverer and spiritual legislator of Israel, and Elijah, a prince among Old Testament prophets. During Old Testament times, these men rescued Israel from bondage and idolatry. They may appear again during the tribulation period to warn Israel against succumbing to the false religion of the antichrist and the false prophet.

Is it possible that the two prophetic witnesses will be Enoch and Elijah?

Some Bible expositors think so. After all, both Enoch and Elijah were upright men who were raptured to heaven. Neither experienced death. Both were prophets—one a Gentile (Enoch) and the other a Jew (Elijah). The church fathers unanimously held to this view during the first 300 years of church history. It may be that God will ordain one of the witnesses to speak to the Jews and the other witness to speak to the Gentiles during the tribulation.

Is it possible that the two prophetic witnesses will be two entirely new prophets?

Yes. Those who hold to this view reason that the text would surely identify famous Old Testament personalities if they were indeed coming back. Because they are not identified, the two witnesses will likely be new prophets that God specially raises up for ministry during the tribulation (see Matthew 11:14).

When—and for how long—will these two prophetic witnesses engage in their work?

Scholars debate whether the ministry of the two witnesses belongs in the first half or the second half of the tribulation. The actual time frame of these two witness is said to be 1260 days, which measures out to precisely three and one half years. This is obviously equivalent to half of the tribulation period. However, it is not clear from the context of Revelation 11 whether this is the first or the last half of the tribulation.

Most prophecy scholars conclude that the two witnesses do their miraculous work during the first three and one half years. They reason that the antichrist's execution of them seems to fit best with other events that will transpire in the middle of the tribulation—such as the antichrist's exaltation of himself to godhood in defiance of the true God and His witnesses.

Why does God let the two witnesses die?

It is only when the two witnesses have finished their ministry that God will sovereignly permit the beast (the antichrist) to kill them (Revelation 11:7). They will not die prematurely. All goes according to God's divine plan.

The bodies of the witnesses lie lifeless in Jerusalem. Jerusalem is figuratively called "Sodom and Egypt" because of its inhabitants' apostasy and rejection of God. The description of Jerusalem as being no better than Sodom and Egypt was to show that the once-holy city had become no better than places known for their hatred of the true God and His Word.

It is apparently by television and the Internet that "the peoples and tribes and languages and nations" will gaze at the dead witnesses for three days. Only modern technology can explain how the whole world will be able to watch all of this.

Note that the refusal to bury a corpse was, in biblical times, a way of showing contempt (Deuteronomy 21:22-23; Psalm 79:2-3; Acts 14:19). Hence, by leaving the dead bodies in the street, the people of the world render the greatest possible insult to God's spokesmen. It is equivalent to the people of the world collectively spitting upon the corpses.

What will be the world's response to the murder of the two prophetic witnesses?

The people of the world will celebrate when the witnesses are put to death (Revelation 11:10). They exchange presents, apparently in relief that the prophets are no longer around. Based on biblical history, it seems that the only prophets people love are dead ones.

What is the purpose of God resurrecting the two prophets in full view of everyone?

Scripture reveals that after the prophets had been dead in the street for days, "a breath of life from God entered them, and they stood up on their feet, and great fear fell on those who saw them" (Revelation 11:11; see also Genesis 2:7). The celebration quickly gives way to fear as the lifeless corpses suddenly stand up in full view of television and Internet feeds. Clips of this event will no doubt be replayed over and over again through various media. It will no doubt go viral on the Internet. This resurrection and ascension of the two witnesses serves as a huge exclamation point to their prophetic words throughout their three-and-a-half-year ministry.

It will be an awesome testimony to God's truth!

16

Religion During the Tribulation Period

What does Scripture reveal about the false religious system that emerges during the tribulation period?

Revelation 17 informs us of religious Babylon, with verses 1-7 providing a description of it and verses 8-18 providing an interpretation of the description. There is much symbolic language here. Babylon is viewed as a great prostitute (or harlot) whose religious unfaithfulness influences the people of many nations. Revelation 17:1 tells us that this prostitute is "seated on many waters," which symbolizes various peoples, multitudes, nations, and languages. Scripture reveals that the kings of the earth commit adultery with this harlot and become a part of the religious system she symbolizes (see Revelation 14:8). This false religious system, then, is pervasive in its influence, working hand in hand with the political system of the end times.

We also read of "seven mountains on which the woman [that is, the prostitute] is seated" (Revelation 17:9). Apparently, the seven mountains symbolize the seven kingdoms and their kings throughout history that are mentioned in verse 10. Mountains often symbolize kingdoms in Scripture (Psalm 30:7; Jeremiah 51:25; Daniel 2:44-45).

These seven kingdoms refer to the seven great world empires—Egypt, Assyria, Babylon, Medo-Persia, Greece, Rome, and that of the antichrist. The biblical text tells us that five of these kingdoms have fallen, one still exists, and one is yet to come (Revelation 17:10). More specifically, at the time of John's writing, the Egyptian, Assyrian, Babylonian, Medo-Persian, and Greek empires had already fallen. Rome, however, still existed, and the antichrist's kingdom was yet to come. Our biblical text thus indicates that false paganized religion has affected—or *will* affect—all these empires.

Based on clues in Revelation 17, we infer that this apostate religious system will be in force in the first half of the tribulation period and will be worldwide in its scope (see verse 15). It will exercise powerful political clout (verses 12-13), will seem outwardly glorious while being inwardly corrupt (implied in verse 4), and will persecute true believers during the first half of the tribulation period (see verse 6).

Does this false religion control the antichrist for a time?

Apparently so. The great prostitute—the false religious system—is said to sit on (and thus control) "a scarlet beast," who is the antichrist (Revelation 17:3). Prostitution is often a graphic metaphor in Scripture that symbolizes unfaithfulness to God, idolatry, and religious apostasy (see Jeremiah 3:6-9; Ezekiel 20:30; Hosea 4:15; 5:3; 6:10; 9:1). It seems fitting that initially a close connection exists between the false religious system and the antichrist, for the antichrist himself is unfaithful to God and idolatrous.

Will this false religion be destroyed?

Yes. Revelation 17:16-18 reveals that the antichrist, along with ten kings who are under his authority, will eventually destroy the false world religion—the prostitute of the end times. There are no textual indicators or clues as to the precise timing of this event. However, it seems most logical and coherent to place it midpoint in the tribulation period, at the same time that the antichrist will assume the role of world dictator by proclamation (see Daniel 9:27; Matthew 24:15). It is logical to infer that at the same basic time, the antichrist will come into both global political dominion and religious dominion, demanding even to be worshipped (Daniel 11:36-38; 2 Thessalonians 2:4; Revelation 13:8,15).

Hence, the false religious system that dominated during the first half of the tribulation will be obliterated now that the antichrist is on religious center stage. The final world religion will be one that involves worship of the antichrist alone.

What is the case for the great prostitute being the Roman Catholic Church?

Some throughout church history have held to this view, which became popular during and following the days of the Reformation. This theory is typically built on the harlot motif (see Revelation 17:1). The very idea of a harlot implies unfaithfulness. Just as a harlot is sexually unfaithful, so, it is alleged, the Roman Catholic Church is unfaithful and has fallen away from the truth of Christianity. Roman Catholicism is viewed as a corruption of Christianity.

Those who hold to this view pay special attention to how the great prostitute (the false religion) is adorned: "The woman was arrayed in purple and scarlet, and adorned with gold and jewels and pearls" (Revelation 17:4). Some suggest that this fits the colors of the robes of both popes and cardinals. As well, the affirmation that the woman was drunk from the saints' blood may point to Roman Catholicism's persecution of Protestant Christians in church history.

What is the case against the great prostitute being the Roman Catholic Church?

Many of those who hold that the harlot is Roman Catholicism also say that the beast of Revelation is Roman Catholicism. This is problematic, since the harlot and the beast are portrayed in Revelation as distinct from each other. By the end of Revelation 17, the beast has destroyed the harlot.

Further, this seems to be a case of commentators reading their current historical experiences into the text of Scripture. This view emerged and became prominent during Reformation times, when men like John Calvin and Martin Luther were taking a stand against Roman Catholicism. It is easy to see how, in such a context, Roman Catholicism could be read into the harlot or beast of Revelation.

Moreover, one must wonder how a theory involving an ecclesiastical institution centuries after Revelation was written could have had any immediate relevance to the original readers of the book of Revelation. Would they have understood the text this way? Many expositors think not. Such a view would seemingly bring more comfort to sixteenth-century persecuted Protestants than to first-century persecuted Christians.

Is it possible that the great prostitute is apostate Christendom?

As was true with the Roman Catholic theory, this theory relies heavily on the harlot motif (Revelation 17:1). Just as a harlot is sexually unfaithful, so, it is alleged, apostate Christianity is unfaithful and is viewed as having fallen away from the truth of Christianity. Some describe it in terms of adultery. Adultery implies that at one time there was faithfulness prior to the infidelity. Apostate Christianity was once *not* apostate, but has since *become* apostate. In this theory, many of those left behind after the rapture will be a part of this apostate Christianity.

If there is a bone to pick with this view, it involves the question of relevance to the original readers of the book of Revelation. Would they have understood the text this way? I don't think so.

Is it possible that the great prostitute could just be some general and broad form of paganism?

Yes, it's possible. Recall that the prostitute (false religion) is said to be seated on "seven mountains"—a metaphorical reference to seven kingdoms: Egypt, Assyria, Babylon, Medo-Persia, Greece, Rome, and that of the antichrist. In Revelation 17:10, the angel tells John that five of these kingdoms have fallen, one still exists, and one is yet to come. Whatever this false religion is, it has affected (or will affect) *all* these empires. We know that paganism has been on religious center stage in Egypt, Assyria, Babylon, Medo-Persia, Greece, and Rome. It is therefore reasonable to assume that some form of paganism will likewise be central in the false religion of the antichrist's time. I think one could make a case that the false religion will mix paganism with apostate Christianity.

What about Jewish religion? Will a Jewish temple really be rebuilt during the tribulation period?

Yes. We know there will be a tribulation temple because Daniel 9:27

speaks of the sacrifices offered in the temple during the first half of the tribulation period. Moreover, Jesus in the Olivet Discourse warned of a catastrophic event that will take place at the midpoint of the tribulation that assumes the existence of the temple: "When you see the abomination of desolation spoken of by the prophet Daniel, standing in the holy place (let the reader understand), then let those who are in Judea flee to the mountains" (Matthew 24:15-16).

This "abomination of desolation" refers to a desecration of the Jewish temple by the antichrist, who will set up an image of himself within the temple at the midpoint of the tribulation. This amounts to the antichrist enthroning himself in the place of deity, displaying himself as God (compare with Isaiah 14:13-14 and Ezekiel 28:2-9). In the book of Daniel (see 9:27; 11:31; 12:11), the term "abomination of desolation" conveys a sense of outrage or horror at the witnessing of a barbaric act of idolatry within God's holy temple. This blasphemous act will utterly desecrate the temple, making it abominable and therefore desolate.

What does the word "blasphemy" mean?

Scripture reveals that the beast was given a mouth uttering haughty and blasphemous words (Revelation 13:5). The root meaning of the Greek word for "blasphemy" can range from showing a lack of reverence for God to a more extreme attitude of contempt for either God or something considered sacred (see Leviticus 24:16; Matthew 26:65; Mark 2:7). It can involve speaking evil against God (Psalm 74:18; Isaiah 52:5; Romans 2:24; Revelation 13:1,6; 16:9,11,21). It can also involve showing contempt for the true God by making claims of divinity for oneself (see Mark 14:64; John 10:33). The antichrist will engage in all these aspects of blasphemy.

When the antichrist first comes into power, he will appear to be a dynamic, charismatic leader who can solve the problems of the world. At the midpoint of the tribulation period, however, he will deify himself. He will set up an image of himself in the Jewish temple, thereby committing the "abomination of desolation" (Matthew 24:15).

Daniel 11:36 confirms that the antichrist "shall exalt himself and magnify himself above every god." We also read in 2 Thessalonians 2:4

that the antichrist ultimately "opposes and exalts himself against every so-called god or object of worship, so that he takes his seat in the temple of God, proclaiming himself to be God." There is no greater blasphemy than this. The antichrist truly is *anti*-Christ, putting himself in Christ's place (see Revelation 13:5-6).

How can we be sure Jesus was not referring to Herod's temple being desecrated in New Testament times?

In Matthew 24:1-2, Jesus affirmed that the great temple built by Herod (the Jewish temple of Jesus' day) would be utterly destroyed: "Truly, I say to you, there will not be left here one stone upon another that will not be thrown down." (This prophecy was literally fulfilled in AD 70 when Titus and his Roman warriors overran Jerusalem and the Jewish temple.) Then Jesus speaks of the desecration of a *different* Jewish temple.

The only conclusion that can be reached is that though the temple of Jesus' day would be destroyed, the abomination of desolation would occur in a *yet-future* temple. This latter temple will exist during the tribulation period (Daniel 9:27; 12:11).

Are preparations being made even now for the future rebuilding of the Jewish temple?

Yes, indeed. Various Jewish individuals and groups have been working behind the scenes to prepare various materials for the future temple, including priestly robes, temple tapestries, and worship utensils. These items are being prefabricated so that when the temple is finally rebuilt, everything will be ready for it.

All eyes are on Israel.

17

The Campaign of Armageddon

What is Armageddon?

Armageddon is a catastrophic war campaign at the very end of the tribulation period (see Daniel 11:40-45; Joel 3:9-17; Zechariah 14:1-3; Revelation 16:14-16). "Armageddon" literally means "Mount of Megiddo" and refers to a location about 60 miles north of Jerusalem. This is the location of Barak's battle with the Canaanites (Judges 4) and Gideon's battle with the Midianites (Judges 7). This will be the site for the final horrific battles of humankind just prior to the second coming of Jesus Christ (Revelation 16:16).

Napoleon is reported to have once said that this site is perhaps the greatest battlefield he had ever seen. Of course, the battles Napoleon fought will dim in comparison to Armageddon. So horrible will Armageddon be that no one would survive if it were not for Christ coming again (Matthew 24:22).

Armageddon will involve an extended, escalating conflict, and it will be catastrophic. There are eight key phases of Armageddon.

What is phase 1 of Armageddon?

Phase 1 involves the allied armies of the antichrist gathering for the final destruction of the Jews. We find this assembling described in Revelation 16:12-16. Demonic spirits are depicted as going "abroad to the kings of the whole world, to assemble them for battle on the great day of God the Almighty...and they assembled them at the place that in Hebrew is called Armageddon." The assembling of these armies actually takes place at the unleashing of the sixth bowl judgment. The Euphrates River will be dried up, thereby making it easier for the armies of the east to assemble.

Contextually, the goal of the massive coalition will be to once and for all destroy the Jewish people. Each member of the satanic trinity will be involved—Satan, the antichrist, and the false prophet. Demons, too, will be involved in summoning the kings of the earth.

What is phase 2 of Armageddon?

Revelation 17–18 reveals that there will be a revived Babylon in the end times, rebuilt by the antichrist. It will be a worldwide economic and religious center. It is noteworthy that when the late Saddam Hussein was in power in Iraq, he spent over 1 billion dollars in oil money to enhance present-day Babylon, which is some 50 miles south of Baghdad—essentially as a monument to himself.

At some point in the latter half of the tribulation period—we are not told precisely when—the antichrist will shift his headquarters to Babylon, which will become a global commercial center. Babylon at this time will likely be in control of the oil fields and the money these fields generate in the Middle East. It is this Babylonian commercial center that is destroyed during phase 2 of Armageddon.

Jeremiah 50:13-14 affirms that because of God's wrath, Babylon will become "an utter desolation; everyone who passes by Babylon shall be appalled, and hiss because of all her wounds. Set yourselves in array against Babylon all around, all you who bend the bow; shoot at her, spare no arrows, for she has sinned against the LORD." Isaiah 13:19 informs us that Babylon's destruction "will be like Sodom and Gomorrah when God overthrew them."

What is phase 3 of Armageddon?

The destruction of the antichrist's capital is not enough to distract him from his goal of destroying the Jewish people. Hence, instead of launching a counterattack against the northern military coalition that wiped out Babylon, the antichrist and his forces now move south to attack Jerusalem. This constitutes phrase 3 of Armageddon. We read about it in Zechariah 12:1-3:

> Thus declares the LORD, who stretched out the heavens
> and founded the earth and formed the spirit of man within

him: "Behold, I am about to make Jerusalem a cup of staggering to all the surrounding peoples. The siege of Jerusalem will also be against Judah. On that day I will make
Jerusalem a heavy stone for all the peoples. All who lift it
will surely hurt themselves. And all the nations of the earth
will gather against it."

Zechariah 14:1-2 adds: "I will gather all the nations against Jerusalem to battle, and the city shall be taken and the houses plundered and
the women raped. Half of the city shall go out into exile, but the rest
of the people shall not be cut off from the city."

What is phase 4 of Armageddon?

Not all of the Jews are in Jerusalem when the antichrist and his
forces attack. Recall that in the middle of the tribulation period, the
antichrist will break his covenant with Israel and exalt himself as deity,
even putting an image of himself in the Jewish temple. Christ, in His
Olivet Discourse, warned of how quickly the Jews must flee for their
lives (Matthew 24:16-31). Many of the Jews apparently flee to the des-
erts and mountains (see Matthew 24:16), perhaps in the area of Boz-
rah/Petra, about 80 miles south of Jerusalem.

This escape from Jerusalem is described in Revelation 12:6: "The
woman [a metaphor for Israel] fled into the wilderness, where she has
a place prepared by God, in which she is to be nourished for 1,260
days [or three and a half years]." Indeed, "the woman was given the
two wings of the great eagle so that she might fly from the serpent into
the wilderness, to the place where she is to be nourished for a time,
and times, and half a time [which is three and a half years]" (verse 14).

It is this remnant of Jews that the antichrist now targets. The Jews
sense impending doom as the forces of the antichrist gather in the rug-
ged wilderness, poised to attack and annihilate them. They are help-
less and, from an earthly perspective, utterly defenseless. This sets the
stage for phase 5 of Armageddon.

What is phase 5 of Armageddon?

Israel is endangered and acutely aware that the forces of the anti-christ have gathered to destroy all the Jews. However, Scripture reveals that their spiritual blindness is now removed and they call out to their Messiah, Jesus Christ. At this point, the remnant experiences national regeneration.

Hosea 6:1-3 indicates that the Jewish leaders will call for the people of the nation to repent—and their collective repentance will take two days:

> Come, let us return to the LORD; for he has torn us, that he may heal us; he has struck us down, and he will bind us up. After two days he will revive us; on the third day he will raise us up, that we may live before him. Let us know; let us press on to know the LORD; his going out is sure as the dawn; he will come to us as the showers, as the spring rains that water the earth.

Just as it was the Jewish leaders who led the Jewish people to reject Jesus as their Messiah, so now the Jewish leaders urge repentance and instruct all to turn to Jesus as their Messiah. This the remnant will do, and they will be saved.

This is in keeping with Joel 2:28-29, which informs us that there will be a spiritual awakening of the Jewish remnant. It would seem that Armageddon will be the historical context in which Israel finally becomes converted (Zechariah 12:2–13:1). The restoration of Israel will include the confession of Israel's national sin (Leviticus 26:40-42; Jeremiah 3:11-18; Hosea 5:15), following which Israel will be saved, thereby fulfilling Paul's prophecy in Romans 11:25-27. In dire threat at Armageddon, Israel will plead for their newly found Messiah to return and deliver them—they will "mourn for him, as one mourns for an only child" (Zechariah 12:10; see also Matthew 23:37-39; Isaiah 53:1-9)—at which point their deliverance will surely come (see Romans 10:13-14). Israel's leaders will have finally realized why the tribulation has fallen on them—perhaps due to the Holy Spirit's enlightenment of their understanding of Scripture, or the testimony of the

144,000 Jewish evangelists, or perhaps the testimony of the two prophetic witnesses.

What is phase 6 of Armageddon?

Phase 6 involves the glorious return of Jesus Christ. The prayers of the Jewish remnant are answered! The divine Messiah returns to rescue His people from danger. The very same Jesus who ascended into heaven comes again at the second coming (Acts 1:9-11).

The second coming will be a universal experience in the sense that every human being on earth will witness the event. Revelation 1:7 says, "Behold, he is coming with the clouds, and every eye will see him, even those who pierced him; and all the tribes of the earth will wail on account of him." And Jesus Himself said, "Then will appear in heaven the sign of the Son of Man, and then all the tribes of the earth will mourn, and they will see the Son of Man coming on the clouds of heaven with power and great glory" (Matthew 24:30).

Old Testament prophetic Scripture reveals that Jesus returns first to the mountain wilderness of Bozrah, where the Jewish remnant is endangered (Isaiah 34:1-7; 63:1-6; Habakkuk 3:3; Micah 2:12-13). Their endangerment is quickly over!

What is phase 7 of Armageddon?

Phase 7 involves the final battle, which will be over in a jiffy. At His second coming, Jesus will confront the antichrist and his forces, and slay them with the word of His mouth. The description of the second coming in the book of Revelation makes it clear that the enemies of Christ suffer instant defeat:

> Then I saw heaven opened, and behold, a white horse! The one sitting on it is called Faithful and True, and in righteousness he judges and makes war. His eyes are like a flame of fire, and on his head are many diadems, and he has a name written that no one knows but himself. He is clothed in a robe dipped in blood, and the name by which he is called is The Word of God. And the armies of heaven, arrayed in fine linen, white and pure, were following him

on white horses. From his mouth comes a sharp sword with which to strike down the nations, and he will rule them with a rod of iron. He will tread the winepress of the fury of the wrath of God the Almighty. On his robe and on his thigh he has a name written, King of kings and Lord of lords (Revelation 19:11-16).

So, instant deliverance comes to the Jewish remnant. The antichrist and his forces are poised for attack against the remnant in the wilderness. The remnant has no chance of survival. The Jewish leaders urge the remnant to repent and turn to Jesus the Messiah, which they promptly do. It is then that the second coming of Christ occurs.

Christ defeats all who stand against Israel. The antichrist will be slain. Habakkuk 3:13 prophesies of Christ's victory over the antichrist: "You went out for the salvation of your people, for the salvation of your anointed. You crushed the head of the house of the wicked, laying him bare from thigh to neck." Likewise, in 2 Thessalonians 2:8 we read of the antichrist that "the Lord Jesus will kill [him] with the breath of his mouth and bring [him] to nothing by the appearance of his coming."

The antichrist will be shown to be impotent and powerless in the face of the true Christ. All the forces of the antichrist will also be destroyed, from Bozrah all the way back to Jerusalem (Joel 3:12-13; Zechariah 14:12-15; Revelation 14:19-20).

Glorious!

What is phase 8 of Armageddon?

Phase 8 involves Christ victoriously ascending to the Mount of Olives. We read about this in Zechariah 14:3-4:

Then the LORD will go out and fight against those nations as when he fights on a day of battle. On that day his feet shall stand on the Mount of Olives that lies before Jerusalem on the east, and the Mount of Olives shall be split in two from east to west by a very wide valley, so that one half of the Mount shall move northward, and the other half southward.

When Christ ascends to the Mount of Olives, some cataclysmic events bring an end to the tribulation period. These include:

- An earthquake of globally staggering proportions (compare with Revelation 8:5 and 11:19). The whole earth will feel its effects. Mountains will be leveled. Islands will vanish. The topography of the earth will be drastically changed.

- Jerusalem will be split into three areas.

- The Mount of Olives will split into two parts, creating a valley.

- There will be a horrific hailstorm, and the sun and moon will be darkened (see Joel 3:14-16; Matthew 24:29).

As these horrific events subside, the tribulation period finally comes to a close.

18

The Second Coming and Subsequent Judgments

What is the second coming?

We touched on the second coming in the previous chapter. To review, the second coming is that event when Jesus Christ—the King of kings and Lord of lords—will gloriously return to the earth at the end of the present age (after the tribulation period) and set up His 1000-year kingdom on earth. The very same Jesus who ascended into heaven will come again at the second coming (Acts 1:9-11).

Can we be sure that the second coming will be a universally visible event?

Most certainly. One key Greek word used in the New Testament to describe the second coming of Christ is *apokalupsis*. This word carries the basic meaning of "revelation," "visible disclosure," "unveiling," and "removing the cover" from something that is hidden. The word is used of Christ's second coming in 1 Peter 4:13: "Rejoice insofar as you share Christ's sufferings, that you may also rejoice and be glad when his glory *is revealed.*"

Another Greek word used in the New Testament of Christ's second coming is *epiphaneia*, which carries the basic meaning of "to appear" or "to shine forth." In Titus 2:13 Paul speaks of "waiting for our blessed hope, *the appearing* of the glory of our great God and Savior Jesus Christ." In 1 Timothy 6:14 Paul urges Timothy to "keep the commandment unstained and free from reproach until *the appearing* of our Lord Jesus Christ."

Christ's first coming, which was both bodily and visible, was called an *epiphaneia* (2 Timothy 1:10). In the same way, Christ's second coming will be both bodily and visible.

We must not forget the clear teaching of Matthew 24:29-30 in support of a visible coming of the Lord:

> Immediately after the tribulation of those days the sun will be darkened, and the moon will not give its light, and the stars will fall from heaven, and the powers of the heavens will be shaken. Then will appear in heaven the sign of the Son of Man, and then all the tribes of the earth will mourn, and they will see the Son of Man coming on the clouds of heaven with power and great glory.

What does *parousia* mean in connection with the second coming?

Parousia is a Greek term often used in connection with both the rapture and the second coming of Christ. Context is the key issue in determining which "coming" is in view.

This word has a number of nuances of meaning, including "present," "presence," "being physically present," "coming to a place," and "arriving." It often denotes both an "arrival" and a consequent "presence with."

For example, *parousia* is used to describe the physical coming and presence of Christ with His disciples on the Mount of Transfiguration (2 Peter 1:16). Likewise, the apostle Paul says in 1 Corinthians 16:17: "I rejoice at the *coming* of Stephanas and Fortunatus and Achaicus, because they have made up for your absence." Paul says in 2 Corinthians 7:6-7: "God, who comforts the downcast, comforted us by the *coming* of Titus." In 2 Corinthians 10:10, Paul relays what some people had said about him: "His letters are weighty and strong, but his bodily *presence* is weak, and his speech of no account." Paul also tells the Philippians: "Therefore, my beloved, as you have always obeyed, so now, not only as in my *presence* but much more in my absence, work out your own salvation with fear and trembling" (2:12). Such usage clearly establishes that *parousia* is often used to communicate the idea of physical presence.

Having said this, it is significant that the term is especially used in connection with the rapture and the second coming of Christ. In both cases Christ will be physically present—in the clouds at the rapture and on earth at the second coming.

In what sense will Christ come again "with the clouds" (Revelation 1:7)?

Clouds are often used in association with God's visible glory (Exodus 16:10; 40:34-35; 1 Kings 8:10-11; Matthew 17:5; 24:30; 26:64). Just as Christ was received by a cloud at His ascension (Acts 1:9), so He will return again in the clouds of heaven (Matthew 24:30; 26:64; Mark 13:26; 14:62; Luke 21:27). Just as Jesus left with a visible manifestation of the glory of God (clouds were present), so Christ will return at the second coming with a visible manifestation of the glory of God (clouds will be present).

How is the second coming described in the book of Revelation?

Revelation 19:11-16 tells us:

> Then I saw heaven opened, and behold, a white horse! The one sitting on it is called Faithful and True, and in righteousness he judges and makes war. His eyes are like a flame of fire, and on his head are many diadems, and he has a name written that no one knows but himself. He is clothed in a robe dipped in blood, and the name by which he is called is The Word of God. And the armies of heaven, arrayed in fine linen, white and pure, were following him on white horses. From his mouth comes a sharp sword with which to strike down the nations, and he will rule them with a rod of iron. He will tread the winepress of the fury of the wrath of God the Almighty. On his robe and on his thigh he has a name written, King of kings and Lord of lords.

In biblical times, generals in the Roman army rode white horses.

Christ on the white horse will be the glorious Commander in chief of the armies of heaven. It signifies His coming in triumph over the forces of wickedness in the world. This is in noted contrast to the lowly colt Jesus rode during His first coming (see Zechariah 9:9).

Our text tells us that "on his head are many diadems" (Revelation 19:12). The many diadems, or crowns, represent total sovereignty and royal kingship. No one will be in a position to challenge Christ's kingly authority.

Jesus is called "King of kings and Lord of lords" (Revelation 19:16). This title means that Jesus is absolutely supreme and sovereign over all earthly rulers and angelic powers (1 Timothy 6:15; see also Deuteronomy 10:17; Psalm 136:3). The long-awaited messianic King has now finally arrived.

The kingship of Jesus is a common theme in Scripture. Genesis 49:10 prophesied that the Messiah would come from the tribe of Judah and reign as a king. The Davidic covenant in 2 Samuel 7:16 promised a Messiah who would have a dynasty, a people over whom He would rule, and an eternal throne (see also Luke 1:32-33). In Psalm 2:6, God the Father announces the installation of God the Son as King in Jerusalem. Psalm 110 affirms that the Messiah will subjugate His enemies and rule over them. Daniel 7:13-14 tells us that the Messiah-King will have an everlasting dominion.

Now the moment has come. Christ the King comes, overcomes all forces of evil, and sets up His kingdom on earth.

Why does it sometimes seem as if the second coming is being delayed?

Second Peter 3:9 instructs us: "The Lord is not slow to fulfill his promise as some count slowness, but is patient toward you, not wishing that any should perish, but that all should reach repentance." God is patient and is providing plenty of time for people to repent. Once Jesus comes, there is no further opportunity to repent and turn to Him.

This is in keeping with God's long track record of immense patience before bringing people to judgment (see Joel 2:13; Luke 15:20; Romans

9:22). We should not be surprised that He continues this patience in the present age.

Sadly, despite God's patience and His desire that none perish, many will refuse to turn to Him and will therefore spend eternity apart from Him (Matthew 25:46). God longs that all be saved (see 1 Timothy 2:4), but not all will receive God's gift of salvation (see Matthew 7:13-14). That is one of the reasons why so many horrific judgments fall on an unbelieving world during the future tribulation period (Revelation 4–18). The people living on earth during that time will have no excuse!

What is the judgment of the nations that follows the second coming?

Matthew 25:31-46 describes the judgment of the nations, which takes place following the second coming of Christ. The believers and unbelievers among the nations are pictured as sheep and goats. According to Matthew 25:32, they are intermingled and require separation by a special judgment. The sheep (believers) will be invited into Christ's 1000-year millennial kingdom. The goats will depart into eternal fire.

Should we interpret the judgment of the nations as the same as the great white throne judgment in Revelation 20:11-13?

No. A comparison of the judgment in Matthew with the one in Revelation makes this view impossible:

- *Different time.* The judgment of the nations occurs at the second coming of Christ (Matthew 25:31); the great white throne judgment follows Christ's millennial kingdom (Revelation 20:11-12).

- *Different scene.* The judgment of the nations occurs on earth (Matthew 25:31); the great white throne judgment occurs (obviously) at the great white throne (Revelation 20:11).

- *Different subjects.* At the judgment of the nations, three groups of people are mentioned: the sheep, the goats, and the brothers (Matthew 25:32,40). The great white throne judgment involves the unsaved dead of all time (Revelation 20:12).

- *Different basis.* The basis of judgment at the judgment of the nations is how Christ's "brothers" were treated (Matthew 25:40); the basis of judgment at the great white throne judgment is a person's works (Revelation 20:12).

- *Different result.* The result of the judgment of the nations is twofold: the righteous enter into Christ's millennial kingdom and the unrighteous are cast into the lake of fire. The result of the great white throne judgment is that the wicked dead are cast into the lake of fire; the righteous are not mentioned (indeed, the righteous are not even there).

We also observe that no resurrection is connected with the judgment of the nations. However, a resurrection does take place in connection with the great white throne judgment (Revelation 20:13).

Clearly, a plain reading of the biblical text indicates that these judgments are not the same.

What is the basis of the judgment of the nations?

The Gentiles at this judgment are evaluated according to how they treated Christ's brothers. In Christ's reckoning, treating His brothers kindly is the same as treating Him kindly. Treating His brothers with contempt is the same as treating Him with contempt. Jesus thus commends the righteous this way: "I was hungry and you gave me food, I was thirsty and you gave me drink, I was a stranger and you welcomed me, I was naked and you clothed me, I was sick and you visited me, I was in prison and you came to me" (Matthew 25:35-36). Conversely, Jesus condemns the unrighteous: "I was hungry and you gave me no food, I was thirsty and you gave me no drink, I was a stranger and you did not welcome me, naked and you did not clothe me, sick and in prison and you did not visit me" (25:42-43).

Who are Christ's "brothers" in this judgment?

A comparison of this passage with the details of the tribulation suggests that "brothers" may refer to the 144,000 Jews mentioned in Revelation 7, Christ's Jewish brothers who bear witness of Him during the tribulation.

Even though the antichrist and the false prophet will wield economic control over the world during the tribulation period (Revelation 13), God will still be at work. God's redeemed (the "sheep") will come to the aid of Christ's Jewish brethren as they bear witness to Christ all around the world. These will be invited into Christ's millennial kingdom.

These saved Gentiles (the "sheep") are not yet given resurrection bodies. They will enter the kingdom in their mortal bodies and continue to have babies throughout the millennium. Though longevity will characterize the millennial kingdom, both mortal Jews and Gentiles will continue to age and die (see Isaiah 65:20). They will be resurrected at the end of the millennium (Revelation 20:4).

What does Scripture say about the judgment of the Jews following the second coming?

The judgment of the Jews is described in Ezekiel 20:34-38. Following are the important facts about this judgment:

- It will take place after the Lord has gathered the Israelites from all around the earth to Palestine.

- Christ will purge out the rebels—those who have refused to turn to Him for salvation.

- Believers among the gathered Israelites will enter into Christ's millennial kingdom where they will enjoy the blessings of the new covenant (verse 37; see also Jeremiah 31:31; Matthew 25:1-30).

- These saved Jews are not yet given resurrection bodies. They will enter the kingdom in their mortal bodies and continue to have babies throughout the millennium, just as their Gentile counterparts will (Matthew 25:46). Though longevity will characterize the millennial kingdom, both mortal Jews and Gentiles will continue to age and die (Isaiah 65:20). They will be resurrected at the end of the millennium (Revelation 20:4).

Will there be an interim period between the second coming of Christ and the beginning of the millennial kingdom?

I believe so—apparently 75 days long. Here's how I arrive at this number.

Daniel 12:11 tells us the image of the antichrist that had caused the abomination of desolation at the midpoint in the tribulation will be removed from the temple 30 days after the tribulation period ends: "From the time that the regular burnt offering is taken away and the abomination that makes desolate is set up, there shall be 1,290 days." Now, keep in mind that the second half of the tribulation lasts precisely 1260 days or three and a half years. Here's some simple math: 1290 days minus 1260 days leaves 30 days beyond the end of the tribulation period.

What about the other 45 days needed for the 75-day interim between the second coming of Christ and the beginning of the millennial kingdom? Daniel 12:12 states: "Blessed is he who waits and arrives at the 1,335 days." The 1335 days minus the 1290 days means another 45 days are added into the mix. It is apparently during this 75-day period that the judgment of the nations (Matthew 25:31-46) and the judgment of the Jews (Ezekiel 20:34-38) takes place.

It is likely that other key events take place during this interval. For example, the antichrist and the false prophet will be cast into the lake of fire (Revelation 19:20). The governmental structure of the coming millennial kingdom will likely be set up (see 2 Timothy 2:12; Revelation 20:4-6). It is also entirely feasible that the marriage feast of Christ—of the divine Bridegroom (Jesus) and His bride (the church)—will take place at the close of the 75 days. Following this 75-day interim, Christ will set up His millennial kingdom (Isaiah 2:2-4; Ezekiel 37:1-13; 40–48; Micah 4:1-7; Revelation 20).

I can't wait.

19

The Millennial Kingdom

What is the millennial kingdom?

Following the second coming, Jesus Christ will personally set up His 1000-year kingdom on earth. In theological circles, this is known as the millennial kingdom (from the Latin word *mille*, meaning "thousand"). Many Scripture passages speak of the millennial kingdom (Revelation 20:2-7; see also Psalm 2:6-9; Isaiah 65:18-23; Jeremiah 31:12-14,31-37; Ezekiel 34:25-29; 37:1-13; 40–48; Daniel 2:35; 7:13-14; Joel 2:21-27; Amos 9:13-14; Micah 4:1-7; Zephaniah 3:9-20).

Do people who become believers during the tribulation period enter into Christ's millennial kingdom?

Yes. Following the second coming of Christ, the Gentiles will face Christ at the judgment of the nations (Matthew 25:31-46). Only those found to be believers will be invited into Christ's millennial kingdom in their mortal bodies—that is, they are not yet resurrected (25:34,46). Likewise, the redeemed remnant among the Jews will be invited to enter into the millennial kingdom in their mortal bodies (Ezekiel 20:34-38).

How do we know that only believers enter into Christ's millennial kingdom?

The book of Daniel informs us that only believers enter into the kingdom. We are told that "the saints of the Most High shall receive the kingdom and possess the kingdom...the time came when the saints possessed the kingdom" (Daniel 7:18,22). The word "saint" in Daniel has the connotation of a divine claim and ownership of the person. It connotes what is distinct from the common or profane. In other words, profane people do not enter into the millennial kingdom. Only those who are God's people—those "owned" by God—enter in.

It would be inconceivable that the wicked and the saints could together inherit a kingdom universally characterized by righteousness (Isaiah 61:11), peace (Isaiah 2:4), holiness (Isaiah 4:3-4), and justice (Isaiah 9:7). The parable of the wheat and tares (Matthew 13:30-31) and the parable of the good and bad fish (Matthew 13:47-50) confirm that only the saved go into the kingdom.

Since these individuals enter the kingdom as mortals, do they still grow old and die?

Yes. Though longevity will characterize the millennial kingdom, Scripture reveals that both mortal Jews and Gentiles will continue to age and die (Isaiah 65:20). Scripture also reveals that married couples among both groups will continue to have children throughout the millennium. All who die during this time will be resurrected at the end of the millennium (Revelation 20:4).

Will some of the children of these believers who enter the millennial kingdom not be believers?

Unfortunately, yes. The fact that only believers ("saints") enter into the kingdom does not stand against the possibility that some of the children of the saints will not be believers. After a few years have passed, there will be children born during the millennium who will grow to adulthood rejecting the Savior-King in their hearts—though outwardly rendering obedience to Him and His government. Some of these will eventually participate in a final revolt against God that takes place at the end of the millennium under Satan's lead (Revelation 20:3,7-10).

Will Israel finally take full possession of the promised land in the millennial kingdom?

Yes. Israel will not only experience regeneration in fulfillment of the new covenant (Jeremiah 31:31-34), but the unconditional land promises in the Abrahamic covenant will finally be fulfilled (Genesis 12:1-3; 15:18-21; 17:21; 35:10-12; see also Isaiah 60:18,21; Jeremiah 23:6; 24:5-6; 30:18; 31:31-34; 32:37-40; 33:6-9; Ezekiel 28:25-26; 34:11-12; 36:24-26; 37; 39:28; Hosea 3:4-5; Joel 2:18-29; Micah 2:12; 4:6-7; Amos 9:14-15; Zephaniah 3:19-20; Zechariah 8:7-8; 13:8-9). It was promised that even though Israel would be dispersed all over the world, the Jews would be regathered and restored to the land (see Isaiah 43:5-7; Jeremiah 16:14-18). This will find its ultimate fulfillment in Christ's millennial kingdom (see Genesis 15:18-21; 26:3-4; 28:13-14; Psalm 105:8-11).

Will Christ actually reign from the Davidic throne during the millennial kingdom?

Yes, He will. God made a covenant with David in which He promised that one of his descendants would rule forever on the throne of David (2 Samuel 7:12-13; 22:51). This is an example of an unconditional covenant. It did not depend on David in any way for its fulfillment. David realized this when he received the promise from God, and he responded with an attitude of humility and a recognition of God's sovereignty over the affairs of human beings.

The three key words of the covenant are "kingdom," "house," and "throne." Such words point to the political future of Israel. The word "house" here carries the idea of "royal dynasty."

This covenant finds its ultimate fulfillment in Jesus Christ, who was born from the line of David (Matthew 1:1). In the millennial kingdom, Christ will rule from the throne of David in Jerusalem (Ezekiel 36:1-12; Micah 4:1-5; Zephaniah 3:14-20; Zechariah 14:1-21). This reign will extend beyond the Jews to include the Gentile nations as well.

Is Christ's millennial rule substantiated in Bible verses aside from the Davidic covenant?

Yes, indeed. Here's a very brief sampling:

- "May he have dominion from sea to sea, and from the River to the ends of the earth!" (Psalm 72:8).

- "To us a child is born, to us a son is given; and the government shall be upon his shoulder, and his name shall be called Wonderful Counselor, Mighty God, Everlasting Father, Prince of Peace. Of the increase of his government and of peace there will be no end, on the throne of David and over his kingdom, to establish it and to uphold it with justice and with righteousness from this time forth and forevermore. The zeal of the LORD of hosts will do this" (Isaiah 9:6-7).

- "I saw in the night visions, and behold, with the clouds of heaven there came one like a son of man, and he came to the Ancient of Days and was presented before him. And to him was given dominion and glory and a kingdom, that all peoples, nations, and languages should serve him; his dominion is an everlasting dominion, which shall not pass away, and his kingdom one that shall not be destroyed" (Daniel 7:13-14).

- "He shall speak peace to the nations; his rule shall be from sea to sea, and from the River to the ends of the earth" (Zechariah 9:10; see also Revelation 20:4).

How does Scripture characterize Christ's government?

Christ's government will be centered in Jerusalem (Isaiah 2:1-3; see also Jeremiah 3:17; Ezekiel 48:30-35; Joel 3:16-17; Micah 4:1,6-8; Zechariah 8:2-3). His government will be perfect and effective (Isaiah 9:6-7), it will be global (Psalm 2:6-9; Daniel 7:14), and it will bring lasting global peace (Micah 4:3-4).

What kinds of physical blessings will Christ bring about in the millennial kingdom?

Scripture reveals that those who enter into Christ's millennial kingdom will enjoy some unique physical blessings. For example:

- People will live in a blessed and enhanced environment (Isaiah 35:1-2).

- There will be plenty of rain and hence plenty of food for animals (Isaiah 30:23-24).

- All animals will live in harmony with each other and with humans, their predatory and carnivorous natures having been removed (Isaiah 11:6-7).

- Longevity among human beings will be greatly increased (Isaiah 65:20).

- Physical infirmities and illnesses will be removed (Isaiah 29:18).

- Prosperity will prevail, resulting in joy and gladness (Jeremiah 31:12-14).

What kind of spiritual blessings will characterize the millennial kingdom?

Christ will bring about great spiritual blessing in His kingdom—all of which relate to the wonderful reality that Jesus Himself will be present with His people on earth. We are told that "the earth shall be full of the knowledge of the LORD as the waters cover the sea" (Isaiah 11:9). Moreover, Satan will be bound during the millennial kingdom (Revelation 20:1-3).

Other key spiritual blessings include:

- The Holy Spirit will be present and will indwell all believers (Ezekiel 36:27; 37:14).

- The Holy Spirit will be "poured upon us from on high" (Isaiah 32:15; see also Isaiah 44:3; Joel 2:28-29).

- Righteousness will prevail around the world (Isaiah 46:13; 51:5; 60:21).

- Obedience to the Lord will prevail (Psalm 22:27; Jeremiah 31:33).

- Holiness will prevail (Isaiah 35:8-10; Joel 3:17).

- Faithfulness will prevail (Psalm 85:10-11; Zechariah 8:3).

- The world's residents will be unified in their worship of the Messiah (Malachi 1:11; Zephaniah 3:9; Zechariah 8:23).

- God's presence will be made manifest (Ezekiel 37:27-28; Zechariah 2:10-13).

Will believers who participated in the rapture take part in reigning with Christ?

I believe so. Scripture promises that Christ will gloriously reign from the Davidic throne. But Scripture also promises that the saints will reign with Christ. In 2 Timothy 2:12, for example, the apostle Paul instructs, "If we endure, we will also reign with him." Those who endure through trials will one day rule with Christ in His future kingdom.

Revelation 5:10 likewise reveals that believers—God's faithful bondservants—"shall reign on the earth." This refers to faithful believers participating in the government during Christ's future millennial kingdom on earth. But this reign extends beyond the millennial kingdom into the eternal state. Indeed, Revelation 22:5 affirms that believers "will reign forever and ever." Luke 19 reveals that a believer's position in the heavenly government will apparently be commensurate with his or her faithful service to God during mortal earthly life.

Reigning with Christ appears to include judging the angels in some capacity. In 1 Corinthians 6:2-3 the apostle Paul asks, "Do you not know that the saints will judge the world?...Do you not know that we are to judge angels?" This is interesting because Psalm 8 teaches that human beings were created lower than the angels. In the afterlife, things will be reversed. Apparently the angels will be lower than redeemed humans and will be subject to their rule.

Will a new temple be built in the millennial kingdom?

Apparently so. Ezekiel 40–48 speaks of a millennial temple being built (see Joel 3:18; Isaiah 2:3; 60:13) and the institution of millennial animal sacrifices (see Isaiah 56:7; 60:7; Jeremiah 33:17-18; Zechariah 14:19-21). The millennial temple will be the final temple for Israel. The dimensions provided for this temple make it significantly larger than any other temple in Israel's history.

This large temple will apparently represent God's presence among His people during the millennium (see Ezekiel 37:26-27). The restoration of Israel as a nation will also entail a restoration of God's presence (and glory) reentering the temple and being with His people visibly. This temple will also be a worship center of Jesus Christ during the entire millennium. It will be built at the beginning of the messianic kingdom (Ezekiel 37:26-28) by Christ (Zechariah 6:12-13), by redeemed Jews (Ezekiel 43:10-11), and even by representatives from the Gentile nations (Zechariah 6:15; Haggai 2:7).

Why will there be animal sacrifices in the millennial kingdom?

This is understandably controversial. Christ's once-for-all sacrifice has taken away sin and has caused the Mosaic law of sacrifices to be abolished (see Hebrews 7–10). Why, then, is the sacrificial system predicted here?

We begin with the observation that Israel and the church are not only distinct today (1 Corinthians 10:32; Romans 9–11), they will also be distinct in the millennial kingdom. We might surmise, then, that temple activities in the millennium relate primarily to Israel (though redeemed Gentiles can also participate) and not to the church (see Isaiah 60–61).

This being the case, some Bible expositors have surmised that the millennial sacrifices will be a kind of Jewish memorial of the awful price Christ—the Lamb of God now living in their midst—had to pay for the salvation of these believing-but-not-yet-glorified Jews. They are yet in their mortal bodies, having entered into the millennial kingdom following the tribulation. The temple system will thus allegedly function much like the Lord's Supper does today, as a memorial ritual (1 Corinthians 11:25-26; see also Isaiah 56:7; 66:20-23; Jeremiah 33:17-18; Ezekiel 43:18-27; 45:13–46:24; Malachi 3:3-4).

The problem with this viewpoint is that Ezekiel says the sacrifices are to "make atonement" (Ezekiel 45:15,17,20). Hence, the "memorial" viewpoint seems to fall short of explaining these sacrifices.

The solution may be that the purpose of the sacrifices in the millennial temple is to remove ceremonial uncleanness and prevent defilement from polluting the purity of the temple environment. According to this view, such ceremonial cleansing will be necessary because Yahweh will again be dwelling on the earth in the midst of sinful (and therefore unclean) mortal people. (Remember, these people survive the tribulation period and enter the millennial kingdom in their mortal bodies—still retaining their sin natures, even though redeemed by Christ as believers.) The sacrifices will thus remove any ceremonial uncleanness in the temple.

Seen in this light, the sacrifices cannot and should not be seen as a return to the Mosaic law. The law has forever been done away with through Jesus Christ (Romans 6:14-15; 7:1-6; 1 Corinthians 9:20-21; 2 Corinthians 3:7-11; Galatians 4:1-7; 5:18; Hebrews 8:13; 10:1-14). The sacrifices relate only to removing ritual impurities in the temple, as fallen-though-redeemed human beings remain on earth.

Will Satan be around to harass God's people during the millennial kingdom?

No. Revelation 20:1-3 speaks specifically of the future binding of Satan:

> I saw an angel coming down from heaven, holding in his hand the key to the bottomless pit and a great chain. And he seized the dragon, that ancient serpent, who is the devil and Satan, and bound him for a thousand years, and threw him into the pit, and shut it and sealed it over him, so that he might not deceive the nations any longer, until the thousand years were ended. After that he must be released for a little while.

Notice that Satan is referred to as a "dragon," an apt metaphor that points to the ferocity and cruelty of this evil spirit being. He is also called an "ancient serpent," apparently an allusion to Satan's first appearance in the Garden of Eden where he deceived Eve (Genesis 3; see also 2 Corinthians 11:3; 1 Timothy 2:14). The "bottomless pit" referred to here serves as the place of imprisonment of demonic spirits (Luke 8:31; see also 2 Peter 2:4). The devil—along with all demonic spirits—will be bound here for 1000 years during Christ's millennial kingdom. This quarantine will effectively remove a powerful destructive and deceptive force in all areas of human life and thought during Christ's kingdom.

Will Satan make one last attempt at deception before being tossed into the lake of fire?

Yes. Revelation 20:7-8 warns that "when the thousand years are ended, Satan will be released from his prison and will come out to deceive the nations." He will move his forces against Jerusalem with fervor.

Deception has always been at the very heart of Satan's activities. John 8:44 tells us, "He was a murderer from the beginning, and does not stand in the the truth, because there is no truth in him. When he lies, he speaks out of his own character, for he is a liar and the father of lies." So when he engages in deception, he is "in character." Deception will be his modus operandi in motivating certain human beings to revolt against Christ.

Who will join sides with Satan?

Even though the millennium will involve the perfect government of Christ, there will still be mortal and fallen human beings who live during the millennium. To be sure, Matthew 25:31-46 is clear that only believers are invited into Christ's millennial kingdom. As noted previously, however, these people will still give birth to babies and raise children, some of whom will choose not to follow Jesus Christ. So long as they do not externally rebel against the government of Christ, they are permitted to live during the millennial kingdom. But all outward rebellion will be squashed instantly.

When Satan is released at the end of the millennium, he will—by deception—succeed in leading many of these unbelieving children in a massive rebellion against Christ. As the text says, "Their number is like the sand of the sea" (Revelation 20:8). This will represent Satan's last stand.

How will Christ respond to the attack?

Jerusalem will be the target city of the satanic revolt. Jerusalem is the headquarters of Christ's government throughout the millennial kingdom (Isaiah 2:1-5). Fire instantly comes down upon the invaders (Revelation 20:9), a common mode of God's judgment (see Genesis 19:24; Exodus 9:23-24; Leviticus 9:24; 10:2; Numbers 11:1; 16:35; 26:10; 1 Kings 18:38; 2 Kings 1:10,12,14; 1 Chronicles 21:26; 2 Chronicles 7:1,3; Psalm 11:6). The rebellion is squashed instantly with no chance of success.

At what point will Satan be cast into the lake of fire?

Revelation 20:10 tells us that following the final revolt against Christ, "the devil who had deceived them was thrown into the lake of fire and sulfur where the beast and the false prophet were, and they will be tormented day and night forever and ever." Notice that our text tells us that all three persons of the satanic trinity—Satan, the antichrist, and the false prophet—will suffer the same dire destiny. More specifically, the antichrist and the false prophet will be thrown into the lake of fire prior to the beginning of the millennial kingdom. They will have been burning there for 1000 years when Satan will join them— and all three will continue to burn for all eternity. They will receive their just due.

20

The Great White Throne Judgment

What is the "intermediate state"?

The state of our existence between physical death and the future resurrection is properly called the "intermediate state." It is an *in-between* state—that is, it is the state of our existence between the time our mortal bodies die and the time we receive resurrection bodies in the future.

The intermediate state, then, is a *disembodied* state. It is a state in which one's physical body is in the grave while one's spirit or soul is either in heaven with Christ or in a place of great suffering apart from Christ. One's destiny in the intermediate state depends wholly upon whether one has placed faith in Christ during one's earthly existence.

The intermediate state of believers is one of bliss and joy, but the intermediate state of unbelievers is horrific to ponder. At the moment of death, unbelievers go as disembodied spirits to a temporary place of suffering (Luke 16:19-31). There they await their future resurrection and judgment, with an eventual destiny in the lake of fire (Revelation 20:11-15).

The intermediate state of the ungodly dead is described in 2 Peter 2:9: "The Lord knows how to…keep the unrighteous under punishment until the day of judgment." The word "keep" in this verse is in the present tense, indicating that the wicked (unbelievers) are held captive and punished continuously. Peter is portraying them as condemned prisoners being closely guarded in a spiritual jail while awaiting future sentencing and final judgment.

What is it like for the wicked dead in the intermediate state?

In Jesus' discussion of the rich man and Lazarus in the afterlife, we discern a number of sobering facts about unbelievers in the afterlife:

- The wicked dead suffer in agony.

- No one can comfort the wicked dead in the afterlife.

- There is no possibility of the wicked dead leaving the place of torment.

- The wicked dead are entirely responsible for not having listened to the warnings of Scripture while on earth.

Probably the worst torment the unbeliever will experience will be the perpetual knowledge that he or she could have trusted in Christ for salvation and escaped punishment. Throughout the endless eons and eons of eternity, the unbeliever will always know that he or she could have enjoyed a heavenly destiny by trusting in Christ while alive on earth.

Is punishment in the intermediate state only temporary?

Yes. The wicked dead will eventually be resurrected (Acts 24:15) and then face judgment at the great white throne judgment. Then their *eternal* punishment will begin in the lake of fire (Revelation 20:11-15).

Will the wicked dead have a second chance?

No. It is sobering to realize that Scripture represents the state of unbelievers after death as a fixed state, and there is no second chance (Luke 16:19-31; John 8:21,24; 2 Peter 2:4,9; Jude 6-7,13). Once one has passed through the doorway of death, there are no further opportunities to repent and turn to Christ for salvation (Matthew 7:22-23; 10:32-33; 25:41-46). Hebrews 9:27 affirms, "It is appointed for man to die once, and after that comes judgment." Woe to those who reject Christ in this life.

Doesn't 1 Peter 3:18-19 indicate that people may have a second chance?

Some Christians wonder whether 1 Peter 3:18-19 points to a second chance after death. This passage says that after Christ died, "he went and proclaimed to the spirits in prison." This does not refer to the wicked dead hearing the gospel again. Many evangelical scholars believe that the "spirits in prison" are fallen angels who grievously sinned against God. These spirits may have been the fallen angels of Genesis 6:1-6 who were disobedient to God during the days of Noah (apparently entering into sexual relations with human women).

The Greek word for "proclaimed" (*kerusso*) in 1 Peter 3:19 is not the word used for preaching the gospel but rather points to a proclamation of victory. This passage may imply that the powers of darkness thought they had destroyed Jesus at the crucifixion, but that in raising Him from the dead, God turned the tables on them—and Jesus Himself proclaimed their doom. If this is the correct interpretation, it is clear that the verse has nothing to do with human beings having a second chance.

Another possible interpretation is that between His death and resurrection, Jesus went to the place of the dead and proclaimed a message to the wicked contemporaries of Noah. The proclamation, however, was not a gospel message but a proclamation of victory.

Still another possible interpretation is that this passage portrays Christ making a proclamation through the person of Noah to those who, because they rejected his message, are *now* (at the time of Peter's writing) spirits in prison (compare with 1 Peter 1:11; 2 Peter 2:5). These imprisoned spirits are awaiting final judgment.

Regardless of which of the above interpretations is correct, evangelical scholars unanimously agree that this passage does not teach that people can hear and respond to the gospel in the next life (see 2 Corinthians 6:2; Hebrews 9:27).

Does 1 Peter 4:6 imply a second chance?

First Peter 4:6 says, "This is why the gospel was preached even to those who are dead, that though judged in the flesh the way people are, they might live in the spirit the way God does." Evangelical scholars suggest that perhaps the best way to interpret this difficult verse is that it refers to those who are now dead but who heard the gospel while they were yet alive. This makes sense in view of the tenses used: the gospel "was" preached (in the past) to those who "are" dead (presently). Seen in this light, the verse does not teach a second chance for the wicked dead.

What is the great white throne judgment?

Unbelievers of all ages will face the great white throne judgment, a horrific judgment that leads to their being cast into the lake of fire (Revelation 20:11-15). The Judge is Jesus Christ, for the Father has committed all judgment to Him (Matthew 19:28; John 5:22-30; Acts 10:42; 17:31).

This throne is "great" because the One who sits on it is our "great God and Savior," Jesus Christ (Titus 2:13-14). It is white, suggesting that the One who sits on the throne is holy, pure, and righteous (see Psalm 97:2; Daniel 7:9).

The judgment takes place after the millennial kingdom, Christ's 1000-year reign on earth. We know it takes place after the millennium because the apostle John, after describing the millennium, states: "*Then* I saw a great white throne and him who was seated on it" (Revelation 20:11).

I must underscore that those who participate in this judgment are here precisely because they are *already unsaved.* Those judged are called "the dead" in obvious contrast to "the dead in Christ."

This means that this judgment will not separate believers from unbelievers, for all who will experience it will have already made the choice during their lifetimes to reject God. The fact that people arrive at this judgment is sorrowful beyond measure, for they have no chance of redemption. They are there because they are unsaved, and they are about to be cast into the lake of fire. I cannot even begin to imagine the sense of dread that will permeate the minds of those who will be there.

How do we know the participants in the great white throne judgment will be resurrected from the dead?

Scripture reveals that those who participate in the great white throne judgment will be resurrected for the very purpose of facing the divine Judge, Jesus Christ. During His earthly ministry, Jesus soberly announced that "an hour is coming when all who are in the tombs will hear his voice and come out, those who have done good to the resurrection of life, and those who have done evil to the resurrection of judgment" (John 5:28-29). Virtually every possible location and place will yield the bodies of the unrighteous dead—the sea, Death, and Hades—and all will be resurrected (Revelation 20:13-14).

Is this related to the "first" and "second" resurrections in the book of Revelation?

Yes. Revelation describes two types of resurrection—the first resurrection and the second resurrection (see Revelation 20:5-6,11-15). These are not *chronological* resurrections but *types* of resurrections. The first resurrection is the resurrection of Christians, and the second resurrection is the resurrection of the wicked.

It is important to grasp that even though all Christians will be resurrected in the first resurrection, not all Christians are resurrected at the same time. There is one resurrection of the righteous at the rapture, before the tribulation period (1 Thessalonians 4:16; see also Job 19:25-27; Psalm 49:15; Daniel 12:2; Isaiah 26:19; John 6:39-40,44,54; 1 Corinthians 15:42). There is another resurrection at the end of the 1000-year millennial kingdom (Revelation 20:4). These are both part of the first resurrection because they all occur before the second (final) resurrection of the wicked. For this reason, we can say that the term "first resurrection" applies to all the resurrections of the righteous, regardless of when they occur.

The second resurrection is a sobering thing to ponder. It is described in Revelation 20:13: "The sea gave up the dead who were in it, Death and Hades gave up the dead who were in them, and they were judged." The unsaved of all time—regardless of what century they lived in, whether before the time of Christ or after—will be resurrected at the end of Christ's millennial kingdom. They will then face judgment at the great white throne judgment. Tragically, the outcome of this judgment is that they will be cast alive into the lake of fire.

What "books" are opened at the great white throne judgment?

Revelation 20:12 tells us that books will be opened at the great white throne judgment. These books detail the lives of the unsaved and will provide the evidence to substantiate the divine verdict of a destiny in the lake of fire. The works that will be judged will include unbelievers' actions (Matthew 16:27), their words (Matthew 12:37), and even their thoughts and motives (Luke 8:17; Romans 2:16).

We also read of another book—*the book of life*. The idea of a divine register containing names goes back as far as Moses' encounter with God on Mount Sinai (Exodus 32:32-33). The apostle Paul speaks of his fellow workers as those "whose names are in the book of life" (Philippians 4:3). In the book of Revelation, the "book of life" is mentioned six times (3:5; 13:8; 17:8; 20:12,15; and 21:27), and it contains the names of all those who belong to God. In Revelation 13:8 and 21:27, the book of life is said to belong specifically to the Lamb of God, Jesus Christ.

When Christ opens the book of life at the great white throne judgment, no name of anyone present at the judgment is in it. Their names do not appear in the book of life because they have rejected the source of life—Jesus Christ. Because they have rejected the source of life, their destiny is to be cast into the lake of fire, which constitutes the "second death" and involves eternal separation from God.

Will degrees of punishment be handed out at the great white throne judgment?

Yes. As a backdrop, all who participate in the great white throne judgment have a horrific destiny ahead. Scripture characterizes their existence in the lake of fire as involving weeping and gnashing of teeth (Matthew 13:41-42), condemnation (Matthew 12:36-37), destruction (Philippians 1:28), eternal punishment (Matthew 25:46), separation from God's presence (2 Thessalonians 1:8-9), and tribulation and distress (Romans 2:9). Woe to all who enter the lake of fire.

Scripture also reveals, however, that there will be degrees of punishment in hell. The degrees of punishment will be commensurate with the degrees of sinfulness.

Scripture provides significant support for this idea. In Matthew 11:20-24, for example, Jesus speaks of things being more tolerable for some than for others on the day of judgment. In Luke 12:47-48, Jesus spoke of the possibility of receiving a light beating versus a severe beating. Jesus also speaks of certain people who will receive a greater condemnation than others (Luke 20:47). In John 19:11, Jesus spoke of greater and lesser sins, and thus greater and lesser guilt (see also Matthew 10:15; 16:27; Revelation 20:12-13; 22:12).

Let us not forget that God is perfectly just. His judgments are fair. So, for example, at the judgment seat of Christ, some Christians will receive rewards while others will suffer loss of rewards. Christ is fair in recognizing that some Christians live faithfully on earth while others do not. His judgment of them will reflect this reality. Conversely, at the great white throne judgment, Christ is fair in recognizing that some unbelievers are more wicked than others. Hitler, for example, will be judged much more severely than a non-Christian moralist. Jesus' judgment of the unsaved will reflect their degree of wickedness.

We might summarize these judgments this way: Just as believers differ in how they respond to God's law and therefore in their reward in heaven, so unbelievers differ in their response to God's law and therefore in their punishment in hell. Just as there are degrees of reward in heaven, so there are degrees of punishment in hell.

Our Lord is perfectly just in all things.

21

The Lake of Fire

What is the lake of fire?

The lake of fire is a place of great suffering that will be the eternal abode of Satan, the antichrist, the false prophet, and all unbelievers (Revelation 19:20; 20:10-15). All residents will be tormented day and night forever. The punishment is eternal.

Jesus often referred to the eternal destiny of the wicked as "eternal fire." Following His second coming, when He separates the sheep (believers) from the goats (unbelievers), Jesus will say to the goats: "Depart from me, you cursed, into the eternal fire prepared for the devil and his angels" (Matthew 25:41). This eternal fire is part and parcel of the lake of fire.

The lake of fire is another term for hell. The Scriptures assure us that hell is a real place. But hell was not part of God's original creation, which He called "good" (Genesis 1:31). Hell was created later to accommodate the banishment of Satan and his fallen angels who rebelled against God (Matthew 25:41). Human beings who reject Christ will join Satan and his fallen angels in this infernal place of suffering.

What are some other terms that describe the horror of hell?

Hell is the place where "the fire is not quenched" (Mark 9:48) and where there will be "weeping and gnashing of teeth" (Matthew 13:42). It is called "eternal punishment" (Matthew 25:46), "destruction" (Matthew 7:13), "eternal destruction" (2 Thessalonians 1:8-9), and "the second death" (Revelation 20:14). The horror of hell is inconceivable to the human mind.

What precisely is the "fire" of hell (or lake of fire)?

Some believe the fire of hell is literal. And, indeed, that may very well be the case. Others believe "fire" is a metaphorical way of expressing the great wrath of God. Scripture tells us:

- "The LORD your God is a consuming fire, a jealous God" (Deuteronomy 4:24).
- "Our God is a consuming fire" (Hebrews 12:29).
- "His wrath is poured out like fire" (Nahum 1:6).
- "Who can stand when he appears? For he will be like a refiner's fire" (Malachi 3:2).
- God's wrath will "go forth like fire, and burn with none to quench it" (Jeremiah 4:4).

Whether the fire of hell is literal or metaphorical, it will entail horrible suffering for those who are there. It may well be that the fire of hell is both literal *and* metaphorical.

What is meant by "weeping and gnashing of teeth"?

Weeping and gnashing of teeth are a common experience in hell (Matthew 13:42; Luke 13:28). "Weeping" carries the idea of wailing, not merely with tears but with every outward expression of grief. The weeping will be caused by the environment, the company, the remorse and guilt, and the shame that is part and parcel of hell.

People gnash their teeth when they are angry. They will be angry at the sin that brought them to hell, angry at what they've become, angry at Satan and demons for their temptations to evil in earthly life, and angry over having rejected their ticket out of hell—salvation in Jesus Christ.

Does the Old Testament term "Sheol" relate to the doctrine of hell?

"Sheol" can have different meanings in different contexts. Sometimes the word means "grave." Other times it refers to the place of departed people in contrast to the state of living people. The Old

Testament portrays Sheol as a place of horror (Psalm 30:9), weeping (Isaiah 38:3), and punishment (Job 24:19).

Does the New Testament term "Hades" relate to the doctrine of hell?

"Hades" is the New Testament counterpart to "Sheol" in the Old Testament. The rich man, during the intermediate state, endured great suffering in Hades (Luke 16:19-31). Hades, however, is a temporary abode and will one day be cast into the lake of fire (Revelation 20:14).

Why is hell sometimes called Gehenna?

One of the more important New Testament words for "hell" (in Greek) is *Gehenna* (Matthew 10:28). This word has an interesting history. For several generations in ancient Israel, atrocities were committed in the Valley of Ben Hinnom—atrocities that included human sacrifices, even the sacrifice of children (2 Kings 23:10; 2 Chronicles 28:3; 33:6; Jeremiah 32:35). These unfortunate victims were sacrificed to the false Moabite god Molech. Jeremiah appropriately called this valley "the Valley of Slaughter" (Jeremiah 7:31-34).

Eventually the valley came to be used as a public rubbish dump into which all the filth in Jerusalem was poured. Not only garbage but also the bodies of dead animals and the corpses of criminals were thrown on the heap where they—like everything else in the dump—would perpetually burn. The valley was a place where the fires never stopped burning. And there was always a good meal for a hungry worm.

This place was originally called (in the Hebrew) *Ge[gen]hinnom* (the valley of the sons of Hinnom). It was eventually shortened to the name *Ge-Hinnom*. The Greek translation of this Hebrew phrase is *Gehenna*. It became an appropriate and graphic term for the reality of hell. Jesus Himself used the word 11 times as a metaphorical way of describing the eternal place of suffering of unredeemed humanity.

How does the New Testament word *Tartaros* relate to the doctrine of hell?

The word *Tartaros* occurs only one time in the Bible and refers to a place where certain fallen angels (demons) are confined (2 Peter 2:4). Most fallen angels are free to roam the earth, engaging in their destructive activities wherever they find opportunity (for example, Luke 8:30). But these imprisoned fallen angels are not free to roam, apparently because they committed an especially heinous sin against God in the past. Perhaps they are the wicked angels of Genesis 6:1-6 who engaged in perverse sin.

Does God really send people to hell?

God doesn't want to send anyone to hell. Scripture tells us that God is "not wishing that any should perish, but that all should reach repentance" (2 Peter 3:9). God sent Jesus into the world specifically to pay the penalty for our sins by dying on the cross (John 3:16-17). Unfortunately, not all people are willing to admit that they sin and to trust in Christ for forgiveness. They don't accept the payment of Jesus' death for them. So God allows them to experience the harsh results of their choice (see Luke 16:19-31).

C.S. Lewis once said that in the end there are two groups of people. One group says to God, "Thy will be done." These are those who have placed their faith in Jesus Christ and will live forever with God in heaven. The second group of people are those to whom God says, sadly, "*Thy* will be done!" These are those who have rejected Jesus Christ and will spend eternity apart from Him.

What is annihilationism?

The doctrine of annihilationism teaches that man was created immortal. But those who continue in sin and reject Christ are, by a positive act of God, deprived of the gift of immortality and are ultimately destroyed. There is no conscious afterlife for them. In this view, there is no eternal suffering in hell.

How do we know annihilationism is a false doctrine?

In Matthew 25:46, Jesus said that the unsaved "will go away into eternal punishment, but the righteous into eternal life." By no stretch of the imagination can the punishment Jesus spoke of be any kind of nonsuffering extinction of consciousness. If actual suffering is lacking, then so is punishment. Punishment entails suffering. And suffering necessarily entails consciousness.

Certainly one can exist and not be punished; but no one can be punished and not exist. Annihilation means the obliteration of existence and anything that pertains to existence, such as punishment. Annihilation *avoids* rather than encounters punishment.

Notice that Jesus said the punishment is "eternal." The adjective *aionion* in this verse literally means "everlasting, without end." This same adjective is predicated of God (the "eternal" God) in Romans 16:26, Hebrews 9:14, 13:8, and Revelation 4:9. The punishment of the wicked is just as eternal as our eternal God.

Is it correct to say that annihilationism is ultimately unjust as a punishment?

I believe so. Notice that there are no degrees of annihilation. One is either annihilated or one is not. Whether you're Hitler or a non-Christian moralist, you both get equally annihilated. The Scriptures, by contrast, teach that there will be degrees of conscious punishment in hell (see Matthew 10:15; 11:21-24; 16:27; Luke 12:47-48; Hebrews 10:29; Revelation 20:11-15; 22:12). These degrees of punishment are commensurate with the level of one's wickedness. Such a punishment is therefore completely just.

Does Scripture communicate a sense of urgency in avoiding a destiny in hell?

Most certainly. Recall that Hebrews 9:27 affirms "it is appointed for man to die once, and after that comes judgment." Notice the order of events. The text does not say that man dies, has a second chance to believe, and then faces judgment. Rather, it says that man dies *and then faces the judgment.*

The fact that we die once and then face the judgment is one reason for the apostle Paul's urgency in 2 Corinthians 6:2: "Now is the favorable time; behold, now is the day of salvation." No one should wait before responding to the gospel, for death could come at any time.

This short life on earth is the only time we have to decide for or against Christ. Once we die, there is no further opportunity (or second chance) to believe in Jesus for salvation.

Ecclesiastes 9:12 tells us that "man does not know his time [that is, the time of death]. Like fish that are taken in an evil net, and like birds that are caught in a snare, so the children of man are snared at an evil time, when it suddenly falls upon them." If this passage tells us anything, it tells us that death often comes suddenly, without warning. The implication is that we must be prepared for the moment, for there are no second chances. A sense of urgency would be unnecessary if we have a second chance following death.

We see this wisdom in Proverbs 27:1: "Do not boast about tomorrow, for you do not know what a day may bring." Each new day may bring the prospect of death. It is therefore wise to turn to Christ for salvation while there is yet time, for there are no second chances in the afterlife. There is no possibility of redemption beyond death's door.

Many people rationalize that they'll have plenty of time to turn to the Lord later in life so they don't need to bother with salvation at the present time. Such a view is full of folly. Consider Jesus' words in Luke 12:16-21:

> The land of a rich man produced plentifully, and he thought to himself, "What shall I do, for I have nowhere to store my crops?" And he said, "I will do this: I will tear down my barns and build larger ones, and there I will store all my grain and my goods. And I will say to my soul, 'Soul, you have ample goods laid up for many years; relax, eat, drink, be merry.'" But God said to him, "Fool! This night your soul is required of you, and the things you have prepared, whose will they be?" So is the one who lays up treasure for himself and is not rich toward God.

Many people today live as if they're entitled to 70 or 80 years. They don't plan on dying younger and don't take the gospel of Jesus Christ seriously in their youth. The reality is that many die young and are unprepared for death and what lies beyond. Again, "now is the day of salvation."

How can we be happy in heaven knowing that people are suffering in hell?

This is a difficult question to answer. In fact, on this side of eternity, we do not have all the wisdom and insight we need to fully answer it. But some scriptural considerations help us keep this question in perspective.

First, God Himself has promised that He will take away all pain and remove all our tears (Revelation 21:4). It is in His hands. We can rest assured that God has the power and ability to do as He has promised. It is a fact that we will be happy in heaven. God has promised it.

Second, we will be aware of the full justice of God's decisions. We will clearly see that those who are in hell are there precisely because they rejected God's only provision for escaping hell. They are those to whom God ultimately says, "Thy will be done."

Third, we will recognize that there are degrees of punishment in hell, just as there are degrees of reward in heaven. This gives us an assurance that the Hitlers of human history will be in a much greater state of suffering than, for example, a non-Christian moralist (Luke 12:47-48).

Finally, it is entirely possible that God may purge the memories of non-Christians (including family members) from our minds. God promises in Isaiah 65:17: "Behold, I create new heavens and a new earth, and the former things shall not be remembered or come into mind."

Let us never forget that God is perfectly wise and just. He knows what He is doing! You and I can rest with quiet assurance in God's wisdom and justice.

22

The New Heavens, New Earth, and New Jerusalem

What are the three heavens mentioned in Scripture?

The Scriptures refer to three heavens. The first heaven is the earth's atmosphere (Job 35:5). The second heaven is the stellar universe (Genesis 1:17; Deuteronomy 17:3). The third heaven is the ineffable and glorious dwelling place of God in all His glory (2 Corinthians 12:2). The third heaven is elsewhere called the "highest heaven" (1 Kings 8:27; 2 Chronicles 2:6).

Why will God destroy our present earth and universe?

After Adam and Eve sinned against God in the Garden of Eden, God placed a curse upon the earth (Genesis 3:17-18). Romans 8:20 tells us that "the creation was subjected to futility." Hence, before the eternal kingdom of glory is revealed, God must deal with this cursed earth. Indeed, the earth—along with the first and second heavens (the earth's atmosphere and the stellar universe)—must be dissolved by fire. The decay, death, and other forms of evil will remain until the One who imposed the curse removes it and creates a new heaven and a new earth. The old must make room for the new.

We must also remember that Satan has long carried out his evil schemes on earth (see Ephesians 2:2). The earth must therefore be purged of all stains resulting from his extended presence. Satan will have no place in the new heavens and the new earth. All evidence of his influence will be removed when God destroys the earth and the heavens.

Is God's destruction of the present earth and heavens taught in both the Old and New Testaments?

Yes. The destruction of the present heavens and earth is taught in both the Old and New Testaments. Psalm 102:25-26, for example, says of the passing of the old earth and heavens: "They will perish...they will all wear out like a garment...they will pass away." Isaiah 51:6 likewise affirms, "Lift up your eyes to the heavens, and look at the earth beneath; for the heavens vanish like smoke, the earth will wear out like a garment." Jesus was well aware of this common Old Testament teaching, for He contrasted the temporal universe with His eternal Word: "Heaven and earth will pass away, but my words will not pass away" (Matthew 24:35).

We receive a fuller revelation of the passing of the present heavens and earth in 2 Peter 3:7-13, where we read these sobering words:

> The heavens and earth that now exist are stored up for fire, being kept until the day of judgment...The day of the Lord will come like a thief, and then the heavens will pass away with a roar, and the heavenly bodies will be burned up and dissolved, and the earth and the works that are done on it will be exposed. Since all these things are thus to be dissolved, what sort of people ought you to be in lives of holiness and godliness, waiting for and hastening the coming of the day of God, because of which the heavens will be set on fire and dissolved, and the heavenly bodies will melt as they burn! But according to his promise we are waiting for new heavens and a new earth in which righteousness dwells.

The good news is that although the present universe, which is stained by sin, will be judged and destroyed, God will create new heavens and a new earth for us to dwell in forever. *It will be glorious.*

In what way will the heavens and earth be made "new"?

The Greek word used to designate the newness of the cosmos is *kainos.* This word means "new in nature" or "new in quality." Hence, the phrase "new heavens and a new earth" refers not to a cosmos that is totally other than the present cosmos. Rather, the new cosmos will stand in continuity with the present cosmos, but it will be utterly renewed and renovated (Revelation 21:1,5). In keeping with this, Matthew 19:28 speaks of "the new world." Acts 3:21 speaks of a coming restoration.

All this means that a resurrected people will live in a resurrected universe! The new heavens and earth, like our newness in Christ, will be regenerated, glorified, free from the curse of sin, and eternal. The new earth, being a renewed and an eternal earth, will be adapted to the vast moral and physical changes that the eternal state necessitates. Everything is new in the eternal state. Everything will be according to God's own glorious nature. The new heavens and the new earth will be brought into blessed conformity with all that God is—in a state of fixed bliss and absolute perfection.

Which of the three heavens become new?

Scripture reveals that the only heavens that have been negatively affected by humankind's fall are the earth's atmosphere and the stellar universe, the first and second heavens. The entire physical universe is running down and decaying, so it will be renewed. The third heaven—God's perfect and glorious dwelling place—remains untouched by human sin. It needs no renewal. This heaven subsists in moral and physical perfection and undergoes no change.

Once the physical universe is cleansed and God creates new heavens and a new earth, all vestiges of the original curse and Satan's presence will be utterly and forever removed. There will be a massive environmental change. We will instantly transition from an environment of pain, suffering, darkness, and death to a new environment of God-focused blessedness.

Will we live forever on the new earth?

Yes, and it will be glorious. In the next life, heaven and earth will no longer be separate realms, as they are now, but will be merged. Believers will continue to be in heaven even while they are on the new earth.

The new earth will be utterly sinless, bathed and suffused in the light and splendor of God, unobscured by evil of any kind or tarnished by evildoers of any description.

"Heaven" will thus encompass the new heaven and the new earth. And the New Jerusalem—the eternal city that measures 1500 by 1500 by 1500 miles—will apparently come down and rest upon the newly renovated earth (see Revelation 21:2). This city will be the eternal dwelling place of the saints of all ages.

Does this mean that the heaven we inhabit in the eternal state will be expanded from what heaven is today?

Apparently so. Many theologians believe that the term "heaven," presently used of God's perfect domain, will one day include the new heavens and the new earth. We might say that heaven will one day include the entire redeemed and resurrected universe (see 2 Peter 3:13; Revelation 21:1).

In that day, the prophecy of Isaiah 65:17 will be fulfilled: "Behold, I create new heavens and a new earth, and the former things shall not be remembered or come into mind." Indeed, as Psalm 9:6 puts it, the wicked will come to an end, and the very memory of them will perish. This is what John describes in Revelation 21:1-5: "Then I saw a new heaven and a new earth, for the first heaven and the first earth had passed away...And he who was seated on the throne said, 'Behold, I am making all things new.'"

Brother and sisters, we have cause to rejoice (1 Corinthians 2:9). We are destined for new heavens and a new earth!

Why will there be no need for the sun in the New Jerusalem, and why will there be no night?

Revelation 22:5 tells us that in the eternal city, "night will be no more. They will need no light of lamp or sun, for the Lord God will be their light." There are two observations I can make about this verse:

First, our present bodies are comparatively weak and need sleep every night in order to recuperate. Our resurrection bodies will apparently not require recuperation through sleep. Our resurrection bodies will never become fatigued. We will never become run-down. Therefore, night becomes unnecessary.

Second, the fact that the glory of the Lord God will light up the eternal city may have a parallel to the Old Testament tabernacle, and later, the temple. Recall that when the tabernacle in the wilderness was completed, the cloud of the Lord's glory settled upon it, preventing human entrance: "The cloud covered the tent of meeting, and the glory of the LORD filled the tabernacle. And Moses was not able to enter the tent of meeting because the cloud settled on it, and the glory of the LORD filled the tabernacle" (Exodus 40:34-35). Likewise, the cloud of the Lord's glory filled Solomon's temple when it was dedicated: "When the priests came out of the Holy Place, a cloud filled the house of the LORD, so that the priests could not stand to minister because of the cloud, for the glory of the LORD filled the house of the LORD" (1 Kings 8:10-11).

Just as the glory of the Lord filled (and lit up) Solomon's temple, so the glory of the Lord will fill and light up the eternal city, the New Jerusalem, itself possibly modeled after the Most Holy Place within the temple. But there is one notable difference. In Old Testament times the glory of the Lord prevented human entrance into the temple. By contrast, Christians, in their upgraded resurrection bodies, will be perfectly comfortable in the New Jerusalem as they bask in the warm glow of the Lord's glory. Our resurrection bodies will be specially suited to dwell in the direct presence of the Lord Almighty.

Why will there be no sea on the new earth?

About three-quarters of the earth's surface is presently covered with water and therefore uninhabitable by humans. In the new earth, by contrast, there will be no sea (Revelation 21:1). This means there will be an immensely increased land surface, making the whole world inhabitable. The life principle in this new earth will not be water but rather *the water of life* (22:1).

Bible expositors observe that for some people, the sea calls to mind the great destructive flood of Noah's time. As well, for many people, the sea constitutes a barrier between loved ones, who may live on opposite sides of the ocean. As the apostle John wrote the book of Revelation, he was exiled on the island of Patmos, surrounded by water on every side and thereby prevented from contact with his loved ones throughout Asia Minor (see Revelation 1:9). There will be no sense of separation on the new earth. Fellowship will never be broken!

What is the New Jerusalem?

The most elaborate description of the heavenly city contained in the Bible is Revelation 21, where we read all about the New Jerusalem:

> I saw the holy city, new Jerusalem, coming down out of heaven from God, prepared as a bride adorned for her husband...having the glory of God, its radiance like a most rare jewel, like a jasper, clear as crystal. It had a great, high wall, with twelve gates, and at the gates twelve angels, and on the gates the names of the twelve tribes of the sons of Israel were inscribed—on the east three gates, on the north three gates, on the south three gates, and on the west three gates. And the wall of the city had twelve foundations, and on them were the twelve names of the twelve apostles of the Lamb...The wall was built of jasper, while the city was pure gold, clear as glass. The foundations of the wall of the city were adorned with every kind of jewel...And the twelve gates were twelve pearls, each of the gates made of a single pearl, and the street of the city was pure gold, like transparent glass...And the city has no need of sun or moon to shine on it, for the glory of God gives it light, and its lamp is the Lamb...and its gates will never be shut by day—and there will be no night there (verses 2,11-14,18-19,21,23,25).

This description of the New Jerusalem is astounding. Presented to our amazed gaze is a scene of such transcendent splendor that the human mind can scarcely take it in. This is a scene of ecstatic joy and fellowship of sinless angels and redeemed, glorified human beings. The voice of the One identified as the Alpha and the Omega, the beginning and the end, utters a climactic declaration: "Behold, I am making all

The New Heavens, New Earth, and New Jerusalem 219

things new" (verse 5). The words of Revelation 21 and 22 represent a human attempt to describe the utterly indescribable.

One thing is certain. The New Jerusalem—the eternal city where you and I will live forever—is designed to reflect and reveal the incredible glory of God. The mention of transparency reveals that the city is designed to transmit the glory of God in the form of light without hindrance. The human imagination is simply incapable of fathoming the immeasurably resplendent glory of God that will be perpetually on display in the eternal city. This is especially so when we consider that all manner of precious stones will be built into the eternal city.

Will the New Jerusalem be a physical city?

Yes, I'm convinced of it. I do not take references to this city to be symbolic of some kind of spiritual twilight zone where believers somehow float around in spiritual fellowship with God. Rather, I take the New Jerusalem to be a literal city, a real place where real resurrected people and a holy God will dwell together. A city has dwellings, order (government), bustling activity, various kinds of gatherings, and much more. There is no warrant for taking the descriptions of the New Jerusalem in Scripture as merely symbolic. Every description we have of the New Jerusalem in the Bible implies a real place of residence.

This makes sense in view of the fact that you and I will have eternal and physical resurrection bodies (1 Corinthians 15:50-55). People with physical bodies must live in a physical place. And that physical place will be the New Jerusalem.

What shape will the New Jerusalem be?

The eternal city could either be cube-shaped or pyramid-shaped—and there are good Christian scholars on both sides of the debate. Some prefer to consider it shaped as a pyramid, for this would explain how the river of the water of life could flow down its sides as pictured in Revelation 22:1-2. Others prefer to consider it shaped as a cube, for the holy of holies in Solomon's temple was cube-shaped (1 Kings 6:20), and hence a cubical shape of the New Jerusalem might be intended to communicate that this eternal city is likened to a holy of holies throughout all eternity.

How large will the New Jerusalem be?

The heavenly city measures approximately 1500 miles by 1500 miles by 1500 miles. Though some interpret these big numbers symbolically, allegedly carrying the idea that "saved people are never crowded," I think the dimensions are intended to be taken literally. The eternal city is so huge that it will cover approximately the distance from Canada to Mexico and from the Atlantic Ocean to the Rockies. That is a surface area of 2.25 million square miles. By comparison, London is only 621 square miles. Put another way, the ground-level area of the city will be 3623 times that of London.

The city is tall enough that from the earth's surface it would reach about 1/159 of the way to the moon. If the city has stories, each being 12 feet high, then the city would have 660,000 stories. That is huge!

A city that large might seem a formidable challenge to those traveling within its boundaries. We must not forget, however, that our resurrection bodies will have amazing capabilities. Some expositors believe our new bodies will have the ability to fly and get places fast. That would be very exciting!

Why are there walls and gates in the New Jerusalem?

Scripture reveals that the New Jerusalem has "a great, high wall, with twelve gates, and at the gates twelve angels, and on the gates the names of the twelve tribes of the sons of Israel" (Revelation 21:12). Moreover, "the wall of the city had twelve foundations, and on them were the twelve names of the twelve apostles of the Lamb" (verse 14).

We could spend days pondering the significance of these facts. For example, why are the angels at the 12 gates? We know from other Scripture verses that angels often functioned as guardians (Psalm 91:11; Matthew 18:10; Acts 12:15), so perhaps they are at the gates to guard the city. Angels in the Bible are also ministering (or serving) spirits (Hebrews 1:14). Perhaps they are at the gates as servants to those who inherit salvation.

Why are the names of the 12 tribes of Israel inscribed on the gates? It's hard to say. We might speculate it is because "salvation is from the Jews" (John 4:22), and the Messiah Himself came from Jewish lineage (Matthew 1:1).

Why are the names of the apostles inscribed on the foundations of the city? Again, it is hard to say. We might speculate that it is because the church itself was built upon the foundation of these men of God, who are therefore worthy of special honor (see Ephesians 2:20).

John himself (the author of the book of Revelation) is one of these apostles. I wonder what his response might have been as he witnessed his own name inscribed on the foundations of the city. I suspect his response was one of great humility.

Scripture reveals that both Jews and Gentiles are a part of God's eternal family (Ephesians 2:11-13). It is therefore quite appropriate that the names of the 12 tribes of Israel and the 12 apostles be singled out in the eternal city.

Is the river of the water of life in the New Jerusalem a literal river?

In Revelation 22:1-2 John says, "Then the angel showed me the river of the water of life, bright as crystal, flowing from the throne of God and of the Lamb through the middle of the street of the city." The biblical text does not reveal much about this river. Some take it to be merely symbolic, though others take it literally. Perhaps the best approach is to take it literally *and* symbolically. Perhaps this is a real river that symbolizes the rich abundance of the spiritual life of the redeemed in the eternal city. Just as a river provides a perpetual outflow of thirst-quenching water on a sunny day, perhaps the river of the water of life symbolizes the perpetual provision of spiritual satisfaction and blessing to the redeemed, who are now basking in the warm glow of eternal life.

What does Scripture say about the restoration of the tree of life in the New Jerusalem?

Revelation 22:2 speaks of "the tree of life with its twelve kinds of fruit, yielding its fruit each month. The leaves of the tree were for the healing of the nations." The tree of life made its first appearance in the first book of the Bible—Genesis 3, where Adam and Eve sinned against God. Paradise was lost, and the first couple were barred from access to the tree. Now, in the last book of the Bible, paradise is restored, and we again witness free access to the tree of life.

In what way do the leaves provide for the healing of nations? Does this imply that in the eternal state the nations will be in need of healing, as if recovering from some kind of conflict? I don't think so. After all, the eternal state will be perfect and ideal in every way. Revelation 21:4 promises that in the eternal state "death shall be no more, neither shall there be mourning, nor crying, nor pain anymore, for the former things have passed away."

It is noteworthy that the Greek word for "healing" in this verse is *therapeia*, from which the English word "therapeutic" is derived. The word carries the basic meaning of "health giving." In the present context, the word carries the idea that the leaves on the tree of life give health to the redeemed peoples of the world. They have nothing to do with correcting any ills for such ills will not exist.

How is the New Jerusalem different from earthly cities?

The New Jerusalem is better in every way:

- Earthly cities constantly have to be rebuilt or repaired, but no repair is ever necessary in the New Jerusalem.

- Believers and unbelievers live in earthly cities, but only believers will be in the eternal city.

- Many people go hungry and thirsty in earthly cities, but no one will hunger or thirst in the New Jerusalem.

- Earthly cities have crime, but there is perfect righteousness in the eternal city.

- Earthly cities often have outbreaks of rebellion, but there is no rebellion in the heavenly city. All are in submission to the divine King, Jesus Christ.

- People in earthly cities have many broken relationships, but all relationships in the New Jerusalem are perfect and loving.

- Widespread disease is common in earthly cities, but perfect health predominates in the New Jerusalem.

- Earthly cities have graveyards, but such are absent in the eternal city. Death will be entirely foreign to our experience in heaven.

- Earthly cities get dark at night, but the eternal city is always lighted.

Our existence in heaven will be completely unlike our experience on earth. The eternal city, the New Jerusalem, is going to be absolutely wonderful, far more so than any human mind could possibly fathom or even begin to imagine. As 1 Corinthians 2:9 puts it, we will experience moment by moment "what no eye has seen, nor ear heard, nor the heart of man imagined."

What kinds of things will never be found in the New Jerusalem?

In heaven we will have resurrection bodies with no sin nature. Satan and demons will be quarantined away from our presence forever. And we will live in a perfectly holy environment. A natural consequence of this wondrous state of affairs is that many things will be foreign to our experience in heaven. The following is just a sampling:

- We will never have to confess a wrongdoing. (There is no sin in heaven that would make confession necessary.)

- We will never experience guilt or shame over any action. (Again, there is no sin in heaven that would bring guilt.)

- We will never have to repair our homes or any other items. (Nothing runs down in heaven.)

- We will never have to defend ourselves before others. (Relationships will be perfect in every way in heaven.)

- We will never have to apologize. (Again, all relationships will be perfect in heaven. Our actions will be focused on others instead of ourselves.)

- We will never feel isolated or lonely. (There will be a perfect expression of love between all the redeemed in heaven.)

- We will never have to go through rehabilitation. (We will remain whole and healthy for all eternity. There will never be any addictions of any kind.)

- We will never be depressed or discouraged. (We will perpetually enjoy the abundant life in heaven.)

- We will never become tired or worn-out in heaven. (Our resurrection bodies will be strong and never need recuperation.)

- There will never be offense (given or received) in heaven. (All our words will be void of sin and full of grace.)

- We will never experience envy or jealousy in heaven. (Our love for others will be utterly complete and perfect, with no unwholesome emotions.)

- We will never experience infidelity in heaven. (The Golden Rule will predominate in heaven. There is no sinful behavior in heaven. Faithfulness will be a hallmark of heaven.)

- We will never again lust after another person. (Our hearts will be pure, with no sin whatsoever.)

- We will never experience a misunderstanding with other people. (No relationships will ever be broken in heaven.)

- We will never have any sense of deprivation. (We will never have to earn money or worry about having enough money to survive. We'll have an overabundance of all we need in heaven.)

- There will be no wars or bloodshed in heaven. (The sinful attitudes that give rise to wars will be nonexistent in heaven.)

I could mention many other things here. The main point is that the absence of all these (and many other) negative things will contribute immensely to our sense of joy and well-being in heaven. We can't even begin to imagine how wonderful it will be.

Is Jesus the Designer and Creator of the New Jerusalem?

Yes, indeed. Jesus is the Creator of all things. Colossians 1:16 says of Jesus, "By him all things were created, in heaven and on earth, visible and invisible, whether thrones or dominions or rulers or authorities—all things were created through him and for him." John 1:3 likewise says of Jesus, "All things were made through him, and without him was not any thing made that was made" (see also Hebrews 1:2).

Jesus made it all—our solar system, our galaxy, and the other galaxies that are staggering distances from each other. It's an awesome thing to ponder. The same Jesus who created the entire universe is creating the New Jerusalem for you and me (see John 14:1-3).

23

Blessings of the Eternal State

Will we experience the direct presence of God immediately upon the moment of death?

Yes—assuming you are a Christian. Upon death, our spirits depart the physical body and are ushered into heaven, where our direct and unhindered fellowship with God begins.

There are many scriptural evidences for this wondrous reality. The thief on the cross who expressed faith in Christ is a good example. Christ—also on the cross—indicated to him that he should not fear death: "Truly, I say to you, today you will be with me in paradise" (Luke 23:43). It is not just that the thief would be in paradise (heaven) after he died. Rather, it is that the thief would be in paradise *with Christ*. And it was to happen *that very day*. In the Greek, the word "today" is in the emphatic position, indicating there would be no delay before the repentant thief would enter heaven following death. As soon as his head dropped in death, his spirit entered the glories of paradise with the Lord Jesus! The same will be true of each of us.

Christ's faithful servant Stephen knew he would enjoy intimate fellowship with Christ upon his death. When he was being stoned for his faithful testimony of Jesus Christ, he looked up to heaven and said, "Lord Jesus, receive my spirit" (Acts 7:59). He knew that once his spirit was in heaven, his direct fellowship with Christ would be perpetual and unhindered.

How intimate will our fellowship be with Christ in the afterlife?

In 2 Corinthians 5:8, Paul indicates that following the moment of death we are "at home with the Lord." The Greek word for "with" in this verse suggests very close (face-to-face) fellowship. It is a word typically used of intimate relationships.

This means that the moment you die and go to heaven, the Lord will not merely wave at you from a distance or perhaps say, "Hi, welcome to heaven," and then walk off. Rather, you will enjoy the direct, unhindered, continued, intimate presence of the Lord. It is for this reason that Christians can see death as something not to be feared (see 1 Corinthians 15:54-55).

When a Christian dies today, we can truly rejoice that he or she is now in intimate fellowship with Jesus Christ. Glorious!

Did Paul have this in mind when he said, "My desire is to depart and be with Christ"?

Yes. The apostle Paul looked forward to heaven. He said: "My desire is to depart and be with Christ, for that is far better" (Philippians 1:23). This verse is incredibly rich in the original Greek. The Greek word for "depart" was used in biblical times to describe a ship being loosed from its moorings to sail away from the dock. The "mooring" that kept Paul from departing to heaven was his commitment to work among believers on earth until his assignment was complete. His ultimate desire, however, was to sail directly into God's presence. And that would happen at the moment of death.

The Greek word for "depart" was also used in biblical times for freeing someone from chains. Here on earth, you and I are chained or anchored to the hardships and heartaches of this life. In death, however, these chains are broken. We are set free for entry into heaven. At the moment of death, the spirit departs the physical body and goes directly into the presence of the Lord.

Scripture further indicates that the fellowship we have with Christ following the moment of death is nearly instant. I say this because "to depart" and "to be with Christ" are, in the original language, two sides of one coin, indicating that the very moment after Paul departs the body at death, he will be with Christ in heaven. It's a quick, two-count event.

Paul communicated this same truth in 2 Corinthians 5:6-8: "We are always of good courage. We know that while we are at home in the body we are away from the Lord…Yes, we are of good courage, and we would rather be away from the body and at home with the Lord." These verses, too, are incredibly rich in the Greek. Without getting too technical, we might paraphrase the present tenses in the first part of this passage to say, "While we are *continuing* to be at home in the body while living on earth, we are *continuing* to be absent from the Lord." In other words, as long as we're on earth in our mortal bodies, we continue to be absent from the direct presence of the Lord in heaven.

In the latter part of the passage, however, we find two aorist infinitives instead of present tenses. We might paraphrase it this way: "We are of good courage, and prefer rather to be *once-for-all* absent from our flimsy, aging, and dying mortal bodies and to be *once-for-all* at home with the Lord in heaven." Death involves an immediate transition from being "at home in an aging mortal body" to being "at home with the Lord."

Will we have a reunion with our Christian loved ones in heaven?

Most certainly. The reuniting with other believers in the afterlife is not just a New Testament hope. It is an Old Testament hope as well. When Ishmael was 137 years old, "he breathed his last and died, and was *gathered to his people*" (Genesis 25:17). When the text says he was gathered to his people, it means he joined other loved ones in the afterlife who were believers.

The same thing happened with Jacob. Genesis 49:33 tells us that "when Jacob finished commanding his sons, he drew up his feet into the bed and breathed his last and *was gathered to his people*."

There are many similar verses in the Old Testament.

- "Isaac breathed his last, and he died and was *gathered to his people*" (Genesis 35:29).
- "The LORD said to Moses and Aaron at Mount Hor, on the border of the land of Edom, 'Let Aaron be *gathered to his*

people, for he shall not enter the land that I have given to the people of Israel, because you rebelled against my command at the waters of Meribah'" (Numbers 20:23-24).

- "The LORD said to Moses, 'Go up into this mountain of Abarim and see the land that I have given to the people of Israel. When you have seen it, you also shall be *gathered to your people*, as your brother Aaron was'" (Numbers 27:12-13).

- "All that generation also were *gathered to their fathers*" (Judges 2:10).

At death, the spirit of the believer departs the body and is reunited with other believing family members and friends in heaven. They are "gathered to" other believers in the afterlife.

This becomes all the more clear in New Testament revelation. Based on the New Testament, we may rest assured that when Christian loved ones die, our communion with them is broken for only a short time. Our fellowship will be eternally resumed soon enough. We will again see their faces, hear their voices, and hug their (resurrected) bodies. We part with them in grief, but will be reunited in never-ending joy.

Consider the Thessalonian Christians. They were very concerned about their Christian loved ones and friends who had died, and they expressed their concern to the apostle Paul. In 1 Thessalonians 4:13-17, Paul assured these believers that there will indeed be a reunion in heaven. He said that at the time of the rapture, both the dead in Christ and those Christians who are alive "will always be with the Lord" in heaven (verse 17). Therefore, Paul said, they ought to comfort each other with this truth.

Will we recognize each other in heaven?

Yes, I'm convinced of it. In 1 Thessalonians 4:13-17, Paul taught the Thessalonian Christians that they would be reunited with their Christian loved ones, and therefore they ought to comfort one another with this reality. What good would a reunion be if nobody recognized anybody else? I can't imagine Paul intending to teach something like this: "Rejoice, for we will be reunited with all our Christian loved ones in heaven—parents, spouses, and children—even though none of us will recognize each other at all." Paul's emphasis on comfort and joy is rooted in the reality that we'll be together again and recognize each other.

Second Samuel 12:23 also comes to mind. When David's son died, he expressed confidence that he would be reunited with him in heaven. "Now he is dead. Why should I fast? Can I bring him back again? I shall go to him, but he will not return to me." The fact that David would "go to him" in the afterlife clearly implies they will recognize each other and rejoice in their reunion in heaven.

Yet another passage that has relevance on this issue is Luke 16:19-31. Here Jesus speaks about the rich man and Lazarus, who died and were in the afterlife. Abraham was also there. The rich man, Lazarus, and Abraham all recognized each other and even knew something of their histories on earth.

Yet another evidence is found in Luke 20:38, where Jesus calls God the God "of the living." In context, Jesus is talking about the God of Abraham, Isaac, and Jacob. Jesus says these patriarchs are alive and well in the afterlife. In effect, Jesus is saying: "Abraham, Isaac, and Jacob, though they died many years ago, are actually living today. For God, who calls Himself the God of Abraham, Isaac, and Jacob, is not the God of the dead but of the living." This clearly implies that Abraham, Isaac, and Jacob are still recognized as Abraham, Isaac, and Jacob in the afterlife.

So—rejoice in the knowledge that you'll recognize all your Christian loved ones in the afterlife.

Will husbands and wives still be married in the afterlife?

Believers will no longer be in a married state in the afterlife. Jesus said, "In the resurrection they neither marry nor are given in marriage, but are like angels in heaven" (Matthew 22:30).

Of course, it will always be true that my wife, Kerri, and I were married on this earth. Nothing will ever change that. And in the eternal state, in the new heavens and the new earth, we will apparently retain our memory that we were married on the old earth. It will be an eternal memory. And what a precious memory it will be.

We should not think of this as a deprivation. It may be very difficult for us to conceive how we could be happy and fulfilled if we are not still married to our present spouse. But God Himself has promised that not only will there be no sense of deprivation, but there also will be only bliss, and there will be no more sorrow or pain.

My wife and I are part of the glorious church, which the Scriptures reveal will one day be married to Christ. Referred to as the marriage of the Lamb (Revelation 19:7-9), this is an event to look forward to with great anticipation.

Will our children still be our children in the afterlife?

Yes. It will always be true that your daughter is your daughter and your son is your son. Receiving a glorified body does not obliterate the fact that in earth-time history, a husband and wife conceived and gave birth to a son or daughter.

But in the eternal state, there is a broader relationship in which we are all equally sons and daughters in God's eternal family. We have each become adopted into His forever family (Ephesians 1:5). We are all children of God!

Will there be any relational conflicts in heaven?

Family reunions often go just great. But let's be honest. If you're from a large family, as I am, at least a few relatives are bound to be a bit grumpy from time to time. I'm happy to report that such will never be the case in heaven. Our eternal reunion with Christian loved ones and friends will be ceaselessly glorious.

Keep in mind that we will no longer have sin natures. There will be no fights among loved ones. There won't be any resentment. There won't be any envy or jealousy or rivalries. There won't be any one-upmanship. There won't be any cross words. There won't be any misunderstandings. There won't be any selfishness. Our relationships in heaven will truly be wonderful and utterly satisfying.

Will we be able to meet and fellowship with believers we've never met on earth?

Yes. And this includes all the believers throughout church history, including Augustine, John Calvin, and Martin Luther. This also includes believers mentioned in the Bible, such as Adam, Noah, Abraham, Moses, Joshua, David, Solomon, Elijah, Elisha, Isaiah, the apostle John, Peter, Paul, and all the others.

Try to imagine it. We can ask Noah what building the ark was like. We can ask Moses to recount parting the Red Sea. We can ask David to describe his battle with Goliath. We can ask Peter what walking on water felt like. We can ask Martin Luther his thoughts as he nailed the 95 Theses to the door at Wittenberg. We can ask C.S. Lewis how he came up with the idea for his Chronicles of Narnia series. This will be a truly fascinating aspect of life in heaven.

What will worship of God be like in heaven?

Certainly one of the highlights of heaven will be the praise and worship of God and Jesus Christ. The Hebrew word for worship, *shaha*, means "to bow down" or "to prostrate oneself" (see Genesis 22:5; 42:6). Likewise, the New Testament Greek word *proskuneo* means "to prostrate oneself" (see Matthew 2:2,8,11). In Old English, "worship" was rendered "worthship," pointing to the worthiness of the God we worship. Such worship is the proper response of a creature to the divine Creator (Psalm 95:6).

We already know that the angels ceaselessly worship the Lord (see Revelation 4:8). The apostle John speaks of a hundred million angels singing praises in unison to the God they adore (Revelation 5:11-12). But one day, countless redeemed humans will join the company of angels in singing praise and rendering worship to God (Revelation 7:9-10; see also 4:8; 5:8-13; 14:2-3; 15:1-4). Revelation 19:1-6 portrays a great multitude of believers worshipfully shouting out "Hallelujah!" before God's throne.

The worship of God in heaven will not be a tedious or contrived experience, as it sometimes is in church services on earth. I'm sure we've all experienced worship on Sunday mornings that has seemed superficial and even (dare I say) boring. Worship in heaven, however, will be utterly genuine, spontaneous, and exhilarating. It will be wondrous. Our lips will be full of adoration to His name. The reality that we will be in our awesome God's direct presence will make all the difference.

Will we continue to learn about God in the afterlife?

I believe so. Redeemed human beings in the afterlife will not be omniscient as God is. Our knowledge and capacity to understand will apparently be greatly increased (see 1 Corinthians 13:12), but we will not be all-knowing. This means that you and I will still be able to grow in knowledge. One area where we are sure to grow is in our knowledge of our awesome God and His countless perfections. Even now, the angels continue to learn about God and His ways (see 1 Peter 1:12). The same will be true of redeemed human beings once we are in heaven.

Ultimately, this means you and I will never be bored in heaven. God has so many matchless perfections that we will always be learning new and wonderful things about Him. We will never come to the end of exploring Him and His marvelous riches. This will be a constant cause of amazement to us.

Will we serve God in heaven?

Yes. Scripture reveals that in addition to enjoying face-to-face fellowship with God throughout eternity, we will be engaged in meaningful service to Him (Revelation 1:5-6). This service will not be toilsome or draining but invigorating and fulfilling. We will find immeasurable satisfaction in our service to God. There will be no drudgery in heaven.

In our service to God, we won't have to rush to fulfill any deadlines. We won't be concerned about any time clocks. There won't be any office politics. There won't be any fear of being fired. We will engage in our service to God without any kind of frustration and without the slightest sense of exhaustion.

This is quite a contrast to our present lives in which we have to be exhorted by Scripture not to grow weary in doing good things (Galatians 6:9). In heaven, such exhortations will be unnecessary. We will be perpetually motivated to do good things. We will find our service to God a truly joyful experience because we will love without measure the One we are serving. Our love for God will be our prime motivation to serve Him.

How do our present lives impact our status in the afterlife?

In Luke 19:11-26, Jesus told a parable to communicate that our service assignment in the afterlife will relate to how faithfully we serve God during our life on earth. In the parable, the master says to his servant, "Because you have been faithful in a very little, you shall have authority over ten cities" (verse 17). The more faithful we are in serving God in the present life, the more we will have entrusted to us in the next life in our service to God. This has profound implications for the way we live our lives today. Faithfulness in the now is preparation for great blessing then.

What is the significance of Satan being forever banished from believers in heaven?

In Revelation 20:10, the apostle John describes Satan's banishment. Satan will never be released from the lake of fire. He will be consigned to hell without possibility of redemption or release. After we've been in heaven with Christ for 100 billion years, Satan will still be confined in the lake of fire, and there he will forever remain.

This is one of the factors that adds significance to Revelation 21:25, which tells us that the gates of the New Jerusalem—the eternal city of the redeemed that will rest on the new earth—will never be shut. Those who dwell in the eternal city will never have any external threat. Satan, demons, and unbelievers will be in eternal quarantine in hell with no possibility of escape.

This also adds significance to the peace, serene rest, and joy that the redeemed will enjoy in heaven (Revelation 14:13). After all, how could the redeemed enjoy peace, rest, and joy in the midst of constant temptations and afflictions from Satan and demons? It wouldn't be possible. But with Satan and demons out of the picture forever, and with sin completely absent, peace, rest, and joy become realities.

Gone forever will be Satan's temptations toward evil. Gone forever will be his attempts to afflict us with bodily ailments. Gone forever will be the seeds of doubt he seeks to sow in our minds.

Awesome and glorious!

24

Death Finally Conquered

Should Christians fear death?

No. Death is a conquered enemy. One of my favorite psalms is Psalm 23, where David the shepherd exulted: "Even though I walk through the valley of the shadow of death, I will fear no evil, for you are with me; your rod and your staff, they comfort me" (Psalm 23:4). One of the important lessons we glean from this verse is that our divine Shepherd is with us not only at the actual moment of death but also *during the process* of dying (as one walks through the valley of the shadow of death). We never go it alone. Our Lord is with us during life, and He will be with us during the process of dying. Once the moment actually comes, we will be with Him face-to-face in heaven (Philippians 1:21-23). It is an event to anticipate with joy.

The truth is, death is not a terminus but a tunnel that leads to a resplendently glorious heaven (see 2 Corinthians 5:1-8). Thus, death for the believer involves a wondrous transition, not a final condition. Death marks the beginning of a wondrous new life in heaven with Christ that will last forever. Death is a gateway into eternal life, and once we are there, death will never again surface among the redeemed.

Recall the apostle Paul's words in Philippians 1:23: "My desire is to depart and be with Christ, for that is far better." Paul was speaking from experience. Second Corinthians 12:2-4 informs us that during his earthly ministry, Paul had been caught up to paradise. The word "paradise" literally means "garden of pleasure" or "garden of delight." Revelation 2:7 refers to heaven as the "paradise of God." Paul said he "was caught up into paradise" and "heard things that cannot be told, which man may not utter" (2 Corinthians 12:3-4).

Apparently this paradise of God is so resplendently glorious, so ineffable, so wondrous that Paul was forbidden to say anything about it to those still in the earthly realm. But what Paul saw instilled in him an eternal perspective that enabled him to face the trials that lay ahead of him. He not only did not fear death, he could hardly wait for it to happen so he could get back to the heavenly paradise (Philippians 1:21-23).

As he recalled and pondered how wondrous and glorious paradise was, he could easily say that he desired to depart this life so he could be with Christ in heaven. No wonder he faced his martyrdom with a cheerful serenity (2 Timothy 4:6-8). He had no worries. He knew where he was going. He knew that in a flash, at the moment of his death, he'd be right back in heaven where he had previously visited.

What will our resurrection bodies be like?

The apostle Paul affirms: "What is sown is perishable; what is raised is imperishable. It is sown in dishonor; it is raised in glory. It is sown in weakness; it is raised in power" (1 Corinthians 15:42-43).

Paul is here graphically contrasting our present earthly bodies and our future resurrection bodies. "What is sown is perishable" is a metaphorical reference to the burial of a dead body. Just as one sows a seed in the ground, so the mortal body is sown in the sense that it is buried in the ground. When our bodies are placed in the grave, they decompose and return to dust.

The exciting thing is what is raised out of the ground—the resurrection body. Paul notes that our present bodies will perish. They succumb to disease and death. We constantly struggle to fight off dangerous infections. We do everything we can to stay healthy, but we nevertheless get sick. Worse yet, we all eventually die. It is just a matter of time.

Our body upgrades, however, will be imperishable. This means that all susceptibility to disease and death will be forever gone. Never again will we have to worry about infections or passing away.

Paul then affirms that our present mortal body is "sown in dishonor; it is raised in glory." Of course, we rightfully try to honor our loved ones when they die. We typically put them in a nice casket with nice clothes. The ceremony is adorned with nice flowers, and loved ones and friends share many kind comments. This is as it should be. Still, the dead bodies are lowered into the ground and covered with dirt. Death—despite our best efforts to camouflage it—is intrinsically dishonoring. After all, human beings were created to live forever with God, not to die and be buried in the ground.

In contrast to such dishonor, our new bodies will be glorious. They will never again be subject to aging, decay, or death. Never again will our bodies be buried in the ground. Our bodies will have awesome strength, energy, and abilities. We will never again have to lament, "I'm too tired." We'll be able to walk and jump with vitality. Our health and strength will never deteriorate or wane.

Finally, the apostle Paul affirms that our present mortal bodies are characterized by weakness, and he seems to be speaking from experience. Perhaps the older he got, the more this truth was confirmed in his own life. From the moment we are born, Paul says, our "outer self is wasting away" (2 Corinthians 4:16). Vitality decreases, illness comes, and old age follows with its wrinkles and decrepitude. Eventually, we may become incapacitated, not able to move around and do the simplest of tasks. That's why nursing homes do such big business around the world.

By contrast, our body upgrades will brim with intrinsic power. We will never have to sleep in order to recoup energy. Never again will we tire, become weak, or become incapacitated.

Words seem inadequate to describe the incredible differences between our present frail bodies and our future resurrection bodies. There will be no more cholesterol buildup, no more heart disease, no more kidney disease, no more diabetes, no more blindness or deafness, and no more aging of skin. We will enjoy perpetual youth with a fullness of vitality and energy.

Will our resurrection bodies be *physical* bodies?

Yes, indeed. Scripture affirms that our resurrection bodies will be just like the resurrection body of Jesus Christ. The apostle Paul said that Christ "will transform our lowly body to be like his glorious body" (Philippians 3:21). John likewise said, "We know that when he appears we shall be like him" (1 John 3:2). This means that we will not be ethereal spirits floating around in a heavenly twilight zone for all eternity. Rather, we will be physically resurrected—just like Jesus—and we will live in a physical place (see John 14:1-3).

If you're wondering how we know Jesus' resurrection body was physical, there's plenty of New Testament evidence:

- Jesus' physical body was missing from the tomb (Matthew 28; Mark 16; Luke 24; John 20).

- Jesus' resurrection body retained the crucifixion scars (Luke 24:39; John 20:27).

- The resurrected Jesus affirmed He was not a spirit but rather had real flesh and bones (Luke 24:39).

- Jesus ate food following His resurrection, thus proving the physicality of His resurrection body (Luke 24:30,42-43; John 21:12-13).

- The resurrected Jesus was physically touched by others (Matthew 28:9; John 20:27-28; see also Luke 24:39-40).

- The word "body" (from the Greek word *soma*), used to describe the resurrection body in 1 Corinthians 15:44, always means a *physical* body in the New Testament when used of individual human beings.

So—you will be resurrected *physically*, just like Jesus.

If we will be resurrected physically, why are we told that "flesh and blood cannot inherit the kingdom of God"?

First Corinthians 15:50 affirms: "Flesh and blood cannot inherit the kingdom of God, nor does the perishable inherit the imperishable." At first glance, it might seem that this verse is arguing against the physicality of our resurrection bodies. But such is not the case. "Flesh and blood" is a Jewish idiom that refers to mortal, perishable humanity. Mortal human beings in their present perishable bodies cannot inherit heaven. Mortal humanity must be made *immortal* humanity in order to survive in heaven. That's why 1 Corinthians 15:53 asserts that "this perishable body must put on the imperishable, and this mortal body must put on immortality." Put another way, the resurrection body will be endowed with special qualities that will enable it to adapt perfectly to life in God's presence.

Will death then be a thing of the past?

Yes, indeed. In Isaiah 25:8 we are told that God "will swallow up death forever; and the Lord GOD will wipe away tears from all faces." This verse contains a Hebrew play on words. The ancient Jews often spoke of death as swallowing up the living, like a big mouth opening in the ground to devour people into the grave. But God promises that one day He will reverse things so that death itself will be swallowed up. When that happens, death will be gone forever.

The apostle Paul, himself an Old Testament scholar well aware of Isaiah 25:8, made the same point related to our future resurrection bodies: "When the perishable puts on the imperishable, and the mortal puts on immortality, then shall come to pass the saying that is written: 'Death is swallowed up in victory'" (1 Corinthians 15:54).

Also, just as Isaiah 25:8 promises that "the Lord GOD will wipe away tears from all faces," we read in Revelation 21:4 that God "will wipe away every tear from their eyes, and death shall be no more, neither shall there be mourning, nor crying, nor pain anymore, for the former things have passed away."

We're in for a big change. Those of us who watch the evening news on television receive regular reports of disaster, death, and mourning. But in heaven, all is life, life, and more life. We will never again be alerted to a sudden and deadly accident of a loved one or friend. No one will ever succumb to an incurable disease. We will never again attend a funeral service. There will be no more hearses. We will never again have to say a final farewell to anyone. We are headed for a glorious, deathless environment.

What should our attitude be toward death?

Scripture provides these insights:

1. Our days are limited, so we ought to live each day to the fullest and be mindful of living for the Lord 24/7. The psalmist prayed, "O LORD, make me know my end and what is the measure of my days; let me know how fleeting I am!" (Psalm 39:4). An awareness of mortality instills in us a desire to make every day count.

2. Though our mortal bodies age and become progressively weaker over time, our inner self—the real us—is renewed day by day as we walk with God. As 2 Corinthians 4:16 puts it, "We do not lose heart. Though our outer self is wasting away, our inner self is being renewed day by day." So regardless of your age, keep your focus on spending time in Scripture and walking with God. Keep the things of the Spirit at the top of your priorities.

3. We ought never to presume we will live a long life, for that is not a guarantee. Proverbs 27:1 tells us, "Do not boast about tomorrow, for you do not know what a day may bring." We have seen that James wrote a similar New Testament exhortation (James 4:14).

4. Scripture reveals that people who obey and honor the Lord live longer, while those who dishonor Him may find their lives cut short. Proverbs 10:27 tells us that "the fear of the LORD prolongs life, but the years of the wicked will be short." Indeed, "the fear of the LORD is a fountain of life, that one may turn away from the snares of death" (Proverbs 14:27). Deuteronomy 4:40 instructs, "You shall keep his statutes and his commandments...that it may go well with you and with your children after you, and that you may prolong your days in the land that the LORD your God is giving you for all time." In the New Testament, Paul writes, "Honor your father and mother...that it may go well with you and that you may live long in the land" (Ephesians 6:2-3). Long life goes hand in hand with living one's life according to God's ways (see Proverbs 3:16; 4:10; 9:11).

Rejoice—a resurrection body awaits you!

An Eternal Perspective

We've had a fascinating journey through Scripture, have we not? Few things are more exciting than coming to understand what Scripture has to say about the future.

I think we've all got a vested interest in the topic. After all, aside from knowing what the end times will look like on planet Earth, we also want to know about our personal future—our *eternal* future.

Eternity is a big concept. We read in the pages of Holy Writ that God has "put eternity into man's heart" (Ecclesiastes 3:11). Though we live in a world of time, we have intimations of eternity within our hearts. We instinctively think of forever. We seem to intrinsically realize that beyond this life lies the possibility of a shoreless ocean of time. It is wondrous to even think about it. We are heaven-bent; our hearts have an inner tilt upward.

From the first book in the Bible to the last, we read of great men and women of God who gave evidence that eternity permeated their hearts. We read of people like Abel, Enoch, Noah, Abraham, and David... each yearning to live with God in eternity (see Hebrews 11).

The psalmist puts it this way: "As a deer pants for flowing streams, so pants my soul for you, O God. My soul thirsts for God, for the living God. When shall I come and appear before God?" (Psalm 42:1-2). David exulted, "I shall dwell in the house of the LORD forever" (Psalm 23:6).

Moses is another great example:

> By faith Moses, when he was grown up, refused to be called the son of Pharaoh's daughter, choosing rather to be

mistreated with the people of God than to enjoy the fleeting pleasures of sin. He considered the reproach of Christ
greater wealth than the treasures of Egypt, for he was look-
ing to the reward. By faith he left Egypt, not being afraid
of the anger of the king, for he endured as seeing him who
is invisible (Hebrews 11:24-27).

It is interesting that the writer of Hebrews said Moses "considered the reproach of Christ greater wealth than the treasures of Egypt,"
because Moses lived at least 1500 years before Christ. It is difficult to
ascertain how much Moses knew about Christ, but our text clearly
indicates that Moses had a personal faith in Christ on the basis of
which he forsook Egypt. God had apparently revealed to him things
invisible to the natural eye. Moses became aware of another King,
another kingdom, and a better reward.

Moses "considered" these things. The Hebrew word translated
"considered" indicates careful thought and not a quick decision. Moses
thought through his decision, weighing the pros and cons. He weighed
what Egypt had to offer against the promises of God for the prophetic
future. He concluded that what God offered in eternity was far supe-
rior to anything Egypt could offer on temporal earth. Moses lived with
eternity in view. He made his decisions based on how they would
impact his existence in the afterlife.

If we were to try to reconstruct Moses' reasoning, we might come
up with something such as this:

God has revealed future things to me—invisible things,
but things of glory, heavenly things. I believe what He says.
At the same time, He has made known to me that I am
His chosen instrument to deliver His people, my fellow
Hebrews according to the flesh, from bondage. But I am
the adopted son of Pharaoh's daughter. To me the throne
of Egypt has been promised, as heir through her. If I follow God's program for me, I must suffer reproach. If, on
the other hand, I remain in the royal court, all the wealth
of Egypt is mine—and how great is that wealth! If I take

the course God has laid out for me, I must suffer affliction with my fellow Hebrews, and I have seen how heavy their burdens are. Whereas if I am ready to be called Pharaoh's grandson, the pleasures of all that Egypt has to offer, the pleasures of sin, may be enjoyed. Each of these things—the affliction of the people of God and the pleasures of sin— is temporal.

It is wiser to look to life after death. In the afterlife, he who has suffered within the will of God will be rewarded, but he who has followed the way of the flesh will be judged. What God has spoken is surely true. I make my choice. I refuse to be called the son of Pharaoh's daughter, preferring by choice to suffer affliction with God's people than to enjoy the temporary pleasures of sin, counting the reproach of the divine Messiah, with its present satisfaction and eventual reward, greater riches by far than the treasures of Egypt.

As He did with Moses, God has also revealed future things to you and me—*from the pages of prophetic Scripture.* And like Moses, we have a choice to make. We can either live for the fleeting pleasures this world has to offer, or we can live in light of eternity, choosing purposefully to live God's way as we sojourn through earthly life toward the heavenly country (Hebrews 11:16). We can live *now* in light of *then.*

I think Moses would have agreed with what the apostle Paul wrote to the Corinthian church: "This light momentary affliction is preparing for us an eternal weight of glory beyond all comparison, as we look not to the things that are seen but to the things that are unseen. For the things that are seen are transient, but the things that are unseen are eternal" (2 Corinthians 4:17-18). *That's* an eternal perspective.

Moses gave up temporal pleasure for the sake of his Savior, Jesus Christ. His priorities were as they should have been. And what joy Moses' commitment must have brought to the heart of God!

Do you not sense within your heart a calling to follow Moses' lead?

The great revivalist preacher, philosopher, and theologian Jonathan Edwards seemed to mirror Moses' commitment. Edwards, who lived from 1703 to 1758, was in the Puritan habit of framing spiritual resolutions to discipline himself. In a number of these resolutions he reminded himself, as he had been taught since childhood, to think of his own dying—or to live as though he had only an hour left before he passed through death's door. In his thinking, his life was a step-by-step journey toward heaven—a journey so important that he ought to subordinate all other concerns of life to it. This heavenly mindset led him to make the following resolutions:

- "Resolved, to endeavor to obtain for myself as much happiness, in the other world, as I possibly can."

- "Resolved, that I will live so as I shall wish I had done when I come to die."

- "Resolved, to endeavor to my utmost to act as I can think I should do, if I had already seen the happiness of heaven and hell's torments."

May the prophetic truths in this book motivate you to make Edwards's resolutions your own.

Bibliography

Ankerberg, John, and Dillon Burroughs. *Middle East Meltdown*. Eugene, OR: Harvest House, 2007.

Block, Daniel. *The Book of Ezekiel: Chapters 25–48*. Grand Rapids, MI: Eerdmans, 1998.

Feinberg, Charles. *The Prophecy of Ezekiel*. Eugene, OR: Wipf and Stock, 2003.

Fruchtenbaum, Arnold. *The Footsteps of the Messiah*. San Antonio, TX: Ariel, 2004.

Geisler, Norman. *Systematic Theology: Church/Last Things*, vol. 4. St. Paul, MN: Bethany House, 2005.

Hays, J. Daniel, J. Scott Duvall, and C. Marvin Pate. *Dictionary of Biblical Prophecy and End Times*. Grand Rapids, MI: Zondervan, 2007.

Hitchcock, Mark. *Bible Prophecy*. Wheaton, IL: Tyndale House, 1999.

Hoyt, Herman. *The End Times*. Chicago: Moody, 1969.

Ice, Thomas, and Timothy Demy. *Prophecy Watch*. Eugene, OR: Harvest House, 1998.

Ice, Thomas, and Timothy Demy. *When the Trumpet Sounds*. Eugene, OR: Harvest House, 1995.

LaHaye, Tim. *The Beginning of the End*. Wheaton, IL: Tyndale House, 1991.

LaHaye, Tim, ed. *Prophecy Study Bible*. Chattanooga, TN: AMG Publishers, 2001.

LaHaye, Tim, and Ed Hindson, eds. *The Popular Bible Prophecy Commentary*. Eugene, OR: Harvest House, 2006.

LaHaye, Tim, and Ed Hindson, eds. *The Popular Encyclopedia of Bible Prophecy*. Eugene, OR: Harvest House, 2004.

LaHaye, Tim, and Thomas Ice. *Charting the End Times*. Eugene, OR: Harvest House, 2001.

LaHaye, Tim, and Jerry Jenkins. *Are We Living in the End Times?* Wheaton, IL: Tyndale House, 1999.

Pentecost, J. Dwight. *Prophecy for Today: God's Purpose and Plan for Our Future*. Grand Rapids, MI: Discovery House, 1989.

Pentecost, J. Dwight. *Things to Come*. Grand Rapids, MI: Zondervan, 1964.

Pentecost, J. Dwight. *The Words and Works of Jesus Christ*. Grand Rapids, MI: Zondervan, 1978.

Price, Randall. *Fast Facts on the Middle East Conflict*. Eugene, OR: Harvest House, 2003.

Price, Randall. *Unholy War*. Eugene, OR: Harvest House, 2001.

Rosenberg, Joel. *Epicenter: Why Current Rumblings in the Middle East Will Change Your Future*. Carol Stream, IL: Tyndale House, 2006.

Ryrie, Charles. *Basic Theology*. Wheaton, IL: Victor, 1986.

Sanders, J. Oswald. *Heaven: Better by Far*. Grand Rapids, MI: Discovery House, 1993.

Showers, Renald. *Maranatha: Our Lord Come!* Bellmawr, NJ: The Friends of Israel Gospel Ministry, 1995.

Toussaint, Stanley. *Behold the King: A Study of Matthew*. Grand Rapids, MI: Kregel, 1980.

Unger, Merrill F. *Beyond the Crystal Ball*. Chicago: Moody, 1978.

Walvoord, John F. *End Times*. Nashville, TN: Word, 1998.

Walvoord, John F. *The Prophecy Knowledge Handbook*. Wheaton, IL: Victor, 1990.

Notes

1. Joel Rosenberg, *Epicenter* (Carol Stream, IL: Tyndale House, 2006), p. 27.
2. George Barna, "The End of Absolutes: America's New Moral Code," May 25, 2016, www.barna.com.

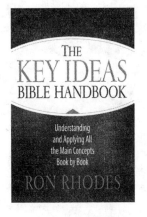

The Key Ideas Bible Handbook

From Genesis to Revelation, the Bible is full of life-changing truth. But to fully experience the power of God's Word, you need to go beyond merely knowing the facts and learn how to let them transform you.

In this dynamic resource, noted author and biblical scholar Ron Rhodes takes you through each book of the Bible, breaking down complex concepts into practical applications and offering helpful insights for each.

For example, key applications found in 1 John include:

- Our fellowship with God hinges on walking in the light as He is in the light.

- When we fall into sin and fall out of fellowship with God, confession to God is the remedy that restores our fellowship.

- When we sin, Jesus is our defense attorney—and He never loses a case in God's court. Our fellowship with God is thereby protected.

Word studies, quotes from famous Christians, cross-references, and more are included in every profound chapter to help you dig deeper into each transformational concept. As you put God's key principles into practice, you'll experience more than ever all the benefits the Bible has to offer.

Other Great Harvest House Books by Ron Rhodes

Books About the Bible

- 40 Days Through Daniel
- 40 Days Through Genesis
- 40 Days Through Revelation
- 90 Days Through the New Testament
- The Big Book of Bible Answers
- Bite-Size Bible® Answers
- Bite-Size Bible® Charts
- Bite-Size Bible® Definitions
- Bite-Size Bible® Handbook
- Commonly Misunderstood Bible Verses
- The Complete Guide to Bible Translations
- Find It Fast in the Bible
- The Key Ideas Bible Handbook
- The Popular Dictionary of Bible Prophecy
- Understanding the Bible from A to Z
- What Does the Bible Say About…?

Books About the End Times

- The 8 Great Debates of Bible Prophecy
- 40 Days Through Revelation
- Cyber Meltdown
- The End Times in Chronological Order
- Northern Storm Rising
- The Topical Handbook About Bible Prophecy
- Unmasking the Antichrist

Books About Other Important Topics

- 5-Minute Apologetics for Today
- 1001 Unforgettable Quotes About God, Faith, and the Bible
- Answering the Objections of Atheists, Agnostics, and Skeptics
- Christianity According to the Bible
- The Complete Guide to Christian Denominations
- Conversations with Jehovah's Witnesses
- Find It Quick Handbook on Cults and New Religions
- Jehovah's Witnesses: What You Need to Know
- The Secret Life of Angels
- The Truth Behind Ghosts, Mediums, and Psychic Phenomena
- What Happens After Life?
- Why Do Bad Things Happen If God Is Good?
- Wonder of Heaven

The 10 Most Important Things Series

- The 10 Most Important Things You Can Say to a Catholic
- The 10 Most Important Things You Can Say to a Jehovah's Witness
- The 10 Most Important Things You Can Say to a Mason
- The 10 Most Important Things You Can Say to a Mormon
- The 10 Things You Need to Know About Islam
- The 10 Things You Should Know About the Creation vs. Evolution Debate

Quick Reference Guides

- Halloween: What You Need to Know
- Islam: What You Need to Know
- Jehovah's Witnesses: What You Need to Know

The Reasoning from the Scriptures Series

- Reasoning from the Scriptures with Catholics
- Reasoning from the Scriptures with the Jehovah's Witnesses
- Reasoning from the Scriptures with Masons
- Reasoning from the Scriptures with the Mormons
- Reasoning from the Scriptures with Muslims

Little Books

- Little Book About God
- Little Book About Heaven
- Little Book About the Bible

AVAILABLE ONLY AS EBOOKS

- Book of Bible Promises
- Coming Oil Storm
- Topical Handbook of Bible Prophecy

To learn more about Harvest House books and
to read sample chapters, visit our website:

www.harvesthousepublishers.com

HARVEST HOUSE PUBLISHERS
EUGENE, OREGON